THE CRITICAL INCIDENT IN GROWTH GROUPS: THEORY AND TECHNIQUE

by

ARTHUR M. COHEN, Ph.D.
Atlanta, Georgia

and

R. DOUGLAS SMITH, Ph.D.
Macon, Georgia

University Associates, Inc.
7596 Eads Avenue, La Jolla, California 92037

Copyright © 1976 by University Associates, Inc.

Hardbound ISBN: 0-88390-101-3
Paperbound ISBN: 0-88390-102-1

Library of Congress Catalog Card Number 75-22510

All Rights Reserved

Printed in the United States of America

$9.50

THE CRITICAL INCIDENT IN GROWTH GROUPS: THEORY AND TECHNIQUE

To Kenneth D. Benne and Warren G. Bennis,
teachers and friends

A special acknowledgment
to Carolyn M. Kilpatrick, M.Ed.,
colleague and friend,
without whose administrative
and technical contributions
this book would not have been published

A leader is best
When people barely know he exists.
Not so good when people obey and acclaim him.
Worse when they despise him.
"Fail to honor people, they fail to honor you";
But of a good leader, who talks little,
When his work is done, his aim fulfilled,
They will say, "We did this ourselves."
Lao-tse

Table of Contents

Introduction	1
Chapter 1: History of Groups	13
Chapter 2: Conditions for Learning and Design Strategy	58
Chapter 3: The Intervention Cube	87
Chapter 4: The Critical-Incident Model: Its Use and Application	114
Chapter 5: A Theory of Group Growth and Development	155
Chapter 6: Some Questions and Answers and an Experience	218
A Selected Bibliography	245
Appendix: Behavioral Characteristics	271
Indexes	
Subject Index	281
Name Index	288

Introduction

RATIONALE

The problem of effectively shaping group growth and development through verbal intervention has been a continuing source of concern to both practitioners and researchers. The essence of the process by which any group develops its potential is the progressive modification of ideas and behaviors through verbal interaction. When an idea is introduced by one of the members of a group, other members may suggest an extension or a different emphasis or may approve or reject the idea. Still others may volunteer their thoughts. Thus, there is an idea-in-the-making: a preliminary statement changed by the work of the group through verbal modification until it represents, more or less adequately, the cumulative, developing, mutual point of view of the group members.

The group leader is an important influence in the acquisition, rejection, or clarification of an idea. The leader alone does not bring about changes in the group or its members. These changes are also effected by group members who assume leadership functions. Although the group leader does not primarily control others, he does initiate verbal and behavioral responses that strongly influence others to perform certain acts that shape the group as a whole. Personality variables, intelligence, physical characteristics, and the like, which have played a very prominent role in studies of leadership in the past, do not by themselves account for influential leadership in human groups. We believe, however, that these characteristics induce desired behavior in others when the member or group leader who possesses them is able to gain the confidence of the group and to respond with leadership acts at the appropriate moments.

Our approach to determining appropriate leadership responses is not characterized by a rigid formality toward interventions, but rather represents an interactional viewpoint of effective group leadership. In this approach, the effective group leader intervenes only after evaluating the interaction among the group's past, the characteristics of its members, the needs of specific group members with whom he interacts, the time limitations involved, and the goals the group seeks to attain.

There are also emotional components to be considered. A decision to intervene, determined primarily by cognitive considerations, may be radically modified by the prevailing mood of the group. For example, a group deeply enmeshed in the process of supporting a member who is risking emotional disclosure may well resent any attempt to deal with this issue intellectually or in any way other than by expressing feelings and sharing concerns. This is not to state that emotional, nonverbal, atmospheric, or mood factors take precedence over cognitive considerations; ideally, each must work in the service of the other. Thus, the nature of leadership intervention is based on something more than either emotional or intellectual considerations alone.

In our viewpoint, effective group leadership requires the discipline of certain specifiable evaluation procedures to analyze ongoing group behavior, together with spontaneity and openness in expressing feelings and implementing actions based on them. We further believe that effective group growth and development is enhanced by a distributive theory of leadership. In this orientation, responsibility for performing functions that are necessary for the group's effectiveness is increasingly shared among all members.

In essence, this is similar to the behavior-therapy term "fading." Fading is a process whereby the therapist helps to initiate certain behaviors and then, following the establishment of those behaviors, begins to withdraw his guidance and influence in small steps. Ultimately, this behavior may well become self-sustaining and autonomous. To the extent that group members are able to perform necessary interpersonal and group functions by themselves, interventions initially made only by the group leader should begin to be expressed by the group members as well.

This objective of "shared group leadership" is based not on any demand for a democratic ethic per se. Rather, it is based on our belief and observation that personal involvement, active and responsible membership, and commitment to group goals are enhanced by this orientation.

CHAPTER 1—HISTORY OF GROUPS

Chapter 1 is divided into two parts to provide a substantive background for the chapters that follow. The first part of this chapter is a survey of the history of the small-group movement. The second part focuses on the development of laboratory training and modern-day encounter and growth groups. In part two the major theoretical and philosophical assumptions of small groups, as well as their specific technological applications, are discussed.

CHAPTER 2—CONDITIONS FOR LEARNING AND DESIGN STRATEGY

In Chapter 2 we propose that before an individual can profit from the advantages offered by participation in any given group, certain conditions for learning must be present. To the extent that these basic conditions are met, actual behavior changes in group members will be facilitated regardless of the theoretical approach of the group leader. Conditions for learning may be defined as those factors or basic assumptions operating in a group that facilitate the acquisition and integrated utilization of knowledge, skills, and values for personal and group growth.

These conditions for learning are not sufficient by themselves to cause change. They do, however, provide a necessary setting for change. Most of these basic assumptions are shared by practitioners of a wide variety of approaches to group work and appear to demonstrate a common validity. Few group leaders would question that appropriate feedback, trust, and involvement are necessary and basic conditions to bring about change in group members.

It is only when group leaders of divergent theoretical approaches attempt to implement in various technical ways these basic conditions for learning that any specific design strategy for interventions becomes obvious. We believe that every concerned group leader has a design strategy, whether it is explicitly articulated in a list of criteria, goals, and techniques, or whether it is primarily implicit but evidenced in his life style and pattern of group interactions.

Design strategy, therefore, is an orientation or philosophy, a way of leading groups so that certain desired events come to pass, and a basic belief that personal and group growth need not be a haphazard process. Regardless of the theoretical stance, design strategy is a conscious attempt to anticipate meaningfully the development of certain critical issues and to plan for their management—that is, the handling of certain problems that seem to be significant.

Depending on the issues and problems they consider to be important, group leaders begin to diverge into various theoretical camps. Each camp has its own rationale concerning proper group leadership procedures. These rationales differ in their explicitness and specificity. Some rationales are quite explicit in proposing rules or guidelines; e.g., "The group should not be allowed to talk about people or events outside the immediate room." Other rationales are more general; e.g., "The leader should so act in every encounter as to enhance those self-actualizing processes the individual may be trying to express." Between these two end points there are design strategies with varying degrees of specificity.

Each design strategy, regardless of group orientation, may be evaluated for its major desired group focus. Thus, a given design strategy may focus on (a) problem-solving tasks and issues that confront individuals, groups, and organizations and/or (b) person-centered activities involving confrontation of the self in relation to others, with an examination of life styles via patterns of social relationships.

Whether problem oriented, person centered, or both, the various intervention approaches are designed to be interjected at times and places likely to influence the group and its individual members most effectively.

At any particular point, groups operate on a number of different levels (or systems of concern). For example, a group might be involved on an intellectual level in discussing alternative plans for solving a political problem. On another level, emotions might be fluctuating between indifference and depression; and yet, on still another level, attempts to take over group leadership might be operating.

Group leaders of different theoretical persuasions attempt to focus on and alter different parts of these ongoing levels. Their particular styles of intervention depend on their beliefs as to which systems of concern are most important. A rational-emotive group leader might prefer to intervene at the cognitive level, hoping to modify faulty basic assumptions and thought patterns. An encounter-group leader would probably place little emphasis on the intellectual level and intervene directly on the emotional level, identifying and dealing with the feelings that inhibit group growth. Other group leaders might prefer to focus on those systems dealing with issues of authority. All the systems operating in a group at any given time are interdependent, and undoubtedly changes in one system will be felt in other systems. Thus it is important to know which system or systems can best be approached by which type of interventions.

Our specific design strategy is an extension of laboratory training. Commitment to this method of training implies an acceptance of certain basic assumptions and specifications of goals, and a certain technological skill development.

However, it is not necessary to accept our specific approach in order to utilize the Intervention Cube and the Critical-Incident Model presented in Chapters 3 and 4. On the contrary, the Critical-Incident Model permits a direct comparison of different theoretical approaches to either the same problems or problems idiosyncratic to specific groups or both.

Chapter 2 is intended to define explicitly our group leadership orientation. It is designed to serve two functions: (1) prescriptively, it suggests certain group procedures found to be effective in achieving group goals; and (2) it differentiates between our prescriptive approach and the descriptive Critical-Incident Model which may be used as an unbiased research and training tool for any type of group.

CHAPTER 3—THE INTERVENTION CUBE

A model of interventions, with specific guidelines for each intervention, is presented in Chapter 3, The Intervention Cube.

A comprehensive model for classifying interventions should serve two functions. First and ideally, it should possess characteristics that would enable the model to be useful as a teaching, training, and research tool. Secondly, an intervention model should possess the generality and flexibility by which any ongoing group could be described.

The Intervention Cube allows any intervention statement to be described and categorized regardless of the group leader's orientation. At the same time, this approach permits a group leader to evaluate the effects of his particular style of intervention on a group.

Briefly stated, any specific leadership response may be classified as to *level of intervention,* i.e., whether the focus is on *group, interpersonal,* or *individual* behavior; *type of intervention,* i.e., whether the intervention is *conceptual, experiential,* or *structural; intensity of intervention,* i.e., the degree to which the choice of response is directed toward the emotional center of the target issue on a continuum from *low* to *medium* to *high* intensity.

Descriptively, the Intervention Cube (along with the Critical-Incident Model) provides a framework for recognizing and describing the salient features of any ongoing behavior and places those important events in a more systematic perspective. For example, from an analysis of intervention responses, using the Intervention Cube, a beginning group leader may find that he is primarily using a series of group-level, conceptual responses of low intensity, especially when faced with a very emotional issue in the group. After evaluation, he may wish to extend his range of responses by trying out other combinations of parts of the Intervention Cube.

Although some may take exception to our specific design strategies and prescriptions for interventions in specific cases, this in no way invalidates the use of the Intervention Cube as an effective tool, regardless of one's theoretical orientation.

CHAPTER 4—THE CRITICAL-INCIDENT MODEL

At one or more points during the interactions among group members, the leader is faced with a critical situation or incident and has to choose an appropriate response. These incidents have different degrees of importance depending on how crucial they are to the development of group solidarity, productivity, and direction.

The concerned group leader must be able to recognize these critical incidents when they occur and have at his immediate disposal an effective rationale for choosing an appropriate intervention response. This would be true regardless of group orientation: the group may be oriented toward the solving of objective problems, as in a work group; toward a discussion of interpersonal dynamics, as in T-groups; or toward an investigation of highly personal disorders involving distress and anxiety, as in traditional group psychotherapy.

While each group is unique, there are certain basic problems or issues invariably present in and common to all groups; certain common critical situations tend to emerge. An attempt should be made to collect and deal with these critical incidents to promote effective individual and/or group growth within each respective intervention approach.

The term "critical incident" was given attention and utilized as a technique by Flanagan during World War II (1947a, 1947b, 1954). The term again appeared in a book by Standal and Corsini (1959), but not in relation to a framework for interventions. According to Flanagan (1954), an incident is defined as any observable human activity sufficiently complete in itself to permit inferences to be made about the person performing the act. A critical incident, then, is an observable human activity of sufficient importance to the group and/or individual(s) to merit an intervention by the group leader.

Chapter 4 discusses the Critical-Incident Model as a means of describing and ordering ongoing group phenomena so as to provide an adequate basis for making leader interventions. Our proposed Critical-Incident Model is a way of arranging data in sequence—from those events that led to and immediately preceded some critical incident to those that are the consequences of certain interventions.

In essence, the Critical-Incident Model should be viewed as an attempt to study ongoing processes. It involves the selection of representative events, the evaluation of their component parts, and the prescription and comparison of alternative responses to be made by the group leader.

The Critical-Incident Model is composed of the following parts: the context within which the critical incident occurred; the behavior and/or conversation that led up to and preceded the point of choice; the surface and underlying issues; the level, type, and intensity of the intervention response; and the results of the intervention on the group.

With this model, the group leader may observe and quickly and accurately classify group behaviors regardless of the theoretical approach or type of group. A selective collection of critical incidents could be used by a trained group leader as a research tool as well as a teaching device for training and improving the effectiveness of group leaders.

This chapter also presents a cross section of several major theoretical approaches to group leadership, preserving the flavor and authenticity of each position by utilizing actual verbatim examples from the group literature. Each of these different approaches to group leadership is embedded in the Critical-Incident Model, thereby allowing a direct comparison of typical intervention responses. Examples have been selected from representative ongoing groups in the following classifications: directive, nondirective, encounter, and T-group. These examples clearly reveal that each theoretical orientation has its own preferred characteristic "style" of intervention responses.

In order to facilitate direct comparisons among these approaches, the same basic issues or group problems are used when possible. This does not imply that different approaches to group leadership have separate and completely nonoverlapping intervention styles. On the contrary, the Critical-Incident Model and the Intervention Cube permit a consideration of the similarities and the differences in group approaches.

The last section of Chapter 4 describes the ways in which the Critical-Incident Model may be used as an effective instrument for teaching, training, and research.

In the teaching and training role, the Critical-Incident Model could be used to collect a series of events considered to be important by practitioners of a particular approach to interventions. A supervisor of beginning group leaders might then present these events to his students in critical-incident form. This could be done with a "fill-in-the-blank" workbook approach by asking the group leader "What would you do if . . . ?" questions. The manual that accompanies this text, *The Critical Incident in Growth Groups: A Manual for Group Leaders*, is especially useful when employing the Critical-Incident Model in a training dimension.

Using another approach, the Critical-Incident Model could be used in a role-playing context in which the significant behavioral events contained in the Critical-Incident Model would be acted out by trainees.

Regardless of the teaching design, the beginning group leader would learn by being confronted with actual events to which he is expected to respond. The nature and adequacy of his responses would allow the student and the supervisor to pinpoint potential strengths and weaknesses. Since these critical incidents have been taken from ongoing groups and have been selected to highlight those issues considered important by a particular orientation, the student would be able to determine the immediate relevance of the interventions to his training.

The Critical-Incident Model can also serve as a kind of viable projective test for interventions in the training of beginning group leaders. If the Critical-Incident Model is used prior to any training on the part of the beginning group leader, he is likely to respond with verbalizations and responses that characterize his personal needs. For example, prior to training, a concept-oriented person might feel very comfortable in handling critical incidents as long as he could intervene conceptually with low intensity responses at a group level. When confronted with critical incidents of high emotional intensity, he might

8   The Critical Incident in Growth Groups

continue to respond in the same rigid manner, become defensive, or even withdraw from the interaction. By using the Critical-Incident Model the supervisor would be better able to design a teaching and training orientation tailored to the characteristics and needs of a specific potential group leader.

The same learning design could also be used by experienced group leaders who wish to experiment with new intervention styles. The Critical-Incident Model and the Intervention Cube together can be used to understand and describe group-leadership behavior and to increase its effectiveness.

CHAPTER 5—A THEORY OF GROUP GROWTH AND DEVELOPMENT

There is no general agreement concerning the development and growth pattern of a group (Tuckman, 1965; Bennis & Shepard, 1956; Kaplan & Roman, 1963; Rogers, 1970). In Chapter 5, we present our own model of group growth and development, divided into ten phases. These ten phases are not mutually exclusive and a degree of overlap exists between and among them.

This model was arrived at through a synthesis of the published work of some fifty investigators and from our own collection of critical-incident and critical-behavior data. The order in which the behavioral incidents of T-group participants flowed suggested the pattern of our model. The model provides a group leader with an overview of the major concepts involved in group phases.

CHAPTER 6—SOME QUESTIONS AND ANSWERS AND AN EXPERIENCE

Chapter 6 consists of a dialogue between a beginning group leader and an experienced trainer. Pertinent remarks made by the trainer reflect our basic philosophy of the Critical-Incident Model and our theory of leadership and conditions for learning. Chapter 6 serves as a personal statement of our beliefs and philosophy and as a summary of the many issues dealt with in this volume. It concludes the book with the account of an actual T-group experience that illustrates a number of these basic issues.

A MANUAL FOR GROUP LEADERS

For each phase that is described in our model of group growth and development (Chapter 5), a number of critical incidents that typify expected important transactions in that specific phase are identified and described in the manual that accompanies this text. These sixty-one critical incidents are indexed according to both phase and major issues. Thus a group leader may read Chapter 5 for an overview of major concepts involved in group phases, either as a series of separate investigations or as a summary of the state of the field, and then decide to focus on one particular phase of group life, e.g., the initial formative stage, and one particular family of issues, e.g., authority problems. The Master Index in the manual will give him a description of this phase as well as references to specific critical incidents that illustrate it and that suggest our intervention responses to such issues. In this manner, intellectual inquiry can be applied directly to ongoing groups.

Conversely, if an investigator records a series of critical incidents all dealing with the same basic issue, he may then refer to Chapter 5 of this text in order to find a detailed description of the suggested phase associated with those incidents.

Each critical incident in the manual deals with emergent issues that are considered to represent a wide range and variety of problems common to laboratory training. Each of these issues is presented through the Critical-Incident Model, along with suggested interventions and optional structural interventions. The phase in which each critical incident is most likely to occur in the life of a group is identified.

SUMMARY

More than most other books on the subject of group leadership, this book has a technological orientation to the nature of interventions. At the same time, however, an attempt has been made to balance concerns for systematization with concerns for individual choice and response style. There are probably some who feel that the more we attempt to specify examples through the use of critical incidents, in order to delineate group movement into phases with certain associated processes and to specify a range of possible interventions appropriate to each of these, the more group leadership will become automated and stilted.

This viewpoint assumes that changes in groups would be programmed, that humanistic values associated with the unique life, drama, viability, and freedom to choose in a group would be lost. This is, in short, the age-old and wrongly perceived antagonism between knowledge and values, between a technological approach and an approach concerned primarily with unspecifiable internal responses.

The differences are more apparent than real. The values that are associated with such terms as "uniqueness" and "freedom of choice" through "spontaneity" are often the very values that offer a limited number of alternatives to the group leader. Freedom of choice for group leaders, in its full sense, means having available all there is to know about a situation, the possible choices, and the consequences associated with those choices.

This value orientation frees the individual by opening a vast range of available options within his own individual style. From this viewpoint, a technological approach as conceived in this book is seen not as intruding on freedom or restricting the domain of choice, but rather as enhancing and enlarging the quantity and quality of available options. It accomplishes this by specifying a wide range of observations, assumptions, alternatives, and probable consequences of certain choices. A refusal to acknowledge the benefits of a systematic and technological approach would be to minimize the importance of the scientific method and further contribute to the "mystique" mythology of the group. Dyer (1963) has stated:

> While it may never be possible or desirable to reduce training to standardized responses, if more trainers are to be developed and training improved, there must be more effort to ascertain what types of trainer style or strategy produce maximum learning. The approach suggested here is to observe and catalogue interventions to see what pattern maximizes certain measured learning goals. (p. 5)[1]

This seems to offer a rational data-based approach to improving the task-solving abilities of all groups.

In searching for ways to enhance personal and group growth, it would be relatively easy to misidentify an impulsive and spontaneous leadership response with the appropriate leadership response. We disagree with the view that spontaneity, "gut feeling," or "simply being oneself" is both necessary and sufficient for effective group leadership (Houts & Serber, 1972).

There are too many instances where being oneself in the group may conflict with the demands of being an effective group leader and doing what is best for the group. For example, a very critical, hostile statement concerning lack of competence, directed toward the group leader by a group member who is generally aggressive, may lead to a number of spontaneous responses by the leader. He may attempt to explain or defend certain policies or behaviors, or he may ignore the statement.

It is quite possible, however, that any of these spontaneous reactions of the group leader to this encounter may be a poor response in terms of promoting personal and/or group growth (Wile, 1972; Banet, 1974) and may actually lead to a loss of confidence in the group leader's abilities. This viewpoint is shared by Fiebert (1968), who states:

---

[1] Reproduced by special permission from *Human Relations Training News*, "An Inventory of Training Interventions," W. G. Dyer, p. 5, 1963, NTL Institute.

To the leader himself the group process is an involving challenge, one in which he attempts to respond selectively to a myriad of interpersonal cues in his effort to crystallize the basic themes of the group and its members. (p. 834)[2]

Even if a group leader acts naturally, like himself, there is no guarantee that an ability to choose an appropriate response will automatically emerge (C. R. Mill, 1972; Lazarus, 1971; Friedman, 1972; Lakin, 1972).

In addition, there are situations when it would be wise not to respond; in these instances the choice should be based on a rational decision rather than on a lack of knowledge. Fiebert (1968), in discussing this point, has further stated:

It seems to this author that with either rationale of group leadership, directive or spontaneous, the leader presents a value orientation which may be contrary to participants' expectations. The critical question is not which value orientation one offers but rather the pragmatic issue of which class of trainer interventions is more effective in group development. At this point it seems a philosophical question dissolves into an empirical one. (p. 837)[3]

This position does not imply that the group leader should stand apart from the group as an interested but detached observer. On the contrary, every group leader has certain personal value orientations that help influence the direction of group movement. If a group leader is to be himself in the group, it must be through the transmission of certain values and ethics to that group, not by substituting spontaneity for technical proficiency. This is not to deny the importance and expression of feelings, but rather to require a creative discipline that allows the group leader to function with the highest degree of effectiveness. The life style and emotional responsiveness of the group leader are probably the *sine qua non*, whose impact, however, may be deepened and broadened by the appropriate use of technological skills (Lieberman, Yalom, & Miles, 1973).

---

[2]Reprinted with permission of author and publisher from Fiebert, M. S. Sensitivity training: an analysis of trainer intervention and group process. PSYCHOLOGICAL REPORTS, 1968, 22, 829-838.

[3]See Footnote 2.

CHAPTER 1

History of Groups

HISTORICAL BACKGROUND

Groups directed at changing ideas, values, and behavior are certainly not new. However, the conscious use of group processes is a relatively new development which emerged during World War II.

The purpose of going back into history—back to the nineteenth century, the seventeenth century, the Renaissance—is to identify the major developments that indirectly paved the way for the current forms of group work.

Beginning Phase

Groups directed at changing ideas, values, and behavior are so numerous and so sketchily recorded that it is neither practical nor fruitful to examine any one group individually. Instead, broad examples illustrating two main approaches will be considered: the intellectual attitude of the Greek philosophers and the emotional orientation of the religious systems, especially those of the Eastern schools. These two are particularly important, not only because they involve groups of people, but because of the trains of thought that emerged from them. Obviously, the Greeks have had a profound influence on Western thought. Similarly, Eastern philosophy, though historically lacking direct influence on the West, is being rediscovered and is very much alive today.

THE GREEK PHILOSOPHERS

The Greeks believed that man and his relation to other men and to the universe could be understood. To them, life was not irrational, subject only to the whims of the gods. It was governed by natural laws which could be discovered and discussed. Man also behaved according to laws that it was thought were analogous to these natural laws. Hence there was a great premium placed on scrutinizing natural phenomena and on the charge to "know thyself."

However, the Greeks were far from content merely to observe the phenomena of nature. Empirical observation alone was considered misleading (Rossides, 1968). Rationality and caution were essential for the human mind to achieve complete understanding.

To some extent, this quest for knowledge was carried on in groups. Rouse (1957) has reported numerous examples of dialogues between two or more individuals in which there was feedback. Socrates would often be surrounded by a group of students examining questions concerning the Good, the Just, Temperance, Moderation, Love, etc. Plato founded a school, the Academie, whose purpose was the intellectual (philosophical) understanding of life.

Concern for Content

In the most general sense, the Greeks used the group approach to understand the universe and interpersonal relations. Content, not process, was the exclusive concern. Groups were formed more for the sake of expediency in learning from one who knew than the use of the group itself or the members themselves via their interactions as teaching agents. They were formed to test ideas rather than behavior. The style of the Greeks was to examine interpersonal relationships intellectually rather than experientially. Each member of the group would present his views, and when the positions of all were understood, improved interpersonal relationships would naturally follow in accord with the "Good." Differences in opinion could only result from faulty knowledge. These differences could be rectified by rationally examining them; when understood, they would vanish. Today, this is considered an unrealistic, optimistic attitude, especially in its disregard of emotional issues. The Greeks were interested in the universal aspects of a problem rather than in the unique qualities of specific incidents.

The Greek mode of inquiry was deduction. Knowledge was derived from broad generalities of thought into which specific observations could be fitted. Empirical knowledge, knowledge from observation, was considered faulty and incomplete, e.g., a straight stick that appeared bent when placed in water. The use of the mind to provide logical conclusions and synthesize perceptions was seen as a safeguard against misleading perceptions.

EARLY RELIGIOUS GROUPS

A good example of the emotional approach to effecting changes in interpersonal behavior can be found in churches and religious schools, but most especially in the monasteries. With the exception of Judaism, all the great faiths have had such schools. Representative schools are the Sangha (Buddhist monastic society), the Sufi orders of Islam, and the monasteries of Christianity.

Like the Greeks, the religious schools did not seek knowledge in the empirical sense, but rather knowledge of the self. Since man was seen as the microcosm of the universe, from this self-knowledge all other necessary knowledge would follow. However, man's salvation and the method of achieving good interpersonal relations was not through reason but, to a large degree, through control over the emotions, especially the negative emotions such as hate, greed, lust, avarice, and vanity.

Vanity—man's identification with himself and his faulty perception of what he is—was seen as the chief factor keeping man from true knowledge of self and thus from knowledge of all else. Vanity was also the cause of negative emotions. It was vanity that allowed man to be hurt, abused, misused, and insulted and that forced him to respond with emotions such as anger, hate, and indignation. Cox (1965) notes that the solution was found in observing and eliminating vanity and replacing it with the understanding that would allow a man to live harmoniously within the world. A large part of this understanding is based on the idea that the majority of man's problems are self-made. This idea is made very explicit in the Eastern religions, namely Buddhism, Hinduism, and Islam. It is also present in Christianity, e.g., in the concept of redemption as man's acceptance of God's offer to absolve him from the "natural consequences of his acts."

The goal of the monasteries was to replace hate with love. This was also one of Judaism's most important goals. One of the clearest examples of this is the Old Testament dictum "Thou shalt love thy neighbor as thyself" (Leviticus 19:18). As Buber (1937) points out, the correct translation of this verse is "Thou shalt act lovingly toward thy neighbor who is like thyself." In essence, love cannot be legislated; nevertheless, individuals can act lovingly. Another important dictum is that of Hillel which became known as the "Golden Rule": "That which is hateful to thee, thou shalt not do to another. This is all of the Law, its entirety. All the rest is commentary. Go and learn." In Buddhism the same negative emphasis is stressed: "Hurt not another with that which causes oneself pain." In Christianity, instead, it is the positive form of the Golden Rule that was given when Jesus instructed his disciples to "Do unto others what you would have them do unto you" (Matthew 7:12).

In Confucianism the same theme appears:

> The *li* are imposed on man from outside. But besides this outer mould we each still have within us something which we may take as a model for our conduct. If we "can find in ourselves a rule for similar treatment of others"; if we do to others what we wish for ourselves, and "do not do to others what we do not like ourselves," then the outpourings of our nature will of themselves be in accord with what is proper. Hence while there are still occasions on which one's own natural uprightness *(chih)* cannot be followed, there is none upon which *jen* (which is one's own uprightness conforming to what is proper) may not be acted

upon. This is why *jen* is the "all pervading" principle of Confucius' teaching and the center of his philosophy. (Fung, 1937, p. 72)

Admittedly, these are idealized goals that can never be reached completely. However, these goals would be achieved easier if a man were a member of a community that held love as a common goal, that placed a great premium on love and tolerance, and that took a very dim view of any outbreaks of opposite feelings. Hence the value of monasteries. This is not to say that monasteries provided the only environment where this type of behavior was possible, but they were generally more effective in doing so than were other institutions.

Judaic ideology resulted in official disapproval of monasticism. "Do not separate yourself from the community" was Hillel's rule, and possibly the Jewish manner of dealing with hostility made it unnecessary to do so. Judaism was akin to the Eastern religions and to Christianity in that it placed a great premium on love; however, the expression of negative feelings was not discouraged. Leviticus 19:17 shows how hostility is to be overcome: "Thou shalt not hate thy brother in thy heart, but surely, thou shalt rebuke thy neighbor." This is possibly one of the earliest recorded prescriptions for confrontation. Also, there was no injunction to love one's enemies in ancient Judaism. Having enemies or feeling hatred was not considered an ideal situation, but it was recognized that it would occur, and methods of dealing with it were prescribed.

In Exodus 23:5, it is written, "If thou shouldst meet thine enemy's ox or his ass going astray, thou shalt surely bring it back to him again. If thou seest the ass of him that hateth thee lying under its burden, thou shalt forbear to pass by him. Thou shalt surely release it with him." This verse appears to be teaching that even though one may entertain feelings of hatred and enmity, he is to treat his enemy civilly. Feelings were recognized and legitimized in ancient Judaism. People were not considered perfectible, and the Law was relied on to make up for the deficit.

The monasteries, however, made attempts toward self-perfection easier. For one thing, a teacher was available who provided the student with a living model of what was proper. Some schools were based solely on the task of attempting to imitate the teacher in everything he did (Cox, 1965). However, many monasteries were extremely rigorous. Their rationale was that demanding almost impossible feats would strengthen the individual. Many practices of Christian and especially Buddhist and Sufi monasteries reflected this idea. There was a rigorous schedule, which included continuous prayer and study, followed by physical work in the fields. During this the individual could not "break"; disobeying, complaining, and expressing anger were not allowed.

However, hard work was not the most demanding aspect of some of the strictest schools. Situations were often deliberately devised in which it was almost impossible for a man to maintain a loving and tolerant attitude (Cox, 1965). For example, the job of one monk might be to hoe beans and not get angry, no matter what occurred. Another monk would be instructed to do everything he could to bring out hostility in the first monk. In this type of environment the only alternative to learning to love your neighbor was to leave.

Comparison with Laboratory Training

When the modern approach to groups, as represented by laboratory training, is compared with that of the monasteries, it is seen that both have the philosophy that a controlled, total environment helps to effect behavior changes. However, laboratory training and other current group methods place great emphasis on the value of feedback, whereas in some of the stricter religious schools, the only feedback one received was to "leave." In fact, "work schools" were explicit about not giving feedback. In these schools a new student might be told, "You are the cook; fix all the meals, clean up, and do not talk." The leader in the monasteries was in control; his word was law, and one simply did not question it. By contrast, the T-group leader actively strives not to be authoritarian. He tries to create an environment in which group members take responsibility for their own actions. Leadership then becomes distributive.

Comparison of the treatment of an individual's feelings also shows a cleavage between the two orientations. In the T-group, encounter, and growth types of groups, the expression of feelings is not only allowed, it is encouraged. The religious work groups were just the opposite. There was no place for the expression of individual feelings. According to Conze (1959a), this stemmed from the rationale that feelings were illusionary and therefore unworthy of attention. There was also the corollary that the expression of feelings, especially negative ones, tended to reinforce the individual's illusions and his identification with them. This is strongly opposed to the current group approaches that view the expression of feelings as leading to increased spontaneity, clarification, and communication, as well as to congruence within the individual members and the group as a whole.

IMPLICATIONS OF THE EMERGENCE OF TRADE

Groups developed as a result of a shift in life style from a rural, agrarian society to an industrial one. While an interdependence has always existed among men, the organization of groups now became formalized. The emergence of guilds, trades, and professional groups dramatized the necessity of intergroup cooperation. The focus gradually moved from individuals within a group to the group itself.

This change did not occur overnight. The trend toward modern industrialism had its roots in the blossoming trade and commerce of the Renaissance. At that time, according to Cassirer (1954), the general mood was based on a humanistic world view that glorified man. To the Renaissance man, it was the creative genius of the individual that was important rather than the external orientations of the natural or supernatural world. This latter view had dominated the Middle Ages; with the dawn of the Renaissance it was as if man had been released, rediscovered, and freed. The focus was not on the group, unless the group was an abstraction of mankind as a whole.

During this age the emphasis was on trade, with the economic corollary that if goods are to be manufactured and sold, people must work to produce, sell, and buy. The process leading to the building of the factories of the Industrial Revolution was a gradual one, but one that was constantly expanding and evolving.

The main outcome was that people were drawn into closer and closer proximity because of the economic necessity for individuals to gather together to produce goods. An excellent example can be seen in the almost lemming-like migration to the budding factory towns of the late 1800's. However, relationships did not end with the association within the work group. Other special-purpose groups evolved to fill the needs of recreation, religion, education, service, etc. Then, as now, these provided the individual with a series of diverse and often conflicting roles, and an increasing identification of self as a part of a larger societal unit. Then, too, there were the more subtle group ties that further defined the individual, giving him added identification within the group framework, as well as limiting and delimiting his very life style, e.g., ethnic groups, class groups, geographical groups.

Due to the pressures of time, space, and proximity, society has evolved into a group society. The individual can no longer see himself only as an individual, isolated and independent; he must view himself in terms of his relationship to and membership in a series of life groups: friends, classmates, colleagues, church members, co-workers, family, political parties, etc. A group seems to have developed for every human interest or need. Since the individual must exist and operate within a group context, interpersonal relationships have become important as necessary subjects of research and practice.

PHILOSOPHICAL FOUNDATION OF GROUPS

As an increasing number of people began to migrate to cities and towns, a concurrent interest in groups and in the knowledge and theory of groups developed. An early example that clearly indicates this trend was the social philosophy of the British Empiricists of the seventeenth and eighteenth centuries.

One of the main controversies of that period was the question of whether ideas were innate or whether they were learned through early experience. The British Empiricists favored the latter view. Thus, from the idea that man was born as a blank tablet, or *tabula rasa*, as John Locke (1894) contended, it was just a short theoretical step for the Empiricist to see the great impact of society on the individual. Then it was but another short step for him to question the whole concept of what constitutes a good society.

Hobbes (1651/1958) was the first of the Empiricists to equate social structure with utility to the individual. However, he made it clear that he did not consider individualism to be compatible with social stability and harmony. It was individualism, he proposed, that gave rise to conflicting interests, conflicting interests being the primary concern of social science. Thus Hobbes recommended that men obtain knowledge by analyzing society the same way they analyzed nature, through the inductive-mathematical-mechanistic method modeled primarily after Newtonian physics. Man was to be studied as the microcosm of the macrocosm of the state.

To further reduce the problem of conflicting interests, Hobbes espoused an absolute state to counterbalance the absolute ego of man. Without government, Hobbes said, "the life of man is solitary, poor, nasty, brutish, and short" (1651/1958, p. 85). Man condescended to form the state only because it was necessary to keep him from killing and being killed. This doctrine of enlightened selfishness, while pessimistic, focused on man and his relation to society. Hobbes not only acknowledged man's negative characteristics but saw them as the driving force of man's submission to government.

Most of the other Empiricists disliked Hobbes. One of these, Locke, was strongly opposed to Hobbes's view that the natural state of man was one of selfishness and war (J. Locke, 1894). Locke held that the original state of man was neither depravity nor goodness, but rather a condition of perfect freedom and equality. He believed, as Aristotle had, that the individual entered the world as a blank tablet.

> Let us suppose the mind to be, as we say, white paper, void of all characters, without any ideas:—How comes it to be furnished? . . . To this I answer, in one word, from EXPERIENCE. (p. 121)

This assumption has far-reaching implications for Locke's social theory. He stated that poor environmental and social conditions were responsible for human misery. It was society's responsibility to provide men with a good experience, and it was up to men to establish a society that could achieve this. Society, said Locke, should be an impartial judge, whose main function is to work for the good of all concerned. Since it is nearly impossible to reach a unanimous decision, it is up to the individual to submit to the will of the majority, once the correct society is established.

Obviously Hobbes and Locke were spokesmen of two very different doctrines. According to Frost (1962), Hobbes's main interest lay in the philosophical justification of the monarchy and rule by divine right, whereas Locke's thrust was to justify a doctrine of political freedom. He opposed rule by divine right and maintained that the power of the state always rests with the people. Both men were wrestling with the idea of the rights of members of a group. Hobbes was pessimistic about the natural state of man, and Locke fairly neutral.

A third philosopher of this period, Rousseau (1762/1952), went to the opposite extreme of unbounded optimism. Man, he felt, if allowed to develop according to his natural inclinations, would automatically become a harmonious and healthy individual. It was poor education and the rigid restrictions placed on children by adult society that corrupted them and caused problems.

Rousseau's solution was to alter child-rearing practices and to change society. He advocated that people look "back to nature" as much as possible. Above all, children should be allowed to develop freely and naturally. Whatever they wanted to do was intrinsically correct. Muuss (1962) cites Rousseau as one of the strongest exponents of educational individualism.

Rousseau's ideas concerning society strongly paralleled his thoughts on child rearing. Here again he advocated freedom above all else. He thought that the best plan would be to rule out even representative government and replace it with direct government by all the people governed. This was where true sovereignty lay. Democracy (government by representation) could be as bad as monarchy. Responsible government was possible only if men were wise, just, and educated—hence his stress on proper child rearing.

> The bounds of possibility in moral matters are less narrow than we imagine: it is our weaknesses, our vices, our prejudices that confine them. Base souls have no belief in great men; vile slaves smile in mockery at the name of liberty. (Rousseau, 1762/1952, p. 420)

This quotation contains the seeds of theoretical concepts such as the self-concept of Rogers (1951) and the faulty basic assumptions of Ellis (1969a). Rousseau was describing the negative conditions that must be removed if learning and change are to take place.

For Locke, as well as the other Empiricists, the most important aspect of humanity was reason; for Rousseau it was feeling. Hume, an associate of Rousseau's, developed an interesting concept that has blossomed in the sensory-awareness groups of today: "The most lively thought is still inferior to the dullest sensation" (1748/1952, p. 455). In other words, the recall of the sensation is at least one step removed from the feeling itself.

Two other outstanding philosophers of this time, who, like Rousseau, were not among the British Empiricists but whose ideas are nevertheless pertinent to the development of current approaches to groups, were James Mill (1869) and his son, John Stuart Mill (1861/1952). J. Mill has been called the Utilitarian philosopher. The basic idea of the Utilitarians is summed up in the maxim "the greatest good for the greatest number."

Mill believed that people are ruled by self-interest, and that social, political, and legal institutions should strive to avoid pain and achieve pleasure for the greatest number possible. Obviously departing from Hobbes, Mill contended, as did Locke and Rousseau, that social institutions not only should be made for the people, but should be beneficial for them. He was raising the question of the state's responsibility to the individual or the group's responsibility to its members.

J. S. Mill's concept that the whole is greater than the sum of its parts has relevance for the rationale of groups. The group is somehow more than merely the summation of its individual members.

The social philosophers of the seventeenth and eighteenth centuries were important in two respects. First, some of their specific ideas had significant effects on later thought. (A case in point is the example of the similarity between the ideas of J. S. Mill and Durkheim [1938].) Even more important, however, is their attitude, their focus on environment. This view had a heavy impact on social philosophers, especially in terms of the important responsibility of society to its members. Such an orientation was the basis from which a science of society evolved. In assessing the quality of government, or group, Mill was concerned with the group's responsibility to the individual.

> We may consider, then, as one criterion of the goodness of a government, the degree in which it tends to increase the sum of good qualities in the governed, collectively and individually; since, besides that their well being is the sole object of government, their good qualities supply the moving force which works the machinery. (J. S. Mill, 1861/1952, p. 337)

Mill also stated that in determining what is in a man's best interest "you must know the cast of his habitual feelings and thoughts" (1861/1952, p. 367).

EVOLUTION AND ITS IMPACT ON SOCIETY

The publication of Darwin's *Origin of the Species* in 1859 was of momentous influence. It reinforced and supported the idea of progress through change. With his concern for the species as a whole, Darwin helped turn attention to the phenomenon of the group. Moreover, *Origin of the Species* highlighted the importance and power of the environment and the necessity of being adaptable to changes within it.

> Hence, as more individuals are produced than can possibly survive, there must in every case be a struggle for existence, either one individual with another of the same species, or with individuals of distinct species or with the physical conditions of life. (1859/1952, p. 32)

The implications of this attitude for an expanding industrial society are obvious and notable. Like Protestantism, the evolution theory helped to support the capitalistic ethic by further implanting the acceptance of competition as a social virtue. Also the concept of evolution through change and struggle became linked with the idea of progress and a sense of social destiny. Society was moving toward a higher level of increased efficiency. Optimism and motivation were among the salient features of the Victorian creed, whose cry could be described as "Success is just around the corner; keep trying and you will succeed." Byron's *Childe Harold's Pilgrimage* (1840) is a good example of how the literature of the period reflected this viewpoint.

Middle Phase

SOCIOLOGY: A SCIENCE OF GROUPS

During the rise of industrialism, as man was drawn into closer contact with other men and became interdependent in his relationships, a need developed for an explicit knowledge of interpersonal relations to cope with the emerging group society. Sociology developed. It was a separate discipline, a science in its own right, concurrent with the boom of industrialism. This development occurred between 1830 and 1842 with the publication of Comte's *Cours de philosophie positive* (1842/1907-08). Though Comte did not create sociology, he did give it a name and a separate place in the social sciences.

What Comte attempted to do with his new science was to extend to history and politics the positive and objective methods of the natural sciences. Positivism is knowledge based on observable scientific facts and their relation to each other and to natural law. It rejects speculation and vehemently outlaws teleological inquiry. Comte believed that the earlier and more elementary sciences, particularly chemistry and physics, had given man control over nature. Sociology was to give man control over himself (Park & Burgess, 1969).

Despite all his talk about social control and—by extension—social change, the thrust of Comte was mainly philosophical and static in nature (Bonner, 1959). His work featured much description and classification, but the society he described was for the most part a static one. Another early spokesman of sociology, Spencer (1899), also dealt with a static society. He believed that society evolved but only according to fixed laws. Any efforts to cause change were not only useless, but detrimental. His idea of change left little room for social control.

During this period, however, steps were being made toward developing a more dynamic sociology. One of the leaders of this development was the American sociologist Ward. In 1883 Ward published his *Dynamic Sociology*. One of the basic ideas Ward propounded was the concept of social telesis— society as a self-directing whole. Social control and social change were indeed possible; in fact, Ward attempted to lay the groundwork for effective social planning.

Up to this point the emphasis had been placed on society as a whole. In Durkheim, we find one of the earliest students of group process. Durkheim's idea of collective determinism held great implications for sociology and, later, social psychology. His thesis was that human behavior can be understood only by knowing the collective structures of the group, its "representations collectives" (1938). These are the results of the union of individuals into groups and represent the common experiences of group members. Durkheim was very emphatic that the process was not an additive one. The whole is definitely different from, and something more than, the sum of the parts;

i.e., a group experience is more than what individual members could have experienced separately. Opposing the concept of a "group mind," however, are critics such as Allport (1924, 1927).

This theory is probably Durkheim's most relevant sociological contribution. However, it should be mentioned that he was a formidable figure in the overall history of sociology. According to Rossides (1968), Durkheim's *The Rules of Sociological Method* (1938) enumerated many of the basic ideas of the modern sociological approach, as well as advocated the functional method and techniques for analyzing social processes. Durkheim frequently emphasized the importance of viewing social phenomena as unique from psychological or other naturalistic orientations.

Another important figure was Simmel (1903, 1950). He viewed society as interaction and interaction as the proper field of sociological inquiry. Society was the pattern of interacting and functional relationships that bound individuals into a unified whole. This type of thinking reveals the beginnings of the concept of "belongingness" and "inclusion" (Bonner, 1959), which plays an integral part in group dynamics. Simmel also did work in the areas of leadership, conflict, and social boundary, all of which are relevant to current group research.

The final figure to be considered is Cooley (1918). He is important because of his work with the primary group. Cooley believed that social processes and social control have their origin in the small face-to-face primary group. It is in the primary group that the individual's personality is developed, that he learns to assume roles, and that he establishes and incorporates group norms. It is also in the primary group that expressions of intimacy and identification are learned and fostered. All of these issues are important, but especially significant is Cooley's emphasis on the value of the face-to-face group.

This brief, selective history of the development of modern sociology reveals the emergence of several sociological trends. There has been a shift in emphasis from society (Comte, Spencer, and Ward) to group processes per se (Durkheim's "representations collectives" and Simmel's interactionalism) to processes within the primary group (Cooley). In the latter cases, it is difficult to determine whether sociology or social psychology is being studied. Increasingly, however, the focus has been on smaller groups rather than on society as a whole. In addition, attempts to study and understand group processes have significantly increased.

THE MEDICAL MODEL EMERGES

The next step in the development of the group's potential is its use for therapeutic purposes. One of the most crucial events in this process was the emergence of the medical model.

There have been three orientations of thought concerning the cause and cure of mental illness. The oldest idea was that a disturbed individual was possessed by a spirit that was either good or evil, depending on the actions of the possessed person. Treatment centered around the exorcism of the spirit. Methods varied from prayer and the laying-on of hands to torture and execution. One early way of dealing with the problem was to make a hole in the skull of the patient, enabling the demon to escape. This method, called trephining, was used as far back as the Stone Age. From the relics that have been found, it is apparent that some individuals survived the operation and lived for many years after it (Coleman, 1964).

Variations of the demonology theory existed from the earliest extant records to the sixteenth century. The Greeks were a notable exception. Although not completely free from the idea that mental illness is to be blamed on the supernatural, the Greeks of the Golden Age seem to have felt that persons who suffered from mental disturbances were not being divinely punished nor deserving of punishment by man. In the main, kindness and tolerance were strongly recommended. For example, Plato (c. 348 B. C./1960) said:

> Someone may commit an act when mad or afflicted with disease . . . let him simply pay for the damage; and let him be exempt from other punishment.

In the Middle Ages, once again, the mentally ill were regarded as being possessed by demons. At first, treatment was rather gentle—mainly prayer, purgatives, and holy water. Later, exorcism became prevalent. The theory developed that if the body were made an extremely uncomfortable habitat, perhaps the demon would give up and leave. Torture was considered an effective means of achieving this end, and, according to Coleman (1964), it appears that exorcisers spared no efforts in their unyielding pursuit of evil spirits.

In the fifteenth and sixteenth centuries, things became worse. People were no longer the unwilling victims of evil spirits; instead, they were viewed as the willing accomplices of Satan. Treatment no longer centered around the cure but around punishment.

As the Age of Reason dawned, the "demon model" was gradually replaced by the "animal model." Rational thought was the only thing that separated men from animals. Therefore, if a man lost his ability to function rationally, he was no more than an animal. While patients were no longer tortured for having demons, the institutions into which they were placed had little advantage over witch hunts except that the ill were allowed to live —chained to a wall in a dungeon or strapped to a bed. With very few exceptions, e.g., Gheel Shrine in Belgium, asylums of the period were a curious cross between a prison and a zoo. According to Coleman (1964), for a penny the public could view some of the more interesting patients.

Slowly this inhumane approach began to change. One of the most dramatic pleas for humanitarian treatment of the mentally ill was made by Philippe Pinel. In 1792, Pinel was placed in charge of La Bicetre, a large hospital in Paris for the mentally ill. Convinced that the inmates of La Bicetre were neither wicked nor bad but, rather, were sick people deserving of kindness and consideration, Pinel ordered that all patients be released from their chains. Dungeons were replaced by sunny rooms; exercising in the fresh air was permitted. Needless to say, the positive effect was staggering.

Deplorable conditions in all hospitals were not rectified immediately. Nevertheless, the humanitarian treatment of the mentally ill as "sick" rather than as "bad" was well on its way. In this climate a therapeutic, curing attitude grew; the emphasis was on helping the disturbed and finding the means of doing so (Morgan & King, 1966).

The medical model encouraged the use of rational investigation to discover the underlying causes of illnesses. Once this idea was accepted, man began to look for quicker, more efficient means of treating more people within a given time period. This, of course, helped lay the foundation for the emergence of group treatment. It is in this tradition that men like Freud and later psychologists developed as therapists.

SOME DEVELOPMENTS IN PSYCHOLOGY

Shortly after sociology emerged as a separate discipline, so did psychology. Wundt is given credit for establishing the first experimental laboratory at Leipzig in 1879; however, the date has been contested, and according to Watson (1968), credit is given to William James's laboratory at Harvard. In any case, psychology was on its way.

The thrust of early psychology, with its extreme, experimental orientation, was very different from the psychology of today. The first psychologists were mainly interested in sensation and perception. Individual difference was not considered to be a particularly legitimate field of inquiry, although it began to come into its own with the rise of the emphasis on testing in the early part of the twentieth century.

World War II gave greater impetus to the testing orientation and prompted the development of the psychologist from an experimenter and tester to a therapist. Demands for therapeutic aid increased. There were not enough psychiatrists to meet the need, and traditional, individual psychotherapy was not practical in terms of the numbers of people who needed help. After the war there continued to be a great need for therapists, in which capacity psychologists have come to serve in significantly increasing numbers.

Forty years before the advent of group dynamics, Triplett (1897) did research with bicycle riders, in which he demonstrated that the riders' speeds were significantly greater when they were paced with other riders. This interest in the effect of a group on the performance of an individual was furthered by Mayer (1903), who found that the work of school children was generally superior when tasks were performed in groups rather than in isolation. Meumann (1913), also working with school children, found that retention of memorized material was greater when children worked in groups.

From these beginnings, and many other examples like them (Bonner, 1959), social psychology emerged as a separate branch within psychology. Consequently, psychology became directly involved with the whole area of the dynamics of groups.

Current Phase

During the Victorian era and the age of technology, there was the widespread belief that life was getting better and easier as man moved to newer and greater achievements. But this optimism was shattered by two world wars and a depression in a single generation.

Theory is influenced by history and by practicality. The economic factor of rehabilitating men and helping them return to productive lives played a decisive role in the blending of the values of humanism and the values of pragmatism needed to design and develop the group approach.

THE BEGINNING OF GROUP THERAPY

The group approach provides an opportunity for creating an authentic parallel to some of the life situations with which the individual has to deal. The group becomes a microcosm of "life on the outside" and thus provides an effective training and testing ground within a realistic, controlled, and supervised environment. Also, there is the possibility of people with similar problems learning from and helping one another. This involves an area of group dynamics, about which there is still much to be discovered. To what extent the group experience produces immediate change and is applicable to outside situations is the subject of current research (Horwitz, 1973; Lazarus, 1971; Lieberman, Yalom, & Miles, 1973).

There are several economic advantages to group therapy. It is possible for one therapist to serve more people than was possible in the traditional individual-therapy situation. Many people who would ordinarily be unable to afford individual therapy can afford group therapy.

Group psychotherapy is more than a type of therapy and more than a methodology. It is a movement in the history of the healing arts and sciences. It has multiple origins, among which are several major influencing forces:

1. the observation that hospitalized patients could be helped by one another as well as by the professional staff (Harris & Joseph, 1973; Powdermaker & Frank, 1953);

2. the post-World War II crisis of too many patients and not enough therapists (Corsini, 1957);

3. the greater acceptability of groups in society, notably influenced by the increasing sense of psychological isolation produced by an advanced technological society (Corsini, 1957);

4. the growing concern with the social aspects of disease—the interpersonal dimension of behavior (Luchins, 1964).

Regardless of the specific reasons for its growth and development, group psychotherapy showed a tremendous growth after World War II. Corsini (1957) published the following account of the articles, books, and theses involving group therapy:

Period	No. of Titles
1906-1910	11
1911-1915	3
1916-1920	5
1921-1925	4
1926-1930	11
1931-1935	20
1936-1940	69
1941-1945	203
1946-1950	536
1951-1955	879

(p. 8)[1]

Despite its short direct history, group psychotherapy has a rather long, indirect past. Some authors cite the healing temple of Epidaurus (600 B.C. to 200 A.D.) as one of the origins, as well as day-long Greek dramas and medieval morality plays (Rosenbaum, 1965). An unusual but interesting reference is given to the Marquis de Sade. While he was in prison he wrote and directed plays through which the other prisoners could act out their feelings. These plays were said to have had a therapeutic effect upon the prison population (Corsini, 1957).

Significant Influences

A number of individuals have significantly influenced the development of group psychotherapy. None can claim the title of its unequivocal father. Mesmer is often cited as the founder of modern group therapy. Klapman (1946) gives credit to Pratt; Bierer (1948) gives the honor to Pratt and Adler jointly; Meiers (1945), to Pratt and Moreno, who gave the field its name, "group psychotherapy," in 1932. The six most often cited as founders of the group psychotherapy movement are Pratt, Adler, Moreno, Burrow, Lazell, and Marsh.

---

[1]From R. J. Corsini, *Methods of Group Psychotherapy*. New York: McGraw-Hill, 1957. Reprinted by permission.

The contribution of Freud must not be overlooked. He may well have been the first to use group analysis (if two or more people are considered a group) and possibly the first to use groups in systematic therapeutic treatment (E. Jones, 1953).

In relating group psychology to the analysis of the Ego, Freud (1921/1952) theorized that the social instinct was not "a special instinct, that is not further reducible" (p. 664), but occurs "in a narrower circle, such as that of the family" (p. 664). Freud was concerned with treating the individual and understanding impinging factors such as "the group mind" as dealt with by LeBon (1896), McDougall (1920), and others. Freud observed that when an assessed individual participated in a group, his behavior often changed. This change occurred as the person assumed the characteristics of a group member, e.g., becoming aggressive by identifying with the leader. Freud dealt with such large-group phenomena as identification, contagion, and suggestion as causal factors.

> We started from the fundamental fact that an individual in a group is subjected through its influence to what is often a profound alteration in his mental activity. His emotions become extraordinarily intensified, while his intellectual ability becomes markedly reduced, both processes being evidently in the direction of an approximation to the other individuals in the group; and this result can only be reached by the removal of those inhibitions upon his instincts which are peculiar to each individual, and by his resigning those expressions of his inclinations which are especially his own. We have heard that these often unwelcome consequences are to some extent at least prevented by a higher "organization" of the group; but this does not contradict the fundamental fact of group psychology—the two theses as to the intensification of the emotions and the inhibition of the intellect in primitive groups. Our interest is now directed to discovering the psychological explanation of this mental change which is experienced by the individual in a group. (Freud, 1921/1952, p. 672)

In its development, group therapy has gone through several stages. Corsini and Moreno have each suggested a division:

Origins	-1899
Pioneer	1900-1930
Modern	1931-Present
	(Corsini, 1957, p. 9)[2]
1910-1945 Period of Discovery	
1945-1963 Period of Controversy and Growth	
1963-Present Period of Integration	
	(Moreno, 1963, p. 129)[3]

---

[2]See Footnote 1.

[3]From GROUP PSYCHOTHERAPY, Vol. XVI, September 1963, J. L. Moreno, M.D., Editor, Beacon House Inc., Beacon, N.Y., Publisher. Reprinted by permission.

A major contention of the historians of the group psychotherapy movement is that the group has characteristics that are unique and need to be considered independently from the traditional individual-therapy model. To clarify this distinction Corsini gives the descriptions for four different types of therapeutic organizations:
1. Autonomous therapy is a system of self-improvement;
2. "Pair" is typically called individual therapy, one therapist and one patient;
3. "Small-group" therapy is usually limited to five or twenty members, but includes the range of three to fifty;
4. "Large groups" include a form of therapy called milieu therapy, a program for an entire community. (Corsini, 1957, p. 4)[4]

When referring to small-group therapy, most people use the term "group psychotherapy." Corsini describes what happens in these groups as

processes occurring in formally protected groups and calculated to attain rapid ameliorations in personality and behavior of individual members through specific and controlled group interactions. (Corsini, 1957, p. 5)[5]

Although he did not start to use groups for therapy, Pratt, a Boston internist, had his tubercular patients meet in groups for weekly lectures on hygiene. Through these group lectures, he noticed a tremendous boost in the morale of the patients and a sense of camaraderie; his patients had seemed to find a "common bond in a common disease" (Pratt, 1949).

Lazell (1921) did not publish any papers on group work until 1921. However, he claimed to have used group methods for several years. Lazell's method was lectures to his patients, followed by discussion periods.

Marsh (1931) did not publish any accounts of his group work until 1931, but claimed to have used groups since 1909. His method was to communicate, via loudspeakers, to the entire hospital population. This was an early form of milieu therapy (Kadis et al., 1963). Marsh openly advocated the use of any technique that obtained results (Mullan & Rosenbaum, 1962). His motto was "By the crowd they have been broken; by the crowd shall they be healed" (Marsh, 1931, p. 328).

Adler (1964) was the first therapist to place primary emphasis on interpersonal relationships: "Interaction is the key . . . the yardstick of social functioning." He had originally used individual therapy but then began to make use of interaction as a technique for training purposes. Instead of the disruptive effect he expected, he found that the members benefited from the presence of others.

Probably the most important individual in the history of group psychotherapy was Moreno. While in medical school in Vienna, Moreno experimented with group methods to help displaced persons, children, and

---
[4]See Footnote 1.
[5]See Footnote 1.

prostitutes (Rosenbaum, 1965). It was his theory that man is spontaneous by nature and that he is creative. Sickness is the loss of this ability to be creative, and the purpose of the group is to help members find and rediscover their lost spontaneity in its natural habitat—in groups (Moreno, 1952). Moreno stated that man is "existentially stuck." Living in groups is a matter of survival; there is no alternative to living in groups. Moreno believed that group therapy goes on "whether by scientific means or not" and that unorganized group psychotherapy can be improved by scientific methods (1959b).

An important aspect of Moreno's contribution is that he provided a theory to account for the structures of the groups with which he worked. This theory of sociometry presented an organized method of exploring the process of interaction. This method in turn expanded the realm of investigation. Dreikurs described the implications of this approach:

> The sphere of application is as wide as life itself. There is nothing that occurs between people that cannot be explored. (1955, p. 29)

In 1931 Moreno founded the first journal devoted to groups, *Impromptu*. This journal was followed in 1937 by the journal *Sociometry*, and in 1947 the first issue of *Sociatry* appeared. It is currently published as *Group Psychotherapy*. Moreno was truly the "indefatigable exponent of the group therapeutic movement" (Corsini, 1957, p. 15).

Burrow (1953) disagreed with Freud and argued that individuals, per se, did not really exist. Groups, according to Burrow, were the key that unlocked patient resistance to the treatment process. By working with others in a group situation, the patient discovered that his problem was not unique; others had similar problems. This revelation alleviated the need for secrecy and isolation.

Corsini (1957) mentions over fifty individuals who have made significant contributions to group psychotherapy.

Schilder (1951a, 1951b, 1951c) was a notable whose wide influence and enthusiasm were of tremendous importance to the growing field. As early as 1934 he was working with groups at Bellevue Hospital in New York City (Schilder, 1936, 1939). He advocated that the therapist must be willing to express his own ideology, capable of expressing it, and able to justify it to the group.

Wender (1936) was reportedly the first therapist to use group therapy in conjunction with individual therapy (Mullan & Rosenbaum, 1962). Although he offered no elaborate explanations, he did comment that hospitalized patients had a greater drive to recover and did in fact get better faster when participating in groups.

For thirty years Wolf (1949) has been an integral part of the group-therapy approach. He was influenced by Schilder and Wender and was reportedly among the first to apply standard analytic techniques to groups (Kadis et al., 1963). He maintains that he does not treat groups, he treats individuals in interaction (Rosenbaum, 1965). He adopted this approach to make treatment available to needy people with lower incomes.

One of the outstanding figures of the group-therapy movement has been Slavson (1947, 1950, 1964). In 1943 he was one of the founders of the Group Psychotherapy Association. He introduced a type of therapy known as activity group therapy. Activity therapy is a situationally based orientation that stresses the acting-out of conflicts. Kadis et al. (1963) credit Slavson with being the strongest driving force in the analytic approach to group therapy. Perhaps the greatest influence he has had was his establishment of a therapeutic foundation for the positive emotional attachments of patients to the therapist and to each other.

Bach (1954, 1957) developed intensive group procedures. His work was reportedly the first attempt to do group work at the level and intensity of individual therapy (Corsini, 1957).

In Great Britain, Bieri (1955) introduced group methods in the mental hospitals. Like Slavson and Moreno, Bieri believed that treatment should be a situational approach. He made the living experience much closer to the outside world by creating a social club. The social club changed the patient from object to subject. Bieri felt that this aided treatment in that it created independent, active, and self-deciding behaviors. Certainly, the social atmosphere was closer to the "real" world as opposed to the typical hospital setting. These clubs were a forerunner of the half-way house, a pause on the road before returning to full community membership (Rosenbaum, 1965).

Another of the significant figures in the group movement is Foulkes. He was a founder of the Group Analytic Society. Foulkes believed that the group is the basis for the study and improvement of human relationships. Since man spends most of his time in a community and man in a community is the major problem of our time, group therapy is the most practical approach (Foulkes & Anthony, 1965). Among Foulkes's important contributions is the concept of design, as summed up by Kadis et al. (1963):

> We have to know what we are actually doing—then we can understand the result of what we are doing. Devise simple situations and stick to them. (p. 15)

Foulkes, like Slavson, advocated the control of group composition according to age and I. Q.

MODIFICATIONS IN GROUP THERAPY

One of the first modifications of the group process was family therapy. Dreikurs, an Adlerian, introduced family counseling in this country (1955, 1967; Dreikurs et al., 1959). He proposed the use of groups as an aid in the treatment of alcoholics, and he was among the first to use groups in private practice. Dreikurs was also one of the first to advocate the use of multiple therapy (1955).

Rogers (1942) and some of his students used a nondirective approach in working with groups. Gordon (1955, 1970) and Hobbs (1949, 1955) added this dimension to the client-centered approach. Although the nondirective approach is just one type of therapy, its widespread use warrants additional attention.

Since its inception, the group approach has been used in many contexts. Some of these involved the treatment of military prisoners (Lipkin, 1948); prison systems (Kassebaum, Ward, & Wilner, 1971; McCorkle, Elias, & Bixby, 1958; Stephenson & Scarpitti, 1974); work with severely disturbed children (Polansky, Lippitt, & Redl, 1950); and milieu therapy (Corsini, 1957). Ackerman (1945) used groups in a variety of settings, e.g., with children, with adults, and with families (see also Ginott, 1961, and Stanford, 1973).

Conjoint family therapy, usually associated with Satir (1964), is a continual expansion and modification of Dreikurs' approach as evidenced in works of Burton (1972), Haley (1963, 1972), Jackson (1959), Sager and Kaplan (1972), and Warkentin (1969).

Wolpe and Lazarus (1966) emphasized the need for locating specific symptoms and using reciprocal inhibition techniques in a group setting when desensitizing phobias. Lazarus (1971) has since adopted a broad spectrum approach, giving emphasis to six modalities. He employs the group as an adjunct to individual therapy.

GROUP THERAPY: EVOLUTION OF THEORY

Moreno aptly called the development of group therapy the third revolution in psychiatry (1959b). The first revolution removed the psychotic from the care of nonmedical practitioners. The second revolution, the Freudian, created an alliance between psychiatry and nonmedical professional people. The aim was to help the large number of neurotics seeking therapy. The third revolution took into account the harmful influences of social forces on mental health and utilized their helpful influences in the therapeutic milieu.

The group movement places importance on the concept of man as a goal-seeking organism. Dreikurs (1955, pp. 30-33) enumerates three ways that the group can aid goal-oriented behavior.

1. A group setting permits experimentation with interactions in the personality make up of each individual. It helps dispel the air of "emotional isolation" and the mutual mistrust that keeps people at a distance.

2. Group therapists have had to accept the fact that therapy does "affect the patient's scheme of values." The focus and realization of this fact speeds the goal-directed efforts of the individual.

3. Group procedures incorporate new methodologies. "A proving ground for various theories," group situations can be recreated, individual therapy

cannot. The group is likely to set up and precipitate problems like those encountered in the real world.

Group treatment has become an important tool in the area of preventive mental health. Many programs have been designed for people with problems of obesity, gastrointestinal disorders, etc. A new major program is the treatment of the parents of handicapped and mentally retarded children (Berkovitz, 1972; Kadis et al., 1963).

Today, training and transitional groups dealing with situational crises such as courtship, marriage, divorce (Krantzler, 1973), death, delinquency, childbirth, child rearing (Dreikurs, 1964; Gordon, 1970), the emotionally disturbed (Rose, 1972), unemployment, and aging, are in evidence. Many of these programs are affiliated with church or social services. Still other groups have emerged to deal with long-term concerns such as isolation, alienation, and stresses on the nuclear family.

Massarik (1972) gives a partial list of the "plethora" of current group approaches. These approaches illustrate the variety of current trends in the group movement.

T-groups	Gestalt groups
sensitivity training groups	bio-energetic groups
recovery groups	Weight Watchers
Alcoholics Anonymous	integrity groups
survival groups	theatre games
Synanon	graphic groups
nude encounter groups	massage experiences
human interaction groups	truth groups
sensory awareness groups	psychological karate
marathons	personal growth labs
psychodrama	human potential groups
sociodrama	confrontation groups
transactional analysis	self-management groups
inquiry groups	Primal therapy groups
conflict-management labs	humanistic "psychotherapy"
life-planning labs	Kraftig Gefuhl
psychosynthesis	Zen
meditation	T'ai Chi
movement groups	yoga
alternate life style labs	(Massarik, 1972, pp. 68-69)

Group dynamics has become an important issue in the theory of group therapy. Some practitioners such as Foulkes and Anthony (1965), Frank (1957), Bach (1957), and Durkin (1957) advocate and use group dynamics in their groups. Others like Slavson, Wolf, and Schwartz say that group dynamics is fine in schools or clubs, but not in therapy (Kadis et al., 1963).

Foulkes and his colleagues agree that each person needs to look at the group gestalt, which includes its dynamics. Every event does involve all the members of the group; the group is the best place to work on interpersonal as well as intrapersonal issues. "Each relationship is developed and is constantly influenced by the existence and pressures of the patient's other relationships" (Kadis et al., 1963, p. 22). All groups follow a "sociogenic law" (Moreno, 1963), which states that higher group forms always proceed from simpler forms, a situation that facilitates therapy (Banet, 1974; Mills, 1967).

Foulkes speaks of groups as collective: ". . . the group tends to speak and react to a common theme as if it were a living entity expressing itself in different ways through various months" (Mullan & Rosenbaum, 1962, p. 14). Although some authors do not give credit to the English Foulkes as having significantly influenced the therapeutic group in the United States (Mullan & Rosenbaum, 1962), the current therapeutic use of encounter groups, T-groups, and Gestalt approaches reflects his influence (Egan, 1970, 1972;. W. F. Hill, 1973). Other English therapists who have been influential in this area are Sutherland (1952), Ezriel (1950), and, most notably, Bion.

Bion (1948) observed the emotional reactions that occur in groups. He noted that individual-group relations could be categorized as valences, or types of interaction, e.g., dependency, fight-flight, or pairing. This approach was unique in that it provided no structure or direction, and the patient's reaction to the lack of structure—his anger or confusion—was the material initially used as data for exploration and analysis. It was a new emphasis that stressed group behavior rather than individual behavior.

Since World War II, Bach (1954) has been instrumental in the application of Lewin's Field Theory to group psychotherapy. He stresses a group orientation but only in its ability to help treat the individual. Bach sees the group's role as creating an atmosphere that helps stimulate self-treatment.

The humanistic therapists stress the significance of the philosophical position that the therapist takes in group therapy. Whitaker and Malone (1953) emphasize the importance of the patient's feelings in an experiential approach. The experiential approaches show a "feeling" for the therapeutic process similar to Rogers' except that he states that the therapist should not impose his values on the patient. Whitaker and Malone advocate that the therapist should be aware of the fact that he *does* impose his ideas on the patient and should acknowledge the extent of this influence. Mullan and Rosenbaum (1962) have advocated the total involvement of the therapist, whereas Van Dusen, Hare, & L. B. Hill (1957), Hare (1962), and L. B. Hill (1958) propose a limited involvement in the application of the existential approach (see also Goldberg, 1973). In general, these variations of the humanistic school are strikingly similar, although they are sometimes at odds with each other.

The use of hypnosis in group settings in the treatment of alcoholics and drug addicts is an approach that was begun in England. Peberdy (1960) and Fox (1960) introduced the technique in the United States.

In conclusion, group psychotherapy is a tremendously influential and widespread movement in the development of psychotherapeutic techniques.

Although the main thrust of the group movement occurred after World War II, the use of therapeutic groups has a long and interesting history.

LABORATORY TRAINING AND THE GROUP MOVEMENT

The complex innovations of the contemporary group movement have given birth to many confusing and imprecise labels. The terms "sensitivity training," "encounter," "laboratory education," and "T-group" are often used interchangeably, ignoring the real differences among these various approaches.

For clarity, we are following Lubin and Eddy (1970) and Egan (1970) in using the term "laboratory training" as a generic term that refers to a range of experience-based learning activities designed and shaped around the learning needs of participants. "Laboratory" refers to the emphasis on experimentation and the testing of new behavior.

The term "growth group" refers to a variety of small-group experiences that focus on the personal and interpersonal development of group members. Growth groups derive from several separate theoretical orientations: the T-group is a type of laboratory training based on the work of Lewin and the National Training Laboratories; the encounter group is a synthesis of many traditions, epitomized by the practice of Schutz (1967, 1973). (Distinctions between T-groups and encounter groups are treated in Chapter 2.) Other types of growth groups include Gestalt, sensory awareness, and the marathon group; collectively, growth groups are referred to as the "group movement." A discussion of differences among growth groups is provided by J. E. Jones (1972).

Early Influences

The origins of laboratory training are part of a long line of social study dating to Spencer, Comte, and others. Although Comte wrote of the possibility of social planning and, by implication, of the possibility of social change, he reportedly never pursued this insight (Bonner, 1959). Spencer's ideas envisioned a rather static society. He saw society's evolution as determined by fixed laws, and he felt that any attempts to oppose these laws were not only ill advised but socially harmful.

While the influence of such great figures as Durkheim, Cooley, Tonnies, Dewey, and Mead is present in a general way, two pre-World War II theorists take precedence as direct progenitors of the concept of laboratory training: Simmel and Lewin. Simmel (1903, 1950) contributed to social experimentation the fundamental concept of interactionism. He viewed society as a pattern of all the functional relationships that bind individuals into an integral whole. Group belongingness is a basic aspect of this field concept. Simmel also stated that conflict was not necessarily negative, but was a restructuring of the organization of a psychological field. The leader and those who are led influence each other so that one cannot function without the other. The leader's influence is limited by the conditions of the total group structure. Thus, superordination is a more accurate term than leadership.

Simmel also contributed his concept of spatiality and social boundary. Spatiality, he explained, is the growth of the individual that takes place in a social circle, which other circles frequently intersect. The wider the area of social participation, the more numerous the intersections of the social circles. Social boundary he defined as a boundary separating one group from another, particularly the "in" group from the "out" group. Boundaries within the individual personality as well as ethnocentrism and intergroup prejudice are all social boundaries. This dynamic concept of social forces was a powerful stimulus to Lewin.

Although Lewin's famous work on field theory was initiated in the late twenties, it was not until he moved to America that the field-theory approach was applied to groups. Using the dynamic concepts of Simmel, with the addition of his own topological concepts of field relationships, Lewin (1951) advanced the concept of action research. It was through his driving force that experimentation moved from the laboratory into the field (society at large) and was directed toward effecting desired changes (Lewin, 1948).

Lewin empirically observed that, regardless of content, the most effective change in attitude is obtained within groups rather than in an individual setting (Lewin, 1943). From action research Lewin also learned that it is only from new emotional experiences that man can gain new knowledge and new insight with which to re-evaluate his older attitudes and sentiments (Marrow, 1969).

As to Lewin's direct influence on laboratory training, Deutsch (1968) said:

> His [Lewin's] article "Conduct, Knowledge, and Acceptance of New Values" (reprinted in Lewin, 1948), and his articles on "Frontiers in Group Dynamics" (reprinted in Lewin, 1951) combined with the research on group leadership and group decisions, represent the intellectual base for the development of the conception of laboratory training groups. (p. 476)[6]

Other generally acknowledged developers of laboratory training are Benne, Bradford, and Lippitt.

---

[6]From M. Deutsch, "Field Theory in Social Psychology," in G. Lindsay & E. Aronson (Eds.), *The Handbook on Social Psychology* (Vol. 1). Reading, Mass.: Addison-Wesley, 1968. Reprinted by permission.

Bradford started his career in the field of adult education. In 1942 he was appointed Illinois State Director of the Works Projects Administration (W.P.A.) for adult education and other educational programs. He was at this time acquainted with Benne, and in 1943 he interested Lippitt in an educational innovation in adult education. During this period he also met Lewin and adapted training techniques from Moreno (Bradford, Lippitt, & Gibb, 1956). This confluence of forces led to the development of laboratory training.

Birth of Laboratory Training

In May of 1946, Bradford held a training conference on adult education in New Britain, Connecticut. Lewin and Lippitt (who had rejoined Lewin at the Research Center for Group Dynamics at the Massachusetts Institute of Technology) attended and, with some of their graduate students, became involved in the project. At this conference, it was observed that the conferees' conversations away from the conference, which were monitored, referred to activities experienced in the small work groups and not to activities experienced in lectures (Bradford, 1967a). This suggested the trial of some new techniques.

The researchers in the Connecticut Workshop Project, as it was called, were Bradford, Lewin, Lippitt, and three research observers, who were graduate students in social psychology, Deutsch, Horwitz, and Seeman (Benne, 1964b).

Early in the conference Lewin arranged evening meetings so that training-staff and research-staff members could study their process observations of the day's meetings. Some of the conference participants who were living on campus asked to attend, and Lewin, reluctant to say no, allowed this (Benne, 1964b). The atmosphere, according to Bradford, became electric as people reacted to data about their own behavior. Before long, all participants were attending these evening sessions (Bradford, Gibb, & Benne, 1964).

The Connecticut experiment—the serendipitous confluence of Simmel's dynamism, Lewin's action research, and a team of innovation-prone educators—gave rise to some important implications: feedback of data about interaction in the group can provide rich learning experiences; role playing can be effective in training change agents, and the process of group building has transfer potentialities to a variety of back-home organizations and community situations.

The excitement of a promising new path gripped all participants, and plans were made to hold another program in 1947. Lewin secured a grant from the Office of Naval Research, and Bradford obtained backing from the National Education Association. The site was the Gould Academy in Bethel, Maine. The academy became the summer home base and training center of the National Training Laboratories, as this new movement came to be called (Bradford et al., 1964). Unfortunately, Lewin did not live to attend the first National

Training Laboratories (NTL) session in the summer of 1947. He died in February of that year.

A training laboratory "is a temporary residential community shaped to the learning requirements of all its members" (Bradford et al., 1964, pp. 2-3). The simultaneous processes of change (training) and innovation (experimentation) are carried on in this global experiential community. Many individual models of group work and many different types of groups are found in this supporting framework.

The special perspective on group work by the founders of laboratory training is described in the following excerpt.

> Every educational innovation represents a set of cultural conditions. First, the innovators perceive needs for learning inadequately met by existing practices. Second, underlying those needs are cherished values seen as threatened in the drift of historical events. These values assume a central role in shaping the new processes of education designed to give them renewed power. Third, new resources in knowledge and skill are seen as available at least in embryo. Such conditions as these motivated the persons responsible for the "laboratory movement" in education. (Bradford et al., 1964, pp. 3-4)[7]

The trilogy so often identified in laboratory training programs—knowledge, skills, and values—was important in the minds of the founders.

Laboratory training is a philosophy, rather than just a technique, that, when applied, creates an environment where innovation on a number of levels may occur—especially on the interpersonal level of change. The T-group is one of the important innovations that emerged from laboratory training.

The Bethel Laboratory in 1947 had as one of its features a Basic Skills Training (BST) Group. In that group, an observer made observational data notes which were then made available for discussion by the group. The trainer, as the group leader came to be labeled, assisted in analyzing and evaluating these data. The initial conception of the BST group was to establish an environment for learning change-agent skills and concepts and for learning to understand and to help with group growth and development. These important ideas were expressed in seven expectations or desired outcomes.

1. To help members internalize more or less systematic sets of concepts.
2. For the group to provide practice in diagnostic and action skills of the change agent and the group leader.
3. That the behavioral content would run the gamut of "human organization" from the interpersonal level and the group level to the intergroup level.
4. That the BST Group would help its members in the application of laboratory learnings to back-home situations and to plan for continuing growth for themselves and their associates.
5. To gain a more objective and accurate view of themselves in their relations to other persons in the group and to the developing group as a whole.

---

[7]From L. P. Bradford, J. R. Gibb, & K. D. Benne (Eds.), *T-Group Theory and Laboratory Method: Innovation in Re-education.* New York: John Wiley, 1964. Reprinted by permission.

History of Groups 39

6. For the participants to develop a clearer understanding of democratic values.
7. For the participants to acquire trainer skills and understandings which will help function adequately as change agents, as group members, and provide them with the ability to communicate these learnings to others. (Benne, 1964b, pp. 86-87)[8]

In 1947, the composition of laboratory groups was heterogeneous; however, there were also a few homogeneous groups. These groups developed in the broader laboratory settings designed for special occupational groups (Benne, 1964b).

During this period, Coch and French (1948) conducted an experiment in the tradition of the Hawthorne studies (see Roethlisberger & Dickson, 1939). Their work substantiated the effectiveness of collaborative participation in increasing industrial production (Coch & French, 1948).

After nine months' work French also reported on a follow-up concerning the effectiveness of the Bethel laboratory.

... the changes (in the participants) were startling. There was a more democratic ideology about human relations, an increased understanding of group dynamics, greater skill in group leadership and membership, a willingness to utilize such specific techniques as role playing, group productivity observers, and action research methods, and a better understanding of the relationship of one participant to another. (French, Sherwood, & Bradford, 1966, p. 47)[9]

The second Bethel laboratory, in 1948, was a refinement of the first in that staff skills were beginning to "jell," and new ideas were being tested against the limited material available from the first laboratory. This second lab focused on a wider spectrum of human organizations—including community and institutional systems. In addition to the direct formulation of "community groups" (later formalized as C groups) for role playing community problems, the lab turned toward the community problems of the laboratories. The 1947 lab met this problem in the style of the New England town meeting. Beginning with the 1948 lab and until 1951, a Delegate Council was formed for representatives of the participants and the staff (Benne, 1964b).

Benne clearly identifies two periods in the history of the T-group and laboratory training. The first is from 1947 to 1955, and the second is from 1956 to 1964. In the first period the main thrust of the lab was to create training formats and technologies to serve learning objectives seen as extraneous to those peculiarly within the province of the BST or T-group. The second period

---

[8]From K. D. Benne, "History of the T-Group in the Laboratory Setting," in L. P. Bradford, J. R. Gibb, & K. D. Benne (Eds.), *T-Group Theory and Laboratory Method: Innovation in Reeducation*. New York: John Wiley, 1964. Reprinted by permission.

[9]Reproduced by special permission from *Journal of Applied Behavioral Science*, "Change in Self-Identity in a Management Training Conference," J. R. P. French, J. J. Sherwood, & D. L. Bradford, p. 47, 1966, NTL Institute.

marks the attempt to reintegrate a T-group experience into the designs of laboratories (Benne, 1964b).

In 1949, an assessment and referral unit was incorporated into the laboratory. At successive periods in the lab this unit collected data from participants concerning back-home problems with which they wished help. The unit then tried to bring together persons with the same problems and resource persons with knowledge and experience of the specific problems (Benne, 1964b).

In the 1950 laboratory a separate group, the A or Action group, was distinguished from the T- (BST had by now been shortened to a simple "T") group. In late 1948 Herbert Thelen, Gordon Hearn, and Siegman Blamberg had been introduced to the staff. Then, in late 1949, a deliberate effort was made to acquire staff members with a more clinical orientation: seven of the ten new staff members were from the field of psychiatry and clinical psychology. A split arose between the clinically oriented staff and the more sociologically oriented staff, a split that was reflected in the T- and A-groups. The T-groups met in the morning, were occupationally heterogeneous and interpersonal, dealt with small-group problems, and were clinical in orientation. The A-groups, instead, met in the afternoon, were occupationally homogeneous, focused on problems and methodologies of change in larger social systems, and were sociologically oriented. A-groups, however, tended to become T-groups, and the involving focus on interpersonal dynamics spilled over into the other group. Eventually, the A-group was discarded (Benne, 1964b).

In 1951, another group technique, called the "skill group," was attempted in the lab. This group participated in a series of exercises in which members were asked to practice various interpersonal, membership, leadership, and change-agent skills. Some members made role-playing presentations while others watched. Analysis and discussion then attempted to make the presentations relevant. These were not geared to the T-group sessions; they were related to previous conceptual input from theory sessions or to other aspects of the laboratory offering. Again, most participants and staff ascribed higher value to the T-group sessions. During this same lab, the more formal C-groups (community) were formed and operated without staff membership (Benne, 1964b).

The scheme in 1952 was to evaluate "large meeting" groups. A large meeting was defined as one in which a platform-audience relationship was established and used. The aim was to study processes of planning, conducting, and evaluating large meetings for the staff and participants (Benne, 1964b). In 1954, mass role playing by the entire laboratory was attempted as an expansion of the A-group procedure, directed toward the process of reaching a decision on a controversial issue.

In both these groups (role playing and large meeting) the skills learned and used seemed to be artificial compared with those in the T-group; there was a tendency toward manipulation and deception in these groups by the same individuals who had learned and were practicing direct communication of open and honest feelings in the T-groups (Benne, 1964b).

Period of Reintegration

The second period identified by Bradford in the history of the T-group and laboratory training is from 1956 to 1964. This period was characterized by the reintegration of the T-group into the laboratory design. Three patterns of reintegration were offered. In the first, the T-group is the center of the laboratory experience. The principal learning objective is clarification of interpersonal and intrapersonal problems coupled with a basic knowledge of small-group phenomena. The second pattern is based on the early, full range of learning objectives; it covers back-home situations and general change-agent skills. In the third pattern, there are different groupings of participants with differing technologies, which are brought together for differing objectives (Benne, 1964b).

One of the important factors in the period of reintegration was the formation of specialized laboratories. Under the auspices of the National Training Laboratories Institute for Applied Behavioral Science, a number of occupationally homogeneous laboratories were developed: American Red Cross workers (1955); industrial managers (1956); Protestant religious workers (1956); Puerto Rican government workers (1956); staff leaders from various national voluntary organizations (1957); public school teachers and administrators (1959); college students and faculty members (1960); leaders in community development (1960); the Protestant Episcopal Church of the U.S.A.; the Methodist Church; the Esso-Humble Oil Company; and the Aluminum Company of Canada (Benne, 1964b).

This period is also noted for the development of regional laboratories. The Western Training Laboratory was begun in 1952 as an adjunct to the University of California Extension. There were soon several others: the Boston University Laboratory in the Development of Human Relations (1954); the Pacific Northwest Laboratory (1954); the Intermountain Laboratory in Utah (1955); the Southwest Human Relations Training Laboratory in Texas (1955); and the Midwest Group for Human Resources (1967). In 1965, the Southeast Regional Laboratory was founded and is presently functioning as Leadership Development Programs, Inc.

Important laboratory additions in this period involved the alumni and foreign-nation programs. The alumni programs were aimed at improving the trainer skills of former laboratory participants. Beginning in 1955, the alumni program was frequently paired with the training of foreign nationals as human relations trainers or back-home change agents (Benne, 1964b).

Drawing on experimental research by Sherif & Sherif (1953), the staff of the Southwest Human Relations Training Laboratory experimented with intergroup conflict between two T-groups. The experiment was productive, and in 1960 an exercise was introduced into the National Training Laboratories Management Work Conference at Arden House in Harriman, New York. The results were positive. Today, the intergroup competition and collaboration exercises have become almost standard laboratory procedures (Benne, 1964b; also see Sherif et al., 1961).

One popular variation of the T-group may be identified with the names of Wechsler, Massarik, Tannenbaum, and the Western Training Laboratory. In this variation, which they called "sensitivity training," laboratory training

> is no longer primarily a technique for the improvement of group functioning, the development of interpersonal skills, the intellectual discussion of human relations problems, or the more surface discussion of neurotic manifestation, . . . Rather, sensitivity training is now pointed in the direction of the total enhancement of the individual. (Benne, 1964b, p. 125)[10]

In another variation of the T-group, the instrumented T-group, the presence of the trainer is considered less important than in other types of groups, and he is removed from direct participation in the group. In his place, several self-administered instruments are introduced (usually paper and pencil tests). The members learn about their group and their membership by becoming an integral part of the processes of collecting, analyzing, and interpreting data about themselves and their group (Benne, 1964b; see also Blake & Mouton, 1964).

One current application of laboratory training involves its use in organization development.

> I think one important theme of the nearly four-year organizational change effort at TRW Systems is that of using Laboratory training (sensitivity training, T-grouping) clearly as a means to an end—that of putting most of our energy into on-the-job situations, real life intergroup problems, real life job-family situations, and dealing with them in the here-and-now. The effort has reached a point where sensitivity, per se, represents only 10 to 15 per cent of the effort, 85 to 90 per cent is in on-the-job situations, working real problems with the people who are really involved in them. This has led to some very important, profound, and positive changes in the organization and the way it does many things including decision making, problem solving, and supervisory coaching of subordinates. (Davis, 1967, p. 5)[11]

If "sensitivity training" is accepted as a generic term, then "laboratory training" can be placed midway between therapy and education (Gibb, 1970).

To recapitulate, laboratory training (including both the T-group with a group emphasis and the T-group with a personal-interpersonal emphasis) retains a strong tie to its origin as an educational method, is concerned with cognitive

---

[10]See Footnote 8.

[11]Reproduced by special permission from *Journal of Applied Behavioral Science*, "An Organic Problem-Solving Method of Organizational Change," S. A. Davis, p. 5, 1967, NTL Institute.

as well as affective learning, and values the ability of the participant to transfer learnings to the back-home situation. It differs from group psychotherapy (the form practiced in many adult outpatient clinics) in that lab participants are seen as relatively well-functioning individuals, repair and restoration of function are not among its objectives, the leader is less central to the process, and the perspective is upon current group developments and interpersonal transactions. (Lubin & Eddy, 1970, as quoted in Golembiewski & Blumberg, 1973, p. 81)[12]

Laboratory training is presently concerned with a number of issues related to its position on the continuum, its goals, and the variations in laboratory experience. One issue of particular concern that involves a number of questions is the selection of participants: how to locate would-be casualties before the program begins; how to minimize hurtful stress while maximizing learning from new behaviors through the process of risk taking; and how to determine what type of people derive the most benefit from laboratory experience (including design and leadership style).

Lieberman, Yalom, and Miles (1973) noted that the casualties in T-group were those participants who had low ego strength and high expectations. They also found casualties to be related to certain leadership styles, i.e., high aggressive stimulation, high charisma, high individual focus, high support, and high confrontation.

In 1969 NTL attempted to deal with policies regarding the purpose of its programs, the selection of participants, and the training of trainers ("Standards for the Use of the Laboratory Method in NTL Institute Programs," 1969). The emphasis was on "being explicit with applicants concerning the purpose and nature of programs" (Lubin & Eddy, 1970 & 1973, p. 72).

To insure voluntary participation, Lubin and Eddy (1970 & 1973) suggested that several optional developmental programs be offered (including laboratory training) for organizations that traditionally support their members in attending laboratory training. As clearly stated by NTL (1969), the program is not designed for people with severe mental or emotional problems, for problem members of an organization whose superior seeks disciplinary measures, or for people who cannot tolerate interpersonal stress.

Argyris concluded that participants who receive the most benefit from laboratory training are "relatively healthy individuals, capable of learning from others how to enhance their degree of effectiveness" (1964, p. 67). He perceived that they had relatively strong egos, defenses low enough to hear feedback, and the ability to communicate, with minimal distortion, their thoughts and feelings (Argyris, 1964; see also Lubin & Eddy, 1970 & 1973).

Laboratory training is experimental in that the environment encourages experimentation with new behaviors. This approach is the "polar opposite"

---

[12]From B. Lubin & W. B. Eddy, "The Laboratory Training Model: Rationale, Method, and Some Thoughts for the Future," in *International Journal of Group Psychotherapy*, 1970, *20*, 305-339. Reprinted by permission.

(Blumberg, 1973, p. 15) of traditional education. It puts "the onus for learning on the individual to create through his own behavior and skills the kind of human situation from which he can learn what is meaningful for him" (Blumberg, 1973, p. 15).

The concept of "quality," when applied to education or training, seems to suggest that above average or superior learning takes place, as viewed by the participant or some other outside authority, e.g., traditional education. The term seems to imply a capacity for transference or generalization to future situations. Overall, a good learning experience is individually designed and well suited to the participant, giving appropriate consideration to his strengths and weaknesses, his desires and needs.

This concept is illustrated in an NTL program. The impetus for such an approach was recognition of the

> importance of group composition and trainer style as determinants of differential participant learning in laboratory education (Harrison & Lubin, 1965; Lieberman, Yalom, & Miles, 1972), and to trainer style in the occurrence of severe stress reactions (Lieberman, 1972; Yalom, 1971). (Heine et al., 1974, p. 3)[13]

Previous to this program, heterogeneity had been the prime concern in preplanning for group formation and trainer assignment. Now a five-phase design was devised for participants to enable them to form their own groups by negotiation; then trainers and participants negotiated for trainer assignment. All members experienced certain facets of group process by making choices based on explicit criteria. The rationale for this design was

> to provide conditions that would encourage participants to value the exercise of choice and to take responsibility for their growth and learning. (Heine et al., 1974, p. 3)[14]

The first, and essential, step of this sequential approach was "developing a sense of self" (p. 3). Other steps included a sense of self in relationship to others, with "commitment to relationships of varying degrees of temporariness" (p. 3) leading to negotiations for group formation and trainer assignment. Heine described and evaluated structural interventions for each step.

Conclusions indicated a lack of severe stress reactions in participants and "considerable modeling of straight talk on both sides."

> The interview and negotiation process provided a crucible in which trainers were confronted with questions that forced them to search deeply for concise statements of their training philosophy, goals, style, and expectations for the group. In addition, the fast-moving, tense, marketplace atmosphere pressured trainers

---

[13]Reproduced by special permission from *Social Change*, "Negotiating for Group and Trainers: The Open Marketplace," C. Heine, B. Lubin, J. Perlmutter, & A. Lubin, pp. 3-6, 1974, NTL Institute.

[14]See Footnote 13.

to confront groups about their expectations and their willingness to engage in a sustained learning effort. (p. 6)[15]

Heine's study illustrates some current issues facing laboratory training and presents at least one design for dealing with these issues. Follow-up studies and duplication of similar and different situations are needed to answer the question "To whom is the group beneficial and under what conditions?"

CONTEMPORARY TRENDS IN THE GROUP MOVEMENT

There are several other contemporary trends in groups that must be identified if the reader is to have an adequate view of the field. Many of these groups may be identified as outgrowths of either the group psychotherapy or laboratory training tradition and most have developed since the Korean War. Their common point seems to be a *Zeitgeist* that is positive, person centered, growth producing, and humanistic (Siroka, Siroka, & Schloss, 1971; Back, 1972). These trends are reviewed briefly here.

The Existential Crisis of Modern Man

The tradition of the growth group has its roots in existentialism; that is, in the existential anxiety created by the increasing pressures on meaningful existence, e.g., two world wars and a depression. With the Industrial Revolution, man had begun to shift his goals and his system of values from a religious framework to an almost reverent attitude toward technology and its potentialities. Deus was replaced by Technos. The future was certain, and man was assured of moving toward a better existence where, through the achievements of science and technology, he would ultimately master the world and solve the problems that had plagued him.

With World War I this philosophy changed. Instead of eliminating problems, technology threatened to destroy man. Though the spirit of optimism revived superficially and temporarily during the twenties, the disillusionment was profound; it became extreme with the depression that followed. Man could no longer believe in the omnipotence and progress of Technos.

Man's existence now became less purposeful and more fearful. The means by which he had intended to master nature had instead mastered him. Whereas the Victorians had focused optimistically on technology and the heights that could be reached through it, the 1930's and the years to follow

---

[15]See Footnote 13.

emphasized the bad side of Technos and the lack of meaning in a life based on it. However, man could not turn back—he had nowhere to turn. He was trapped. Trapped, betrayed, afraid, and desperate—these were the "Hollow Men" described by T. S. Eliot. Their habitat was the brittle, noisy meaningless cage of *The Waste Land* (1922).

It was during this period that the philosophy of the early existentialists began to increase in popularity. It had evolved as a reaction to the extreme rationalism of the nineteenth century and the increasing depersonalization of the mid-twentieth century. Like the period of the depression, this existentialism reflected despair. Life was not rational. It had no meaning save the meaning of an individual's existence to himself. Although this view, while pessimistic, at least offered the possibility of meaning, it was difficult, if not impossible, to find that meaning in a forty-hour-a-week meaningless job. The basic dilemma was still the same: man was in a state of transition in which the values that had formerly given a framework of excitement and meaning to life —reason, competition, religion—had become suspect and even outmoded without being replaced by new values.

Even with the lessening of the economic depression, despair still hovered as a sort of gray dullness. Despite the return of relative financial security, there was no wide-scale rekindling of the fires of adventure and success. It took another war to break the depression's hold. Anger began to be expressed as the dilemma of the individual lost in a society whose mechanics were beyond his control or understanding. Interpersonal relationships were called superficial as the traditionally strongest bastions of meaning—job, family, and religion—succumbed to the impact of bureaucracy; the mobile, disjointed life of the suburbs; and disbelief. During the fifties and early sixties, the cry was one of despair at the lack of meaningful communication and understanding.

This is the plight of the new "Hollow Men" described by Rollo May. Lost and afraid, they turn to others to help them structure existence in a meaningful way. However, the others are no better off (May, 1953); life takes on a rather incomprehensible, chaotic tenor which May calls the schizoid world (May, Angel, & Ellenberger, 1958). The result is a terrible loneliness which man tries to alleviate by frantically reaching out for human contact (Burton, 1972). But the more he identifies with others, rather than taking an active role, the more he loses his sense of self and becomes trapped in a superficial existence without meaning or communication. This is a world characterized by loneliness and anxiety (May, 1969). If the anxiety is too much to bear, the individual suppresses the conflict completely at the expense of genuine feeling, leaving only the mechanical shell of existence (May, 1953).

In reaction to this dilemma, the philosophy of existentialism and existential psychology has developed with increasing popularity. Recently existentialism has departed from the more despairing views of Nietzsche (1909) and Kierkegaard (1941). Rather than the individual being seen as lost and left to his own devices, he is seen as being able to take the responsibility for shaping his environment into a personal world of meaning (May et al., 1958). The emphasis is on growing and on fulfilling one's potential.

Thus, there has developed a real need for the development of skills in communication—especially communication within and between groups. This is seen as one of the main routes to alleviating loneliness and the feeling of being lost in an incomprehensible and overpowering mass of people with whom there is no apparent common bond. Re-education in the expression of feelings is also needed. The feelings that modern man has been taught to distort and hide must be brought into the open if the "hollow" man is ever to break his shell and become a creative, spontaneous, and healthy individual. Laura Perls (1970) succinctly describes the existential dilemma in this manner:

> I am deeply convinced that the basic problem not only of therapy but of life is how to make life livable for a being whose dominant characteristic is his awareness of himself as a unique individual on the one hand and of his mortality on the other. (p. 128)[16]

The Human Potential Movement

In the last half of the twentieth century, society found itself pressed against a wall of human issues which, historically, it has tended to neglect. With increasing concern, people began to ask certain questions: How can we learn to live authentically? How can we be aware of and sensitive to ourselves and others? How can we integrate our thinking selves and our feeling selves? How can we recognize and reach the untapped human potential within ourselves? Although the pressures of the economy, wars, and domestic concerns have forced man to deal with "practical" issues, recent social developments have encouraged him to be aware of a deficit in his life. With more leisure time and better living conditions, an easing of the Calvinist tradition of hard work and little pleasure was apparent. There was a subtle but respectable trend toward seeking enjoyment. The so-called sexual revolution, the concerns about increased leisure time, and a more relaxed, liberal approach toward life have all contributed to the acceptance of what is known as the human potential movement.

ENCOUNTER GROUPS

The roots of the encounter movement are many and varied. Its history stretches into antiquity; however, a discussion of its important modern roots should include Moreno, Perls, Reich, and Schutz.

---

[16]Perls, L. "One Gestalt Therapist's Approach." In J. Fagan and I. L. Shepherd (eds.), GESTALT THERAPY NOW. Palo Alto, California: Science and Behavior Books, 1970. Reprinted by permission.

Moreno emphasized the significant encounter, a central focus in modern growth groups.

> In the beginning was the encounter. And when you are near I will tear your eyes out and use them instead of mine, and you will tear my eyes out and use them instead of yours, then I will look at you with your eyes and you will look at me with mine. (Einladung zu einer Begegnung, Vienna, 1914, as quoted in Moreno, 1959a, p. 234)[17]

His work with psychodrama may be considered an important predecessor of today's encounter groups. Here-and-now behavior, the central role of the therapist, and the use of auxiliary individuals as helpers are prominent factors in Moreno's therapy, which can currently be seen in work by Yablonsky (1972) and Van Meulenbrouck (1972).

> Is it any wonder, then, that so many groups which focus on personal, intrapsychic material (as opposed to pure group process) find themselves reenacting a group member's familial relationships? Especially in psychodramatically oriented groups, the roots of a person's interactional problems with his peers are usually sought and found in the family. Whether one examines Janov's primal therapy, the bioenergetic therapy of Lowen and others, or the garden variety encounter marathon, he is likely to find group members attempting to resolve unmet needs for affection from parents, risking the forbidden expression of anger or frustration or defiance toward them, or pleading for acceptance in spite of a failure to measure up to parental expectations. (Sorrells, 1972, pp. 318-319)[18]

Psychoanalysis, largely through Reich, has been another influence on contemporary growth groups. Reich (1949) deviated from orthodox psychoanalysis by replacing pedagogical measures with analytic interpretations (p. 40). In his therapy the manner or form of relating rather than verbal content was emphasized. He used a technique of constantly confronting the patient with a specific character trait until the patient could look at it objectively and then take the responsibility for using this new knowledge to change his character (p. 50). Reich, who emphasized the present-day effect of the trait instead of etiology, may have utilized a technique that was a precursor of "feedback" as it is currently defined in terms of groups, i.e., the process by which an individual finds out how others see him.

One of Reich's most important contributions is the concept of "character armor," a defensive system of the whole organism geared toward maintaining a familiar and comfortable, but confining, way of perceiving the world. However, a value system favoring risk and involvement is quite central to the whole concept of personal growth groups (Blumberg, 1973). These groups

---

[17]From PSYCHODRAMA VOL. II, 1959, J. L. Moreno, M.D., Author, Beacon House Inc., Beacon, N.Y., Publisher. Reprinted by permission.

[18]From J. Sorrells, "Groups, Families and the Karass," in L. N. Solomon & B. Berzon (Eds.), *New Perspectives on Encounter Groups*, pp. 318-319. San Francisco: Jossey-Bass, 1972. Reprinted by permission.

attempt to penetrate and modify the individual's character armor through certain structured experiences, significant encounters with others, and even the fatigue that develops in "marathon" groups (Levitsky & Simkin, 1972). Maslow, who helped change the emphasis of applied psychology from the pathological to the normal individual, makes the point well:

> Supposing you have attained a nice stabilization of forces and you are adjusted? Perhaps adjustment and stabilization, while good because it cuts your pain, is also bad because development toward a higher ideal ceases? (Maslow, 1968, p. 6)[19]

Contemporary encounter groups incorporate techniques from many approaches: nonverbal communication, psychodrama, massage, meditation, T'ai Chi, psychosynthesis, structural integration (rolfing), the Feldenkrais exercises, Gestalt therapy, theater and dance. Schutz (1967, 1971, 1973) provides accounts of the encounter movement's history, theory, and application.

EASTERN INFLUENCES

A major impact on modern growth groups came from Eastern thought. According to Watts (1961), the process in which the guru and the student involve themselves during the student's search for enlightenment may be analogous to the process of personal growth in groups. Watts states that the guru puts the student in a therapeutic double-bind situation, orders him to be spontaneous, and does not allow him to break the double-bind by trying to escape. When the student is thoroughly exhausted, when he can no longer block, he may give in to spontaneity, which leads to a sudden "flip" and a new dimension of consciousness. In this sense, spontaneous action is that which is not blocked by a social control mechanism such as the ego.

Watts suggests that no matter what psychological theory is involved, the guru-student relationship is the process that actually occurs in Western therapy. It is clear why this process may be intensified in the unfamiliar, unstructured group situation, thus pushing the participant to a new level of consciousness. The contemporary Westerner's double-bind in relating spontaneously to a group can be seen as analogous to the Easterner's bind, which relates spontaneously to the aged authority figure, the guru. Aside from this analogy, Westerners have evidenced a mistrust of the physical world and alienation from the organism, whereas Eastern thought makes clearer the ultimate unity opposites, e.g., the mind and the body, the doer and his psychological world.

The recent liberal movement in society has led to a renewed interest in Eastern thought, to an awareness that man has forgotten how to let things happen. Perhaps the spiritual hunger of the times created a vacuum ready to receive these new ideas. Although drugs have made an initial impact and have

---

[19]From *Toward A Psychology of Being* by Abraham H. Maslow, © 1968. Reprinted by permission of D. Van Nostrand Company.

caused a cultural shift in attention, they have not been found to be a permanent or satisfactory answer to man's problems. Instead, new groups and social institutions have surfaced to try to replace the missing elements (Gustaitis, 1969).

GESTALT THERAPY

Gestalt therapy, originated by the late Fritz Perls, can be looked at as a fertile meeting of Eastern and Western thought and is of importance to the personal growth movement. One of its sources was Gestalt psychology, developed in the early twentieth century through the work of Wertheimer (1923, 1945), Kohler (1929), and Koffka (1928, 1935). Kohler (1929) observed that "other people seem to recognize our experiences from without more clearly than we are able to observe them from within" (p. 129). The attention of the early Gestaltists was usually restricted to the phenomena of conscious awareness and to the experiential fact that consciousness cannot be broken into parts.

Gestalt psychology drew heavily from the theories of the phenomenologists, William James (1890), Jaensch (1929), and Katz (1937). The phenomenologists' emphasis on the free description of immediate experience illustrates how past theory contributes to present practice.

Gestalt therapy is essentially a form of existential therapy. Its immediate aim is to restore awareness; its ultimate aim is to make the individual whole and to release his potential (Naranjo, 1968). Its target is the total organism in interaction with the environment. The figure shifts, but in meaningful relation to the ground. According to Gestalt therapy, the individual must regain his awareness, his wholeness, his contacting of the environment in order for learning to occur. In reaching this goal the person is offered methods of invading his own privacy and the opportunity to observe himself in action (Perls, Hefferline, & Goodman, 1951).

The point at which growth is blocked or ceases has been called the impasse point. Perls, whom Gustaitis (1969) called the "Prophet of the Now," strove in his awareness groups to move each individual past his impasse point (Perls, Hefferline, Goodman, 1951). Perls had been influenced by Freud and Reich but had abandoned psychoanalysis in favor of Gestalt techniques. Trained by Max Reinhardt as a theater director, Perls used props, role playing, and video tape, and encouraged physical expressions of inner conflicts (Perls, 1969).

The method that Perls used to conduct an experiential workshop for the American Association of Humanistic Psychology in 1964 was enthusiastically received. Maslow (1968) often speaks of a "Third Force" of humanistic psychologists whom he sees as spreading the values of personal growth.

ESALEN

Since 1962, Esalen Institute at Big Sur, California, has been an important center of the human potential movement. The action-oriented workshops run by Esalen are experimental and experiential; they focus on the feeling man, though the thinking man is not ignored. Esalen is not an institution for sick people, but for normal people seeking personal growth, a place where they can find the existential, the here-and-now.

After living in an experimental community in India, Michael Murphy, Esalen's founder, came to the conclusion that the West lacked a "way," and that the new way would of necessity involve sensory-awakening and growth-producing human relationships (Gustaitis, 1969).

Murphy founded Esalen Institute (Murphy, 1969) to implement Huxley's idea of education in the nonverbal humanities. The Institute grew quickly, possibly because the movement needed a hub; a comprehensive program was begun in 1962 and a full, nine-month curriculum in 1967. Since its founding, other institutions in its image have appeared across the country, but Esalen remains as the single most important center in America that attempts to synthesize the various growth disciplines.

DIFFERENCES BETWEEN THERAPY AND PERSONAL GROWTH GROUPS

Frank (1964) has made some interesting distinctions between group psychotherapy and growth groups. Therapy-group members are seen by themselves and others as needing help, whereas growth-group members are seen as well-functioning individuals interested in increasing their knowledge and skills. Attitudes that are in need of modification by therapy usually concern deep-seated resistant feelings involving significant figures in the patient's life; growth groups attempt to deal in the here-and-now with individuals who are relatively peripheral to each other. The therapist in a therapy group has a central significance as a leader, whereas the growth-group leader attempts, over a period of time, to establish a shared or distributive leadership.

The main focus of growth groups is on increasing the individual's awareness of, and sensitivity to, himself and others through direct interpersonal contact. Support and encouragement are given to the recognition and direct expression of inner feelings. The published accounts of growth groups, however, are primarily anecdotal and/or autobiographical, e.g., Howard (1970), and do not contain a clear statement of theory or method. Schutz (1958) is an exception, since he has attempted to present his work in encounter groups within a three-dimensional theory of inclusion, control, and affection. Schutz (1967) describes the encounter-group process in the following terms:

> An encounter group has no preset agenda. Instead, it uses the feelings and interaction of group members as the focus of attention. The process of achieving

personal growth begins with the exploration of feelings within the group and proceeds to wherever the group members take it. A strong effort is made to create an atmosphere of openness and honesty in communicating with each other. Ordinarily, a strong feeling of group solidarity develops and group members are able to use each other very profitably. (p. 21)[20]

In amplifying this point, Burton (1969) has stated:

I have attempted from time to time to offer interpretations to my encounter groups and found them uniformly rejected by the participants . . . this does not mean that interpretation has no place in encounter, but it does have very little place. Encounter is experientially introjective rather than interpretative and it places little premium on intelligence with its function of rapidly manipulating symbols and placing and displacing them. (p. 14)[21]

This viewpoint and approach is in contrast to those of T-groups, which place a high premium on conceptualization about participants' experiences, and to those of psychotherapy groups, which place heavy emphasis on interpretation and symbols (McLellan et al., 1970).

Perhaps one of the most important distinctions to be drawn between T-groups, encounter groups, and therapy groups comes from the report of the Task Force on Recent Developments in the Use of Small Groups of the American Psychiatric Association, *Encounter Groups and Psychiatry* (1970):

T-groups springing from the field of social psychology have behind them a long tradition of research in group dynamics. No comparable body of knowledge has been generated by group therapy, a field notoriously deficient in any systematic research. Thus, what is presently known of the basic science of group psychotherapy stems almost entirely from social-psychological research with task groups and T-groups. Psychotherapy owes to the T-group much of its systematic understanding of such factors as group development, group pressure, group cohesiveness, leadership, and group norms and values. Furthermore, T-group research has elaborated a wealth of sophisticated research techniques and tools of which the group-therapy field is now slowly availing itself. The variegated new forms of the encouter group are, of course, even less research oriented than the group psychotherapy field. (p. 23)

Appley and Winder (1973) also discuss in detail the differences between growth groups and therapy groups.

Criticism

The group movement has been subject to some criticism. Sometimes participants are not carefully screened for serious pathological problems (Lubin &

---

[20]From W. C. Shultz, *Joy: Expanding Human Awareness.* Copyright © 1967 by William C. Schutz. New York: Grove Press, 1967. Reprinted by permission of Grove Press, Inc., and Souvenir Press Ltd., London.

[21]From A. Burton (Ed.), *Encounter: Theory and Practice of Encounter Groups.* San Francisco: Jossey-Bass, 1969. Reprinted by permission.

Eddy, 1970 & 1973; Reddy, 1972; Yalom & Lieberman, 1973). Groups can become a fad, the popular leisure-time sport for the upper-middle class. They can attract opportunists; sick, self-styled leaders; and individuals who use the group to define their existence. The method lacks a coherent theory (Bennis & Shepard, 1956; Hampden-Turner, 1966). Furthermore, an ethic applying to all the variously trained leaders has not been developed, although it is particularly needed because of the drug problem and the fact that some of the leaders attract a large personal following (Burton, 1969; Lakin, 1973). Some critics feel that groups may be seen as a panacea for all ills: "Certain Esalen type and Synanon oriented marathon groups, for example, wittingly or unwittingly teach their participants they are worthwhile people if other members of the group will give them a bear hug" (Ellis, 1969b, p. 196).

These are the growing pains of a new and valuable structure for society. Groups challenge the tradition that intimacy occurs only in twos; they provide possibilities for warmth and intimacy not offered by society (Burton, 1972). They distribute widely the values of caring and responsibility and the need for taking risks to reach one's potential (Bebout & Gordon, 1972; Walton, 1973).

The leaders of today's groups include educators and behavioral scientists, as well as psychiatrists and analysts. The rise of this kind of group may signify the gradual demise of the medical model, since the problem for normal individuals is not disease but a lack of joy and a blocked path to self-realization and fulfillment (Rogers, 1970; Schutz, 1967). Personal growth groups may be the logical successors to Freudian-based psychotherapy, which met modern man's first rush of existential anguish (Burton, 1969; Horwitz, 1973; Lieberman, Yalom, & Miles, 1973).

Teaching people to find personal growth in group situations and to understand group processes is quite relevant to the needs of the times (Appley & Winder, 1973; Maslow, 1971). In the complex modern world, man is finding himself relating to others in groups at work and at play (Etzioni, 1964, 1968). In fact, McLuhan (1964; McLuhan & Watson, 1970) sees man as having come to another tribal stage along the evolutionary path and as having entered it this time with his eyes open. Group methods, in general, are in tune with the times and are part of a trend toward interrelationships of greater complexity among individuals (Hyman & Singer, 1971; McLuhan & Quentin, 1967), hence their particular efficacy in serving the needs of the people (Bosco, 1972; O'Banion & O'Connell, 1970; Schutz, 1971).

Other Influences

THE PHYSICAL SELF

Another contribution to the enhancement of the total person has been the work done by Rolf. Through working with the physical being she has helped realign the emotional, teaching people to stop wasting energy by fighting gravity. In giving her rationale for studying physical man, Rolf (1958) states that not only does man project ideas from within himself to the outer world but he has also

> quite literally projected into a physical world that he himself has created externally, the mechanical world in which he lives unconsciously, that from this universe which exists within his own skin he has revived the prototype for the levers, the wheels, the communicating mechanisms which now constitute his material world. (p. 3)[22]

Rolf takes the position that the physical body is the personality rather than the expression of the personality and that by working directly on this physical body (manipulating body parts into a proper distribution with gravity) a "structural integration" is achieved. The subjective results of structural integration, according to Rolf (1958), are greater self-awareness and a feeling of physical lightness.

Gunther (1968, 1969, 1971) teaches sensory awakening, his approach to body awareness and encounter. His method involves intense experience and resensitization through the release of chronic muscular tension and the body armour. Gunther typically uses a wide range of techniques, verbal and nonverbal, to increase self-awareness and sensitivity to others. However, he offers more than just a series of techniques or exercises. He offers an attitude—an orientation that is a blend of Eastern meditation and Western hedonism. It is an attempt to rediscover, enjoy, and integrate the physical, sensory qualities of our existence with the practical cognitive-verbal expressions of our lives—i.e., to "get out of your minds and back into your bodies." (See also Fisher, 1970, 1973; Fast, 1970; Spiegel, 1974.)

THE ARTS

Two people who have utilized art in groups as an effective means of awakening should be mentioned. The first is Rhyne, an art therapist and group leader who, in 1966, organized a group using art as a method of personal growth (Rhyne & Vich, 1969). Her method is based on spontaneous free expression, intense sensory awareness, and interpersonal experiencing. The second individual using the art experience in groups is Halprin, who founded and directs the San Francisco Dancers Workshop, where she teaches encounter and sensory awareness as well as dance and theater (Gustaitis, 1969). Rubin, a student of Lee Strasberg, Fritz Perls,et. al., and the founder and director of the Theatre of Encounter, currently employs Rhyne's and Halprin's approach in encounter groups (Denny, 1974).

---

[22]From I. Rolf, "Structural Integration: Gravity, An Unexplored Factor in More Human Use of Human Beings." *Systematics*, 1958, *1*(1), 3-20. Reprinted by permission.

THE MARATHON

The marathon is a type of encounter group utilizing a twenty-four- to thirty-six-hour continuous session (Kaplan & Sadock, 1972). This method was first developed by Bach (1966, 1967) and Stoller (1967, 1968a, 1968b, 1968c). The marathon grew out of Stoller's earlier experience with sensitivity training. It aims at achieving as much self-education, exploration, and feedback within the short time span as can possibly be handled by the participant. The phenomena that usually appear in encounter groups, which meet over a longer period of time, show up in intensified form in marathon encounters. In the beginning hours, participants tend to present themselves behind the fronts they are accustomed to displaying in public, and later, as time goes on, the fronts begin to dissipate. Participants may find themselves having to resolve the conflict of whether to retreat or become more involved. If most of the individual conflicts are resolved in the direction of greater involvement, then the last portion of the marathon is usually characterized by rare and unguarded intimacy and sharing among the members (Mintz, 1967, 1971; Stoller, 1972).

NON-BEHAVIORAL-SCIENCE GROUPS

The experiential group is not restricted to the behavioral sciences. For example, the San Francisco Zen Center teaches living in each moment; the goals at the Zen Mountain Center at Tassajara Springs, California, are the same, but the means of accomplishing these goals are hard work and discipline. Perhaps the best-known group approach outside the realm of the behavioral sciences is Synanon, founded in 1958 by Charles Dedrich. The purpose of Synanon is to resolve pressing social problems, such as addiction, through group processes (Endore, 1968; Yablonsky, 1965). The participants at Synanon forcibly, but without physical violence, break each other's protective illusions and simultaneously release their pent-up aggression, blasting each other out of their excuses and into responsibility and maturity. This method has also been found helpful for nonaddicts. (The area of aggression and violence has recently been dealt with by May, 1972.)

Focus on the Individual-Within-a-System

In many areas where practitioners seek to achieve change, such as organization development and community mental health, emphasis is being shifted from changing the individual to focusing on the individual-within-a-system. There is growing evidence that re-education and behavior change within the individual are likely to be blunted or to wither from disuse without support and reinforcement from the system. Unless the system is established or organized with the idea of continuing the individual's personal growth, any creative process is likely to be blocked. The development and modification of back-home system norms through the involvement of key organizational departments should be explored more thoroughly. While there are numerous theories of organization development, there are no comprehensive studies that investigate the optimum interfacing of T-groups and organizations for maximum change. Priorities and guidelines need to be established for the various organizations using T-groups, since laboratory training methods will probably be applied with increasing frequency and sophistication to help organizations effectively use their own resources for organizational problem solving (Davis, 1967).

Perhaps equally important in the future of small-group development is the study of temporary systems. There are many committees and team relationships that are formed to achieve temporary but vital goals. The knowledge gained from observing small-group interactions should be applied to these temporary systems. Team relationships need to establish mutual trust, emotional cohesion, and clear communication in order to reach productive solutions to their problems. Specific training programs, designed to build effective teams, will have increasing value in the future.

The use of small groups in dealing with social issues such as civil rights, law and order, war, and government continues to grow. Almost any polarized group, when placed within the characteristics of a larger system, experiences pressures to shift in both attitude and behavior (Nadler, 1968; Shellow, Ward, & Rubenfeld, 1958; Rubin, 1969). The inherent dangers of close contact among polarized groups would seem equally important to explore. There are undoubtedly specific approaches and techniques that could be very useful in dealing with intergroup relationships (Golembiewski & Blumberg, 1973).

Conclusion

Finally, it is suggested that small-group leaders, whether directing their energies toward group therapy, group dynamics, group creativity, or organizational efficiency, experiment with the techniques developed in the different approaches. The plea is for discriminating eclectic empiricism. In an eloquent summary statement that reflects the present authors' feelings, Parloff (1970) has stated:

> Man's ultimate motivation appears to be that of finding and maintaining a state of happiness. It is not surprising, therefore, that over the centuries various proposals have been put forth for the achievement of this goal. What is surprising is how few proposals have emerged and how recurrent these few are. The encounter group movement appears to proffer only one of the classical views. Necessarily, it conflicts with other classical prescriptions. I will not presume

to enter into the debate over which is the true summum bonum. I suggest only that concepts such as the reification of openness and honesty, the celebration of the body, and regard for one's inner experiences deserve no less respect than the set which urges the benefits of self-denial, self-discipline, and self-mastery as prerequisites to the joys of competence, intellectual achievement, and productivity. Both views are due the reverence accorded to age and survival. Neither has led to a Golden Age. However, the individual who has access to alternative views and alternative routes to happiness may be less despairing when he finds himself at a road block. (p. 301)[23]

---

[23]From M. B. Parloff, "Group Therapy and the Small Group Field: An Encounter." *International Journal of Group Psychotherapy*, 1970, *20*(3), 267-304. Reprinted by permission.

CHAPTER 2

Conditions for Learning and Design Strategy

All group leaders operate on the basis of certain basic assumptions that they believe underlie effective functioning in groups. Some of the assumptions presented in this chapter are offered as being valid and generally applicable to all groups, regardless of their theoretical orientation; other assumptions seem to apply only to a specific group approach. A discussion of the implications of such assumptions should encourage group leaders to explore the assumptions underlying their respective positions.

There are two parts to the chapter. Part one considers the basic conditions for learning that appear to be fundamental to all groups and includes a general statement of the underlying assumptions and the rationale for these conditions necessary for individual and group learning. Part two compares four different orientations to groups: directive, nondirective, T-group, and encounter group. Each of these orientations is discussed in terms of its distinctive basic assumptions, characteristics, and design strategies.

BASIC CONDITIONS FOR LEARNING ACROSS GROUPS

Individual growth in groups depends on certain conditions for learning. Design strategy may vary from group to group, depending on the issues to be emphasized; however, certain basic conditions for learning are necessary—conditions that facilitate the acquisition and, most importantly, the utilization of knowledge, skills, and values for personal and group growth. Conditions for learning do not cause change; they make it possible for change to occur. They tend to be either problem oriented—concerned with human issues confronting individuals, groups, and organizations—or person oriented—centered on facilitating fruitful encounter between one's self and others through an examination of interpersonal styles and patterns of social relationships.

Basic Assumptions: Individual

Personality consists of a blend of many different levels of organization. The authors of this text reject the idea of a one-to-one relationship between cause and effect, but we accept a "field theoretical" perspective in which multiple causes are assumed. These multiple causes may involve the personal history of the individual, a recognition of his needs—which may vary from situation to situation and from time to time—as well as the here-and-now interactions between the individual and other members of his group. The result of these multiple, interdependent forces is specific behavior that is partly unique to that individual and partly common to other individuals in the group. To the degree that other group members understand and support individual idiosyncratic behavior, the individual is strengthened in his uniqueness and individuality. To the extent that other group members identify with those causes and behaviors common to all in the group, the group will grow and develop. Ideally, both individual growth and group development operate as mutual facilitators.

An individual's perception of a situation influences his behavior. In turn, a person's perception is influenced by his view of himself (his self-concept), his history, and his needs. One individual's perception of a given event may not correlate with another's perception of the same event. As the group members share their perceptions, the discrepancies that emerge become an important and even crucial aspect of group development.

The above assumptions lead to an important conclusion: behavior is a consequence of the person and his environment. In essence, what a person does can be determined (1) almost completely by his own skills and capabilities, (2) almost completely by some aspect of his environmental situation, or (3) some combination of both. Although this last situation is probably the most common, certain developing group techniques may allow an individual's responses to be predicted from the potent demand characteristics of the particular group exercises.

Basic Assumptions: Group

The essential nature and character of a group is dynamic. There is a continuous evolutionary process in which issues, conflicts, and encounters rise to the surface, are recognized, and are resolved. As a result of this process, changes occur in the group. Moreover, certain problems and issues arise with differential frequencies; e.g., although many topics are considered during initial group meetings, dependency issues frequently occur, only to submerge and then rise in a less-pronounced form in later sessions.

An important function of the group is to create certain conditions that enhance the probability that change will occur in individuals. This is accomplished by the establishment of group standards and norms through which strong influence can be brought to bear upon individuals. Conversely, the individual is encouraged to utilize his abilities and resources in bringing about productive change in the group. The group setting, with the specific type of atmosphere it generates, leads to the observation that the whole is greater than the sum of its parts.

What a leader does or does not do in a group significantly influences the conditions for learning. The group leader, regardless of orientation, helps to bring about change by interacting with group members on important emerging issues—significant events or *critical incidents*. These events or incidents require responses from the group leader. The manner in which he responds largely influences the direction and movement of the group.

The group serves as an appropriate basic unit in which to study, experience, and apply new values, skills, and knowledge. Thus, an individual may experience his group as embodying those aspects of his relationship with others that cause him difficulty. If his problems are worked through appropriately in this group, the results can be applicable to other groups such as the family, school, or organizations.

Changes in knowledge, skills, and values occur through the investigation of individual and group processes. Processes, as distinguished from the content of interactions, are the feelings and perceptions that underlie intrapersonal, interpersonal, and group-level behaviors. Process issues are always present in connection with what group members are saying and doing to each other. Process is generally studied in the service of some task or goal. For example, in a management team, the task may be to resolve conflict over certain substantive issues dealing with manpower allocations. Critical decisions cannot be reached, however, without sufficient attention to the underlying dynamics among the team members as they try to resolve their conflicts and work effectively as a group unit. On the other hand, in a T-group, for example, the major task may be the study of intrapersonal, interpersonal, and group processes. As opposed to the management group, where process is analyzed to achieve content goals, the T-group considers content a means of understanding process.

Specific Conditions for Learning

The above assumptions about the individual and the group provide a foundation from which to explore specific conditions for learning. The basic conditions for learning are the following.[1]

1. *Feedback:* This condition for learning specifies that group members need to receive information from others about the impact of their behavior. This helps determine the adequacy of existing styles of behavior and points out possible

---

[1] These conditions have been developed in association with National Training Laboratories, particularly through the work of Kenneth D. Benne and Leland P. Bradford.

directions for change. This condition underscores the importance of adequate communication, adequate in the sense that it must be given in such a manner that the recipient is free to explore its meaning and suggestions. The following are criteria for useful feedback:

a. It is descriptive rather than evaluative. By describing one's own reaction, it leaves the individual free to use it or not to use it as he sees fit. By avoiding evaluative language, it reduces the need for the individual to react defensively.
b. It is specific rather than general. To be told that one is "dominating" will probably not be as useful as to be told that "just now when we were deciding the issue, you did not listen to what others said and I felt forced to accept your arguments or face attack from you."
c. It takes into account the needs of both the receiver and giver of feedback. Feedback can be destructive when it serves only our own needs and fails to consider the needs of the person on the receiving end.
d. It is directed toward behavior which the receiver can do something about. Frustration is only increased when a person is reminded of some shortcoming over which he has no control.
e. It is solicited, rather than imposed. Feedback is most useful when the receiver himself has formulated the kind of question which those observing him can answer.
f. It is well timed. In general, feedback is most useful at the earliest opportunity after the given behavior (depending, of course, on the person's readiness to hear it and the support available from others).
g. It is checked to insure clear communication. One way of doing this is to have the receiver try to rephrase the feedback he has received to see if it corresponds to what the sender had in mind.
h. When feedback is given in a training group, both giver and receiver have opportunities to check the accuracy of the feedback with others in the group. Is this one man's impression or an impression shared by others? (NTL, 1967, p. 47)[2]

Feedback, then, is a way of establishing a "helping relationship" in a group. It is a corrective mechanism for the individual who wants to learn how well his behavior matches his intentions.

2. *Disclosure.* Disclosure is the degree to which an individual is willing, behaviorally, to react to others openly as well as to allow others to react to his own behavior. Typically in the early sessions of a group, few people are willing to disclose themselves by expressing their authentic thoughts and feelings. Later, members become intimate and are frequently willing to disclose their feelings and thoughts and to express their honest reactions. Unwillingness to risk disclosure makes it impossible to receive useful feedback and thus impossible to change behavior. Willingness to risk disclosure is increased by appropriate feedback and a supportive climate.

---

[2]From *Feedback and the Helping Relationship* (NTL Institute Reading Book). Washington, D.C.: Author, 1967. Reprinted by permission.

There is a high positive correlation between feelings of intimacy, closeness, or "emotional cohesion," and the willingness to disclose oneself in an open, straightforward manner—to become transparent. Disclosure is positively affected by other factors and conditions: the length of time members have been exposed to one another, the extent of personal or impersonal discussion, appropriate feedback, and a supportive climate. While many traditional group leaders prefer to use primarily verbal means of inducing intimacy and disclosure, other group leaders have utilized certain nonverbal sensitivity exercises as a shortcut to the same goals.

3. *A Supportive Climate.* In order for disclosure to occur, and to prevent feedback from being threatening or ignored, an atmosphere of help and respect must be fostered. In a supportive climate, a group member is able to accept and utilize feedback because he knows that he controls its application to himself. Certain additional factors are necessary for the establishment of a relatively threat-free environment.

    a. Mutual trust may be encouraged by discussions of confidentiality, commonality of goals, and respect for the position of each individual. Any behavior that encourages belief and confidence in others should be supported as an indicator of developing trust.

    b. Recognition that the helping situation is a joint exploration among all members reduces exploitative and defensive behavior and makes it easier for other individuals to listen and to receive help in a constructive manner.

4. *Experimentation.* Even though the conditions for learning have been firmly established, behavior does not always occur automatically. On the basis of feedback and other conditions for learning, a group member must be willing to experiment with different ways of behaving, to observe the effects of his behavior on other members, and to help determine change directed toward effective behavior.

In T-groups, members are encouraged to try out new styles of behavior while in the group. The group is then able to give feedback suggestions for future experimentation. This process of experimentation increases the repertoire of behaviors available to an individual when he faces a variety of situations, thus leading to increased interpersonal effectiveness.

5. *Practice and Application.* New or modified behavior requires frequent and relevant practice before it becomes internalized and enduring. Furthermore, the changes that occur in the learning situation are fundamentally useful only as they become transferable to "real world" situations. T-groups, for example, often provide occasions for giving a member a "behavior prescription," i.e., a specific way of behaving that is believed to be constructive for that individual. The group may then expect the member to practice and apply this behavior within the group. As this occurs, members give feedback concerning the impact of the new behavior on the group and

possibly suggest future refinements. The individual can thus adjust comfortably to his new behavior in order to try it out in the "real world."

Basic Design Strategy

More than a definition of a set of operations, basic design strategy is a philosophy, a way of looking at groups so that group growth and development does not become a haphazard affair but instead emerges as an orderly and evolving process, a process that is observable and amenable to change.

Design strategy is a conscious attempt to plan meaningfully for the development and resolution of certain critical issues and for the handling of certain problems that seem to be significant within a particular orientation. The nature of these problems and issues varies, depending on the theoretical orientation of the group. One group, for example, might be concerned with the interpersonal behavior of one individual toward another at a given moment; another group with the exploration of an individual's ideal self; a third with the issue of relationships to authority.

Each of these situations involves distinctly different issues and, consequently, different design strategies to resolve them. Even the same issue, e.g., authority, may be attacked at different levels depending on the type of group. An encounter group might deal with the problem primarily at the affective level, focusing on conflict between two or more dominating members; a T-group might deal with the affect as well as a conceptual analysis of authority issues; a psychoanalytic group might elicit biographical material from a member's past and use this within an analytic explanatory framework.

Group leaders usually operate on the assumption that certain issues are more important than others and that certain issues develop sooner than others. Effective group leadership is enhanced when group leaders make their basic assumptions, issues, and goals more explicit and more concretely accessible to their own awareness.

The Critical-Incident Model, the Intervention Cube, and our model of group growth and development, as attempts to organize and understand the complexities of group behavior, are relatively simplified and systematic frameworks that are amenable to empirical evaluation and utilization. The alternative to making such attempts is to bemoan the incredible complexity of group processes and thus avoid the burdens and challenges of developing rigorous research, better knowledge building, and a valid evaluation of group leadership.

In considering the technology of leadership effectiveness, a number of systems operate in ongoing groups at any given time. For example, a heated discussion among group members over which of two alternatives to choose to resolve an issue may be approached on a number of different levels. At one level, the focus could be on the substantive issues to be decided. At another level, the focus could be on the nature of the conflicts and the means of resolving them. On still another system level, a leader might choose to focus on personal styles and emotional expressions among members.

Various group orientations—T-groups and psychotherapy groups—use different techniques in dealing with different systems. Yet these different group orientations could attend to the same system, e.g., interpersonal conflict, with similar techniques.

There is enough distinctiveness among certain different group approaches to justify the identification of their characteristic design strategies. The group approaches discussed here are the directive, the nondirective, laboratory training (T-group), and the encounter group.

THE DIRECTIVE GROUP

Directive groups are distinguished by the central role played by the group leader. According to Wolberg (1967), directive approaches put the therapist in an active role in determining which of the basic problems of the individual to attack, the immediate and remote objectives to be considered, and the promotion of a plan of action. These tactics are often seen as persuasive and commanding.

The directive approach is most importantly characterized by a body of knowledge and a theory of group development that strongly influences the direction of the group. In a psychoanalytic group, interpretations are made within a clearly prescribed structure of psychoanalytic theory. In a psychodrama group, the leader is directive in investigating relationships within sociometric theory.

Group leaders often develop a directive stance and central role without necessarily becoming directive group leaders in the sense of overtly and consciously intervening within one theoretical framework. In encounter groups the individual talents and leadership abilities of such leaders as the late Fritz Perls, Will Schutz, and Bernard Gunther are highly valued. Each of these leaders assumes a centralized role in groups, directing the members in certain well-defined activities. However, partially to avoid the pitfalls inherent in dogmatic leadership and to foster greater self-reliance, encounter leaders refuse to describe their functions in terms stronger than "facilitator," "guide," or "helper."

Traditional, directive-group leaders attempt to utilize their personality in the service of an accepted framework of theory concerning group behavior; that is, leader and member behavior in the group is interpreted within the stated theoretical assumptions of that approach, whether it be psychoanalytic, transactional analytic, or rational-emotive.

In contrast, encounter-group leaders adopt an approach that is idiosyncratic to their personality and in which the life style determines the direction of the group. These group leaders are highly valued, and their encounter workshops are usually chosen on the basis of the individuals leading them, and not on the issues involved (Lubin & Eddy, 1970 & 1973). However, as the encounter group movement begins to develop a coherent theory to explain the phenomena observed in these groups (Burton, 1969; Schutz, 1967), the distinctions between traditional directive and encounter groups will decrease.

Three group leaders representative of the directive approach are Nathan Ackerman, Eric Berne, and Albert Ellis. Ackerman was a psychoanalytically oriented psychiatrist whose group work ranged from child therapy to family therapy. His general approach was that the therapist must be forthright and, at times, even blunt in order to make free and undefensive use of himself in the service of a goal (Ackerman, 1949).

Ellis is much more definitive. He specifies actual commands to be given to the group by the leader, on a regular timetable of experiencing (Ellis, 1969b).

Berne, who developed the transactional analytic framework of Parent, Adult, and Child in conflict (Berne, 1966), allows for some degree of freedom within the group, but he clearly specifies guidelines, courses of action, and limitations on statements by the transactional therapist.

Ackerman (1945) lists four important goals: (1) to improve adaptation to specific situations; (2) to relieve certain forms of acute emotional stress; (3) to change personality organization; and (4) to bring about a change in social re-education. Ellis (1959) states his goals as (1) showing the person how his irrational, unrealistic perceptions and thoughts are blocking effective personality change; (2) helping the person to uncover these assumptions and to understand them; and (3) helping him to cast these aside and to accept more reasonable and logical philosophies of life. Berne's goals are simply to help the patient tolerate and control anxiety. The adult ego state is taught to take control of all social maneuvers (Berne, 1966). Although all these goals are remarkably similar, it is interesting to note the ways in which they diverge when specific design strategies are considered.

General Design Strategy and Specific Techniques

Ackerman, Berne, and Ellis propose representative guidelines to help the group leader make interventions that are appropriate and well timed: (1) no gimmicks or deception should ever be used (Berne, 1966; Ellis, 1967) since the leader must personify the goals and methods of the group as a participant and as an observer; (2) the group must offer a varied social reality against which the members can test their unreasonable ideas, new feelings, and insights (Ackerman, 1949; Ellis, 1967), and in addition, participants may learn to laugh at their own defensive social maneuvers (Berne, 1966); (3) there is a need for multiple relationships (Ackerman, 1949) coupled with a maximum amount of encounter in a minimum amount of time (Ellis, 1969b), until the person is ready to face his own behavior with a rational frame of mind (Berne, 1961); (4) Ellis (1969a) states that one important approach is to allow the person the means to cope with the inescapable traumas of life that lead to anxiety. Ackerman (1954) and Berne (1966) attempt to reduce the level of anxiety within and outside the group.

The question of when to intervene is handled by each of these directive leaders in the following representative statements. The leader should intervene:

1. when the person, not the defense, will respond (Berne, 1966);
2. to "fix" information that the person will later deny (Berne, 1966);
3. if the person is deceiving (Berne, 1966; Ellis, 1969a; Ackerman, 1945);
4. to teach theory as emotions become calm following a crisis (Berne, 1966; Ackerman, 1945);
5. to stimulate empathy (Ackerman, 1945, 1954; Berne, 1966);
6. to show persons what they are telling themselves (Ellis, 1967);
7. to relieve acute emotional stress (Ackerman, 1955; Berne, 1966);
8. to help the group move continually back and forth between social reality and inner emotional life (Ackerman, 1949)—shifting to keep Parent, Adult, and Child interested in the situation (Berne, 1966);
9. to encourage use of intellect rather than intellectualizing (Berne, 1966).

The more important question of how to intervene, i.e., what areas or specific issues to focus on, is represented by the following statements.

1. The leader should force the patients to look at what they tell themselves, be active and directive in giving homework and in commanding certain behaviors, constantly confront the patient with any irrational behavior, not allow transference, and give the patient three insights—present behavior has antecedent causes, the past is disruptive because irrational beliefs are maintained, and a person must continually challenge his own value system (Ellis, 1967).

2. The leader must strip away the protective guard and achieve a personal definition of the problem; this is done by organizing the group processes and promoting mutual support and mutual constructive interpretation of all conflicts (Ackerman, 1954, 1955).

3. The leader should indicate crossed communications (Parent to Child, Adult to Parent) as they occur, by diagnosing the use of ego states as a defense. The leader should teach the theory of transactional analysis so that the person involved is a participant-observer of his behavior (Berne, 1966; James & Jongeward, 1971).

There are a number of other directive leadership orientations described by Thorne (1950). For example, the patient may be exposed to the therapeutic use of conflict in order to face certain situations that demand constructive decisions and actions. At other times the patient may be given educational assistance in order that he may re-evaluate his attitudes. Thorne advocates an open, eclectic approach, bringing to bear many therapeutic devices for change. Furthermore, the extent of directiveness must be evaluated for each patient, according to his needs. It may vary from domination to a participative relationship.

Haley (1963) evolved specific strategic interventions for long-term and short-term directive treatment. Haley assumed that the dynamic function of symptoms is that of power motivation, but that the therapist should be oriented toward wresting control from the patient. The therapist accomplishes this by encouraging the resistances and symptoms of the patient. Ultimately the patient is required to repeat the symptoms in such a manner that they become so offensive he cannot continue to indulge in them. For example, a compulsive eater might be commanded to eat nothing but a favored food until a point of revulsion is reached. Only then is permission given *not* to eat that specific food. Such methods of self-punishment and aversive control are designed to benefit the patient. In many of these methods, the tactics of satiation and counterconditioning are quite evident.

There are other directive methods designed to enable a patient to face "reality." Glasser (1965) developed a strategy termed "reality therapy," in which there is a constant encounter between therapist and patient. During these encounters, reasons for behavior are not explored; inner conflicts, dynamics, and the unconscious are ignored, and excuses for deviant behavior are not accepted. The last phase of this therapy deals with the patient's acceptance of full responsibility for his behavior; with this acceptance, relearning begins. The therapist remains very active, emphasizing the patient's strong points, encouraging adaptive behavior, and planning for future actions. These actions are designed to place the patient in a better-functioning relationship with reality.

Within the relatively structured and stable theoretical system of directive-group approaches, such as group psychoanalysis, answers to questions involving specific interventions for specific phenomena at specific points in the life of the group are surprisingly vague. There are inadequate specifications for the various types of conflict, authority, and resistance issues. With proper specifications, the phenomena would facilitate the systematic learning of intervention skills for a variety of anticipated issues.

One general criticism of the directive approaches is that they foster dependence on the therapist and inhibit the patient's self-sufficiency. This criticism should be evaluated to determine if temporary increases or decreases in dependence are helpful or harmful—suggesting the need for greater emphasis on a technological approach to interventions.

THE NONDIRECTIVE GROUP

Nondirective groups are distinguished by the central role played by the patient or group member as opposed to the role of the group leader. The goal of therapy is not to solve a particular problem but rather to enable a client to develop improved ways of dealing with his life. The group leader helps the client do this by providing an atmosphere of total acceptance and by avoiding value judgments. This procedure encourages the client to look to himself rather than to the therapist for direction and the solution of his personal problems.

Carl Rogers (1942) is recognized as the prime figure in the conception of nondirective or client-centered therapy. He states that the therapist using the nondirective method must have genuine interest in the patient, be willing to listen to him carefully to understand him, and provide an atmosphere of total acceptance or "unconditional positive regard" (Rogers, 1951). Rogers believes that every individual has within himself the potentiality of growth, which can be utilized under appropriate psychological circumstances. In this approach, there is a great deal of confidence in the unique capacity of the client to discover and solve his own problems. The therapist respects the individual and allows him to discover himself. In a very real sense, the direction of the therapy is set by the client, and the therapist follows this direction. Since the therapist sets more limits on himself than on the client, nondirective methods differ significantly from directive methods, which place more limits upon the patient.

Raskin (1948) pointed out that Rogers translated the philosophical concepts of individual responsibility, respect for the integrity of the individual, and confidence in the capacity of the individual to be responsible for himself into a therapeutic procedure that is consistent with what the therapist actually does in therapy. In Argyris's terms (1972), Rogers translated his "espoused theory" into a "theory in action."

The goal of the nondirective or client-centered approach is to bring clients into a greater awareness of their present feelings. This is usually accomplished by presenting each individual with the feelings and thoughts he communicates to the therapist. Interpretation, as it is traditionally held, is not important in this setting. Instead, awareness and reflection of feelings are the criteria for nondirective interchange.

Increased awareness of attitudes and feelings and an openness to experience without damaging preconceptions and "shoulds" are also intended products of this improved communication process. The client becomes aware that the locus of evaluation is not external but rather within himself. There is a deliberate attempt to promote the individual's growth so that he may be able to deal with present and future problems in an integrated and mature fashion.

Rogers has suggested several specific goals as a result of movement in therapy. These goals are *"symptom to self," "environment to self," "others to self,*" and "*past to present.*" In successful therapy the person learns that it is safe to leave the less dangerous consideration of his symptoms, others, the environment, and the past, and to focus on the discovery of "me, here, and now" (Rogers, 1951, pp. 135-136).

General Design Strategy and Specific Techniques

If the therapist provides a certain type of relationship, the client will discover the capacity to use that relationship for growth; change and personal development occur. There are three basic conditions for growth in groups utilizing this approach. First, the leader must communicate an attitude of unconditional positive regard for the person; i.e., he must accept all the client's feelings, whether positive or negative, and thereby create a warm and supportive climate for the group members. This gives the client the freedom to explore his various inner feelings without evaluation or judgment by the therapist.

Secondly, the client chooses his own goals. He learns from the consequences of the choice and grows toward autonomy and self-direction. Most importantly, he listens to himself and his own internal psychological and physiological messages rather than depending on outside messages—values, directions, goals.

Finally, the client chooses his own values. The role of the therapist is to help him to establish his individual value system. The therapist allows other group members to present alternative values which the client is free to accept or reject (Rogers, 1951).

The following summary of specific operations and techniques characteristic of the client-centered therapist is based on a list drawn up by Hobbs (1955, p. 16)[3] and on his elaboration of these and other points.

1. When the patient is engaging in some defense mechanism (projection, rationalization, etc.), the therapist responds to what the client says without pointedly calling attention to these defenses.

2. The therapist should encourage maximum participation of all group members. This leads to effective group functioning since all members are drawing from a larger resource pool.

3. Group members should be encouraged to take responsibility for themselves as well as for leadership functions.

4. The most effective therapist is one who presents the expressed feelings of the clients by clarifying and/or rephrasing those feelings.

---

[3]From N. Hobbs, "Client Centered Therapy." In J. McCary & D. E. Sheer (Eds.), *Six Approaches to Psychotherapy.* New York: Dryden Press, 1955. Used by permission.

5. In addition to clarifying comments by various group members, the leader relates new comments to previous comments earlier in the life of the group.

6. Structured interventions (role playing, subgrouping, etc.) are not advised, for this kind of action may be interpreted by the group as directive and forced.

7. The leader usually attempts to understand and communicate the intent of a member's message. In order to do this, he may have to resort to rephrasing. If a client, for example, expresses withdrawal and reluctance in both verbal and nonverbal behavior, the leader might state, "Perhaps you feel you did not want to come here today."

8. Whenever a group strays from the topic of conversation, the group leader points this out, thereby allowing the group to make its own choice as to its direction.

9. The therapist does not stress his authority, admonish or give moral advice, or argue with the client. Rather, he helps the person talk and think through the implications of the client's statements.

10. All feelings explicitly and implicitly displayed by the client are to be accepted by the therapist. Tolerance of the client's feelings of hostility, antagonism, or resentment may clear the way for further expression by the client.

11. The therapist may answer questions and give information when such responses are relevant to treatment, but he refrains from giving information when the issue of dependency is involved in the question.

12. Most importantly, the therapist conveys to the client, verbally and nonverbally, a sense of acceptance and confidence in the ability of the client to handle his own problems.

The clearest contrast to be drawn between the strategies of nondirective versus other group approaches is seen in what the client-centered therapist does not do (Hobbs, 1955).

1. No prescriptions or diagnoses of the client's condition are given by the therapist. Instead of striving for what he is not, the client finds that there are advantages in being what he is and in the further development of the possibilities he now has.

This distinction is not shared by T-groups and encounter groups. They frequently devote several sessions to the diagnosis of problem areas and the construction of specific behavioral prescriptions for their members. T-groups and encounter groups, however, stress the development of the individual's full potential. This is termed the humanistic bedrock of all the approaches that view man as striving for self-fulfillment.

2. The leader does not advise, moralize, praise, blame, or teach. Neither does he plan programs of activities or the agendas of group meetings; the group members determine what direction the group will take.

This prohibition is in sharp contrast to the general strategies of other group approaches. It is quite common to find T-group leaders teaching, advising, and planning programs of activities to clarify some important facet of group dynamics. T-groups sometimes begin with explicit agendas. Encounter groups also teach, advise, and structure activities, but seldom above an affective or visceral level. On the other hand, encounter groups seldom begin with a preplanned agenda, as in T-groups, but rather go with the prevailing feelings of the group. In this respect they resemble nondirective groups. In still another contrast, directive group leaders—particularly those using behavior-modification principles—have begun to discover the advantages to be gained by appropriate praise (reinforcement) and blame (extinction or punishment) in accelerating group growth and development (Liberman, 1970a, 1970b, 1970c).

3. The nondirective leader does not attempt to promote insight directly, nor does he ask probing questions or suggest areas for exploration. The directive group leader, by contrast, directly attempts to provide insight by asking probing questions, suggesting areas for discussion, and making direct interpretations. This is not to state that the nondirective group leader avoids the use of insight. Insight, when it occurs, must emerge as a consequence of client inquiry and self-revelation without external pressure. Encounter-group leaders provide insight through a variety of directive methods, verbal and nonverbal. For example, members may be directed to engage in a fantasy exercise, discuss its personal meanings, and then act out the consequences nonverbally. In the nondirective approach, the leader waits until the proper statements reflecting growth have first been emitted by the group member. The leader then attempts to reward and encourage this personal growth by allowing it to continue to grow without interference.

The directive, encounter, and T-group approaches are more inclined to elicit certain desired responses on the part of group members by appropriate questions and exercises. Once these responses are elicited, they are appropriately encouraged.

4. In a painstaking and insightful analysis of the role of the nondirective therapist, Telschow, Gorlow, and Hoch (1950) found that the effective group therapist is one who succeeds in maintaining a minimum level of anxiety in a group while encouraging members to assume the role of the therapist. Encounter groups share this belief, but set about achieving it by maintaining high levels of group anxiety through certain structured activities.

In a similar manner, anxiety is used as a tool in directive groups and T-groups to stimulate members to explore areas that are threatening but necessary to personal growth. It is evident that different strategies are involved in attaining similar goals. The nondirective group leader feels that as little anxiety as possible provides the therapeutic atmosphere that results in an open discussion of problems. Directive-, encounter-, and T-group leaders feel that anxiety is necessary for learning and, when heightened and utilized properly, important for growth and change.

In conclusion, the design strategies utilized by nondirective-group leaders are quite explicit. Furthermore, they follow directly from the theory and rationale postulated by Rogers. Client-centered methods appear to be most useful with individuals who are responsive to "unconditional positive regard" and are of relatively sound personality structure. The method appears to be less effective with persons manifesting strong anxiety symptoms or psychotic disorganization (Wolberg, 1967). Thus the choice or rejection of client-centered therapy seems to depend on the depth of the individual's disturbance, the existing degree of ego strength, and the nature of the problem.

Client-centered therapy has, however, made important contributions to psychotherapy through research into the basic elements of interviewing, understanding of process, and outcomes of therapy. It has stimulated a considerable amount of professional literature in attempting to spell out the management of certain important phases of group treatment. It is worthwhile to mention at this point that Rogers (1967, 1970) has recently turned his attention to the area of group sensitivity training, considering it to be compatible with his belief in the need for the development of human potential.

LABORATORY TRAINING (T-GROUP)

The primary objective of the T-group is to mobilize group forces to support the growth of members as unique individuals and as collaborators in interpersonal processes. Although there are many similarities with traditional therapy groups, there are also some important differences. The T-group generally adheres to the ongoing current dynamics of interaction (process) as opposed to genetic causes. Furthermore, the T-group deals with conscious and preconscious behavior rather than with unconscious motivation. It makes the important assumption that persons participating are well rather than ill (Bradford, Gibb, & Benne, 1964). Since T-groups are composed mainly of normal people, there is less emphasis on therapy than in the traditional directive groups.

"Laboratory" has been used on occasion as a synonym for T-group. It should be noted, however, that the T-group is simply one important component of the laboratory and is crucial for certain types of learnings. It is one of the groupings referred to by Benne (1964b), but the term must not be used as an equivalent to the overall laboratory approach. Excellent summaries of the laboratory approach have been written by Yalom (1970), Gottschalk and Pattison (1969), and Lakin (1972).

T-groups have as a major goal the growth of the individual. This is achieved by increasing the individual's ability to integrate knowledge, skills, and values about himself in relation to others. Knowledge is acquired by participation in a group that attempts to offer a balance between experiencing and knowing, i.e., a group in which conceptual and visceral understanding of either an individual or group experience is highly valued. It is commonplace to observe skill sessions in which individuals attempt to put into action knowledge learned about the group and about the self.

In contrast to typical encounter groups, in a T-group the understanding of group dynamics and group process is held to be an important goal that may provide insights into back-home situations. To initiate and facilitate change, major values, such as the democratic ethic, the helping relationship, and science are stressed in attempts to operationalize approaches for the leader and participants in a group.

T-groups are quite flexible in their approach and goals. T-groups have been used at the personal level to help reduce defensiveness and increase openness and honesty in dealing with current and real concerns. T-groups having an interpersonal focus deal with improved communication with others as well as new ways of working with others. T-groups designed for intergroup activities deal with the diagnosis and management of intergroup problems, including improvement in handling conflict.

T-groups may be utilized to deal primarily with team building at the group level. This is done within subunits of large organizations in order to understand and resolve problems unique to that department, task force, team, or class.

General Design Strategy and Specific Techniques

It is generally agreed that in laboratory training, the T-group or training group is the heart of the entire experience. Laboratory training, however, is dedicated to a triad of learnings that are referred to as *knowledge, skills,* and *values*. The skills are the experiential learnings that take place within the T-group. The knowledge is conceptual and theoretical, imparted to the participants in general sessions or as spontaneous inputs by the trainer. The values permeate the entire laboratory and are lived and transmitted during all the sessions and activities. The major value shared by trainers is that of the democratic ethic which translates itself into a distributive theory of leadership.

Most laboratories begin in a general session, with participants gathering as a community. Some broad objectives of the program are stated, and participants are assigned to T-groups. This general session is brief, and little attempt is made at education. This is in keeping with the underlying theory of laboratory training, which is in contrast to traditional educational theory. In the traditional educational situation, knowledge and theory are given to the student, and he is to apply what he has learned to "real life" experiences.

Laboratory training focuses initially on the experiential; real life is lived and experienced within the T-group. Conceptualization and theorizing are delayed until immediately after the experience or are examined concurrently with the experience. Indeed, this approach is well named a "laboratory": each group within the laboratory is an experiment in which the participants are the materials and ingredients. Initially, the trainer is the interpreter of the actions and reactions of the participants as they mix and jell within the group; however, the trainer recognizes that he is also a very important part of the experiment itself and of the mixture that will soon become a group.

At the beginning of the life of a T-group, the trainer eschews the role of the traditional leader or educator, and the group members find themselves in a position of ambiguity without direction and leadership; there is a void which causes some anxiety. The skill of the trainer is of great importance; too much anxiety may immobilize the group, whereas too little may not allow the necessary conditions for learning to develop. The trainer must recognize the importance of anxiety as a prelude to learning. The void perceived by the participants, the lack of direction, the absence of traditional leadership, the apparent lack of goals, the absurdity of a group of people sitting together with nothing to do, serve to engender enough anxiety to let the participant project his own needs, desires, and feelings into the situation.

Since the goal of the laboratory is behavior change, the first condition for learning is disclosure. The anxiety that has been engendered helps the participant to "behave," if for no other reason than just to fill the void. And if a person is to receive information on the effects of his current behavior, it is necessary for him to behave sufficiently so that others will react to his behavior. The reaction of others to this behavior is termed feedback.

In order to learn what effects his behavior is having on others, a person must receive feedback. When he receives adequate information he is in a position to determine whether changing his behavior is a desirable goal. If it is, he is also in a better position to decide what changes are necessary to achieve that goal. Thus the participant can decide his own direction for performance improvement. In order to achieve these ends, however, a supportive climate is necessary.

A supportive climate is one in which the learner does not feel threatened and does not become defensive about his behavior. Such an atmosphere exists in the T-group to the extent that each member feels that he is among more than friends—he is among people who really care about him and want the best for him. Everyone in the group is grieved by the sadness of other members; all rejoice in the happiness of one another. There is no fear of being hurt by anyone in the group. Every member of the group is a source of strength and support to every other member. In such an atmosphere, the learner finds it easier to shed old dysfunctional behaviors and attempt new and more useful behaviors.

These behavioral changes are not automatic occurrences. After feedback is received on current behavior—if the feedback is specific, descriptive, and nonjudgmental—the participant may want to experiment with other types of behavior and test their effects on others.

This process can be enhanced by members of the group giving one another "behavior prescriptions," something that is usually attempted fairly late in the life of the T-group. Through this process the participant is in a better position to determine appropriate and effective behaviors. As the participant becomes more comfortable with his new behavior and has examined its functionality with himself and other members of the group, he has an opportunity to practice it. The more positive feedback he receives from the group members, the more internalized and enduring the behavior becomes. The T-group provides an excellent climate for such practice.

Changes in behavior tend to be painful, and it takes courage to change and to maintain the changes. The T-group provides an atmosphere that makes it less difficult to change; it is far more difficult to apply new behaviors to other and possibly less supportive situations. However, as these changes are fundamentally useful only as they become transferable to outside situations, the learner and the learning group are encouraged to apply their new behaviors outside the T-group. In some T-groups emphasis is placed on utilizing negative feedback in outside situations in which mutual feedback is not always possible, e.g., an encounter between a superior and a subordinate in a business situation. Specific skills are practiced within the group to facilitate transference (Porter, 1974).

One of the most important factors in the growth of a T-group is that of norm development. While norms may not be stated explicitly by the participants, normative issues such as inclusion-exclusion, participation-observation, and dependency-counterdependency are always present in the group. How much a group member should disclose concerning a problem confronting all members and whether someone will be hurt by direct feedback and, if so, whether he and/or the group will reject the giver of the feedback are other normative issues that are of importance to group members.

The problem of norms is a complex one. There are general norms that most trainers would agree on, e.g., openness, direct expression of feelings, feedback, group involvement. There are other group norms that appear to depend on the goals of the group and the leadership bias of the trainer, e.g., his orientation toward the individual, a group, or an organization. Some trainers, for example, urge their groups to explore and establish norms in the areas of leadership and authority problems; other trainers tend to emphasize personal norms involving disclosure, intimacy, and trust; and still others devote a majority of time to the resolution of organizational conflicts. This does not imply that there is no overlap. However, specific design strategy is the point at which trainers begin to exhibit their individual styles. There is little empirical evidence, unfortunately, as to which group norms facilitate group growth and development.

Specific techniques of intervention usually involve assuming the role of a facilitator or guide rather than a leader. Verbal and nonverbal techniques may be used to facilitate and encourage understanding of an ongoing process. From time to time the trainer may conceptualize what has just occurred in the group. At other times, he may sense the need to sum up the important themes present in the group and point to possible future directions. This latter technique is usually carried out during the beginning or ending moments of a group.

A number of general trainer techniques are identified by Bradford (1964). The suggested techniques are quite general in nature and consequently have limited value to the beginning group leader. Statements such as "The trainer avoids group dependency on him" and "The trainer should bring conflict or competition to a head if it becomes immovable and blocks further group action" are quite common. Such statements, found throughout the T-group literature, offer little concrete advice as to the specific operations the trainer uses in intervention activities.

Another important aspect of laboratory training (of which the T-group is a central part) is the emphasis on group building and community building. A group, much like the nuclear family in society, is not an encapsulated, isolated entity. If the individual and the group are to function fully they must function within a larger society. Thus, the entire laboratory becomes a society or a community in itself. Community sessions are held and community activities are not only encouraged but built into the program.

Within laboratory training, learnings come from many sources and focus on a number of different levels. Learnings are concerned with (1) intrapersonal development; (2) two dimensions of interpersonal development—the individual within his group and, on a larger scale, within his community; (3) intragroup development—the group members as a group; and (4) intergroup relations—the group interacting with other groups and the community at large.

THE ENCOUNTER GROUP

Encounter groups are distinguished by a number of considerations that set them apart from traditional directive, nondirective, and T-groups. Unlike other groups, cognitive understanding and group theory are minimized, if not ignored. The encounter has been defined as

a sudden, spontaneous, intuitive meeting with another person in which there is an immediate sense of relatedness. (Moustakas, 1967, p. 45)

The sense of immediacy, intuitiveness, and spontaneity appears to have acquired value at the expense of inhibiting theory development. Burton (1969) comments on this point:

> interestingly enough, those in the vanguard of the encounter movement, the leaders and group facilitators themselves, have been notoriously unresponsive to the self-demand for theoretical clarification. (p. ix)[4]

Encounter groups vary from those that emphasize nonverbal physical awareness exercises (Gunther, 1968) to those that are primarily verbal (Schutz, 1967; Otto, 1968). The encounter group exists as a framework or environment in which encounter activities take place. Unlike T-groups, the group is not the object of study, nor are its dynamics. Another distinction, described by Lubin and Eddy (1970) is that the

> T-group with a personal-interpersonal emphasis resembles some encounter groups in some of the methods that are used, but deals less with personal-historical material and has more of an educational focus. (p. 331)[5]

This again points to the need for clarification of goals and characteristics in these overlapping approaches.

In the rapidly growing field of encounter groups, it is difficult to select only a few prominent individuals for discussion since the area is in a constant state of change. Representatives range from those who endorse primarily nonverbal avenues of sensory awareness (Gunther, 1969) to those who use both verbal and nonverbal and other art media (Otto, 1968) to practitioners like Will Schutz (1967) who conceptualize group growth and development and work within such a framework. Moreover, other therapists such as Rogers (1970) and Ellis (1969b) are applying their approaches to the group encounter area.

Burton (1969) reviewed a wide range of encounter-group practitioners. These ranged from those who preferred a highly personal, spontaneous, idiosyncratic approach (Cahn, 1969; Warkentin, 1969) to those who established a fairly rigid (and atypical) agenda (Ellis, 1969b) to at least one attempt at theory application from T-groups (Gibb & Gibb, 1968a). Both Burton (1969) and Otto and Mann (1968) indicate the diverse, individualistic, affect-oriented nature of the field.

---

[4]From A. Burton (Ed.), *Encounter: Theory and Practice of Encounter Groups*. San Francisco: Jossey-Bass, 1969. Reprinted by permission.

---

[5]From B. Lubin & W. B. Eddy, "The Laboratory Training Model: Rationale, Method, and Some Thoughts for the Future." *International Journal of Group Psychotherapy*, 1970, 20, 305-339. Reprinted by permission.

General Design Strategy and Specific Techniques

The overriding goal of encounter groups is to actualize individual potential, usually through nonintellectual means (Lieberman, Yalom, & Miles, 1973). Members may attend encounter groups for many reasons, ranging from a desire to receive help on a specific problem to the pleasure of "encountering" as a popular pastime. The overall "mission" of the encounter group is to move society toward being less repressive and restrictive by altering many psychological and interpersonal relationships within that society. Encounter also attempts to utilize human potential by correcting the overemphasis on intellectual awareness at the expense of feelings and emotional awareness.

In general, encounter groups are intended to provide opportunities for participants to achieve (a) warmth, trust, and closeness among members; (b) openness and authenticity by living in the present; (c) a return to concerns with body wisdom; (d) an emphasis on positive values and enhanced creativity, and, finally, (e) the acquisition of insight as an integration of knowing and feeling. The specific nature of each of these goals and of the paths to their achievement varies among encounter-group leaders.

WARMTH, TRUST, AND CLOSENESS AMONG MEMBERS

The attainment of warmth, trust, and closeness among encounter-group members appears to be a basic goal prerequisite to all future group growth. Otto (1968) proposes that our social masks be dropped to enable members to see each other as humans with real human feelings. In order for the basic conditions to occur, members must share intimate and deep aspects of their current personal lives. Alienation must be removed and interpersonal trust developed; sensitivity toward other members must be present. Members should be open to new, intimate, and close relationships (Otto, 1968). The group must come to grips with problems of inclusion and affection. Feelings of rejection and abandonment must be uncovered and resolved (Schutz, 1967, 1971).

The question now arises as to how the encounter-group leader is able to encourage warmth, trust, and closeness among group members. There are a number of techniques and design strategies directed toward achieving a relatively quick sense of intimacy and closeness; e.g., members are instructed to have certain experiences, to discuss their reactions, and to ask each other questions (Otto, 1968). In the least concept-oriented groups like Gunther's (1968), members are directed to have certain experiences and to carry out instructions even if they seem silly. They are promised that the activities will make sense after being performed. Members are asked to give and request personal information and to participate in group activities that require the exchange of this personal information. In addition, members are told the value of directly expressing or receiving feelings through physically touching other group members (Otto, 1968; Schutz, 1967; Gunther, 1968, 1969, 1971). Conflict is implicitly encouraged by providing nondirective outlets for the safe expression of hostility in confrontations.

There is a wide variety of techniques and structured activities that help the leader create an atmosphere of warmth, trust, and closeness. Direct verbal statements of feelings create emotional bonds among group members in direct proportion to the intensity of expression. This suggests that leaders who rapidly legitimize and require the direct expression of feelings (not attitudes, thinking, or opinions) create an atmosphere of warmth and closeness in an abbreviated period of time. The leader must take care to involve as many group members as possible in this process or the group may be too threatened to continue and may freeze (Schutz & Seashore, 1972). The influence and example set by the leader's behavior at this point is crucial to further development.

Several encounter books (Schutz, 1967; Gunther, 1968, 1971) have a number of activities specifically designed to dissolve these resistances and to "loosen people up." Traditional groups that allow members to become familiar through verbal discussions of attitudes, opinions, and intellectualized feelings take longer to achieve a state of strong emotional cohesion.

OPENNESS AND AUTHENTICITY BY LIVING IN THE PRESENT

Openness and authenticity are desired as continuing personal characteristics, and are not limited to one particular group or situation. Gunther (1969) states that members must be open to experience, to intense feelings and emotions, and to the feeling and expression of hostility and aggression. In addition, members must be open to pain and conflict, which must frequently be worked through if learning is to occur (Schutz, 1967). In order to achieve authenticity, members must learn to utilize their senses and intuition to deal directly with experience, rather than responding only to rigid preconceptions (Burton, 1972). Members are encouraged to avoid intellectualization. Authenticity arises from simple, direct, and undistorted responses to all the experiences one encounters.

While the term *authenticity* is not explicitly anti-intellectual, it nevertheless encourages the direct use of intuition, spontaneity, and raw experiences, an approach that is often implicitly antithetical to the day-to-day intellectual approach to problem solving. Authenticity is also encouraged by the stress placed on living in the present.

Living in the present appears to sensitize group members to current experiences by focusing their entire attention on the here-and-now. In this approach, members are not allowed to become preoccupied with past events or events that have occurred outside the group—the there-and-then. The leader's continual requirement that all members deal with the here-and-now increases emotional intensity within the group and thereby fosters identification and resolution of encounters among members. The emphasis on the here-and-now is also characteristic of T-groups.

In order to create an awareness of authenticity and living in the present, the leader may use the techniques of sensory-awareness exercises (Gunther, 1968) or may recommend the nonverbal communication of feelings (Schutz, 1967) or a literal acting-out of feelings. In one sensory technique, the leader requires every member to report only what he experiences or feels, right now, in this room, as it relates to others in the room, i.e., talking in the here-and-now. Discussing people or events outside the group is forbidden, since it deals with the there-and-then. Members whose discussions within the group seem irrelevant or tangential are asked to show what such discussions have to do with what is occurring in the group at that time.

With the insistence on dealing with phenomena in the here-and-now, typical forms of resistance such as intellectualization and rational abstractions tend to be made inoperative. To avoid increased exposure, one could withdraw from discussion or leave the group. However, group pressures tend to prevent this from happening, since many typical resistances to exposure involve the use of there-and-then defenses.

A RETURN TO CONCERNS WITH BODY WISDOM

The majority of encounter-group proponents agree that there is an imbalance in the everyday world that favors cognitive, rational, intellectual development at the expense of experiential awareness. Learning in an encounter group, therefore, involves sensory-awareness exercises which teach body wisdom (Gunther, 1969). Gunther feels that members must relearn the body wisdom of childhood through a sensory re-awakening. In essence, members are asked to get back in touch with their bodies, to experience and be aware of the sensations and feelings that their bodies are feeding them. In general, there must be optimal sensitivity and functioning of the body, since improved body functioning leads to improved emotional functioning (Schutz, 1967).

In order to promote body wisdom, the leader must bring the members to the point where they can touch each other. This is done in order to dispel feelings of alienation and to legitimize the process (Schutz & Seashore, 1972). This last factor is most important, as western culture generally has a taboo against touching as a form of expression. Touching is strongly associated with, and conditioned to, expressions of strong feelings toward another loved object. The leader may spend considerable time discussing the taboos in society against tears, anger, and physical touching (Forer, 1972). Members are generally encouraged to enjoy the experience of being touched (Howard, 1970). Any guilt at doing this is dispelled once members learn that the sensuous and erotic ability to feel is not limited to the sexual sphere (Gunther, 1969).

The return to body wisdom, including the ability to express and receive feelings from other group members through physical contact, does not occur at once. Members are led through a series of structured activities and techniques that increase their self-awareness and, later, their awareness of others. For example, early in the life of the group, the leader might ask members to relax, to uncross their legs and arms, and to take a deep breath. Soon thereafter, he might ask them to concentrate on their bodies and report all sensory experiences regardless of how trivial they may be. Attention is given to concentrating, listening, smelling, tasting, and using the entire body in communicating with others. The leader might show the members how to stimulate their own bodies and their partner's body by slapping, tapping, shaking, lifting, or stretching. Following the experience, they are given the opportunity to express their reactions to the physical contact. The degree of contact may then be increased to wrestling and hugging and even extended to other group activities (Gunther, 1969).

Body wisdom is an important goal in encounters as it represents the Eastern concerns with body awareness, meditation, and the need to be in touch with the environment. The underlying principle is that physical proximity leads to psychological intimacy. This principle appears to be strengthened by the observation that members who are initially distrustful, hostile, or even indifferent toward one another find themselves experiencing a strong shift in feelings as a result of a directed activity involving positive physical contact. Sometimes this emotional shift occurs as a result of a single potent physical-contact exercise. The positive, pleasurable aspects of this physical contact override previous intellectual or rational attitudes and present a shift or modification of feelings. It is also believed that previous societal conditioning that legitimizes pleasurable physical contact only with a love object can be counteracted by the rapid emotional changes occurring through structured encounter activities. It is not suggested that a sudden, drastic change will result that completely reverses previously held feelings and attitudes on the part of members. However, carefully planned physical-contact exercises among group members tend to promote body wisdom, define members' feelings toward one another, and produce a psychological intimacy that apparently emerges more quickly through nonverbal techniques than through traditional verbal approaches.

AN EMPHASIS ON POSITIVE VALUES AND ENHANCED CREATIVITY

Encounter groups place a high value on spontaneity and living to one's full potential. Some encounter groups assume that if one achieves warmth, trust, closeness, openness and authenticity, a return to body wisdom, and insight as an integration of knowing and feeling, enhanced creativity must somehow follow. Other groups take a more direct approach and utilize creativity workshops where members are encouraged to develop creative expressions in various verbal and nonverbal media. A member may be asked to create, in paint, clay, or other natural objects, himself, his feelings toward others, or his world. As in the nonverbal physical-contact exercises, each member is asked to put himself into his work and to feel what he is doing. This results in the emergence of strong, emotionally expressive products. The creativity workshops led by Rhyne (Rhyne & Vich, 1969) illustrate such attempts to encourage positive creative efforts on the part of the individual.

THE ACQUISITION OF INSIGHT AS AN INTEGRATION OF KNOWING AND FEELING

In encounter groups, *insight* represents a viable balance between feeling and knowing. However, although this appears to be the theoretical definition accepted by many encounter leaders, in reality, *knowing* does not imply traditional cognitive or intellectual information. This is probably a reaction to the fact that the world favors and even overemphasizes the cognitive, rational approach at the expense of or even exclusion of feelings. The majority of encounter leaders would probably accept "experiential knowledge" as a definition of *knowing*.

There are a number of ways in which encounter leaders attempt to foster insight. Group discussion, for example, typically follows structured activities (Otto, 1968). After a significant catharsis by a group member, the leader usually intervenes to help him understand what has happened (Gunther, 1969). In groups that enjoy a longer life, the leader encourages members to carry through with simple and easily accomplished action programs. These programs are directives issued by the group to a particular group member in order to facilitate his personal growth in the real world. The value of this approach is that the group supports the members in relating the experiential knowledge gained in the group to the outside world.

In general, insight takes many forms throughout the life of a group. In the beginning stages, insight may consist of a gradual awareness of greater contact with the body and its sensations. Later, insight may broaden to include increased knowledge of interpersonal effectiveness. When members become receptive to new feelings and behavioral alternatives, insight represents the adoption of a more productive life style.

The design strategies utilized by encounter-group leaders appear to be a gathering of many games or skill activities designed to highlight personal or interpersonal processes. Although some attempt has been made to systemize these techniques (Schutz, 1967, 1973), there is no comprehensive theory of the encountering process. A recent study by Lieberman, Yalom, and Miles (1973) attempted such a comprehensive effort by examining group variables among various trainer orientations. Schutz (1974) has questioned

Conditions for Learning and Design Strategy 83

the validity of the study, its conclusions, and whether the study has any relationship to encounter groups as they are defined by the authors themselves.

Both this study and the review of it illustrate some of the problems involved in design strategies in group research. A more general perspective of recent studies in group training (Gibb, 1974) concludes that the quality of research is improving sufficiently for such research to be considered seriously.

A review of the current techniques and design strategies reveals at least three important psychological principles that account for the majority of the observed effects.

1. Direct verbal statements of feelings create emotional bonds among group members in direct proportion to the intensity of expression.

2. Insistence on dealing with phenomena in the here-and-now and the general avoidance of there-and-then discussions enable resistance to be minimized or avoided.

3. Physical proximity, in the social island of a group, leads to psychological intimacy.

These principles deserve empirical investigation and partially form the basis for future theorizing.

Table 2.1 presents an overall summary of the major issues and characteristics that distinguish therapy groups (both directive and nondirective), T-groups, and encounter groups.

Table 2.1. Similarities and Differences in Group Approaches

Therapy Groups (Directive/Nondirective)	T-Groups	Encounter Groups
1. Members see themselves as maladjusted or sick.	Members see themselves as essentially "normals" who are seeking self-improvement but may also come for specific problem areas.	Members see themselves as essentially "normals" but may also come for specific problem areas.
2. Members are not particularly concerned with group dynamics; the group is simply the medium through which problems are solved.	Members are specifically interested in the study of group dynamics as an important goal.	Members are not particularly concerned with group dynamics: the group is simply the medium through which other members are experienced.
3. The group leader is the central person throughout the life of the group, whether facilitating or directing activities.	The group leader is, initially, the central person, but this gradually evolves into distributive leadership over the life of the group.	The group leader is the central person throughout, whether facilitating or directing activities.
4. The group leader seldom gives any formal theory input, although feelings and events are often reflected within a particular personality-theory framework.	The group leader frequently gives brief theory input on such issues as feedback and authority, as they reflect current group feelings and events.	The group leader does not give any formal theory input. Ongoing feelings and events are discussed at their lowest common level, i.e., in terms of basic primary feelings.
5. In the directive approach there is prior staff planning, usually on an individual basis, to match the patient need with a range of educational and therapeutic techniques. No prior staff planning occurs in the nondirective approach.	There is prior staff planning to match client learning needs with a range of educational and experiential technology.	There is little staff planning in general. Members themselves determine their needs by interaction. Staff provides a wide range of experiential techniques.

Conditions for Learning and Design Strategy 85

Table 2.1.(cont.)

	Therapy Groups (Directive/Nondirective)	T-Groups	Encounter Groups
6.	The group typically deals heavily in there-and-then discussion, including genetic material.	The group typically deals in here-and-now discussions, with little genetic material.	The group deals almost exclusively with here-and-now discussions. Genetic material is avoided.
7.	The group has no preset agenda. Group behavior decides the direction of group discussion.	The group sometimes begins with inputs or activities, but typically does not. Group behavior decides the directions of group discussion.	While the group may sometimes begin with a warm-up activity, no preset agenda is used. Group behavior decides the group direction.
8.	The emphasis is on experiencing affect in relation to the understanding of a problem. Understanding is usually based on psychological theory (directive) or a philosophy of self-growth (nondirective).	Emphasis is on experiencing affect and on being able to conceptualize and understand the experience.	Emphasis is on experiencing the affect as an end in itself. Discussion of the feeling is permitted, but abstract conceptualizing is discouraged or ignored.
9.	Stress is placed on the importance of accurate communication through appropriate techniques of feedback, support, and disclosure.	Stress is placed on the importance of accurate communication through appropriate techniques of feedback, support, and disclosure.	Stress is placed on the importance of accurate communication through appropriate techniques of feedback, support, and disclosure.
10.	There is emphasis on personal adjustment and the solving of personal problems through primarily verbal activities.	There is emphasis on personal growth and creativity through multimedia verbal and nonverbal activities.	There is emphasis on personal growth and creativity through multimedia verbal and nonverbal activities.

Table 2.1. (cont.)

Therapy Groups (Directive/Nondirective)	T-Groups	Encounter Groups
11. The focus is on individuals achieving new insight or new motivations in order to change behavior in the real world outside the group.	The focus is on increasing interpersonal effectiveness and on trying out and experimenting with new behavior in the group.	The focus is on trying out and experimenting with new behavior in the group.
12. The focus is on unconscious or motivational material, rather than on conscious statements or actions.	The focus is on current, conscious, interpersonal data rather than on unconscious material.	The focus is on current, conscious, interpersonal data, but with heavy use of fantasy methods.
13. The complete emphasis is on promoting the transfer of therapeutic knowledge gained in the group to back-home situations.	The emphasis is on promoting the transfer of knowledge, skills, and values gained in the group to back-home situations.	There is little discussion of the transfer of knowledge to back-home situations. Group experiences are often considered their own justification.
14. There is a strong emphasis on the research evaluation of techniques and outcomes.	There is a strong emphasis on the research evaluation of techniques and outcomes.	There is little emphasis on the research evaluation of techniques and outcomes. The emphasis is on affective concerns and developing new techniques to get at feelings.
15. The orientation is primarily therapeutic and only incidentally educational.	The focus is primarily educational, directed toward interpersonal learning, and only incidentally therapeutic.	The focus is primarily therapeutic and only incidentally educational.

CHAPTER 3

The Intervention Cube

The Intervention Cube was developed to meet the need for a model that can be used to observe, categorize, and analyze interventions by group leaders, regardless of theoretical and/or practitioner orientation. The Intervention Cube is composed of dimensions that provide an exhaustive system for the classification of interventions by group leaders. It is atheoretical in that it is not biased toward any single approach to group work; it is neutral in that it does not have special value-oriented prescriptions for interventions. It serves as a systematic observation technique and as a content-analysis technique. It requires a relatively low level of inference. Its focus is on behavior. It is a manageable system of twenty-seven combinations of dimensions. Its three basic categories—level, type, and intensity—are mutually exclusive, as are the three subcategories within each of these.

The Intervention Cube is applicable to any group, regardless of its goals, composition, situational characteristics, and leadership orientation. It can be used as a research tool in rigorous experimentation. It can also be used as a potent vehicle for training group leaders, providing it is integrated with a particular theory of practice.

There has been serious attention paid to the interventions of group leaders, especially in the last fifteen years, and the literature presents a great variety of material relating to interventions. Yet, a search of this literature reveals no adequate comprehensive model of interventions that serves the purpose and meets the criteria that are identified in this chapter. (See also Chapters 4 and 5.)

All interventions presented in this book may be classified according to the components of a matrix called the Intervention Cube. Briefly stated, the Intervention Cube consists of the *level of intervention,* i.e., whether the focus is on group, interpersonal, or individual behavior; the *type of intervention,* i.e., whether the intervention is conceptual, experiential, or structural; and the *intensity of intervention,* i.e., the degree to which the choice of response is directed at the emotional center of the target issue on a continuum from *low* to *medium* to *high*. These three response dimensions are conceptualized as the Intervention Cube. (See Figure 3.1.)

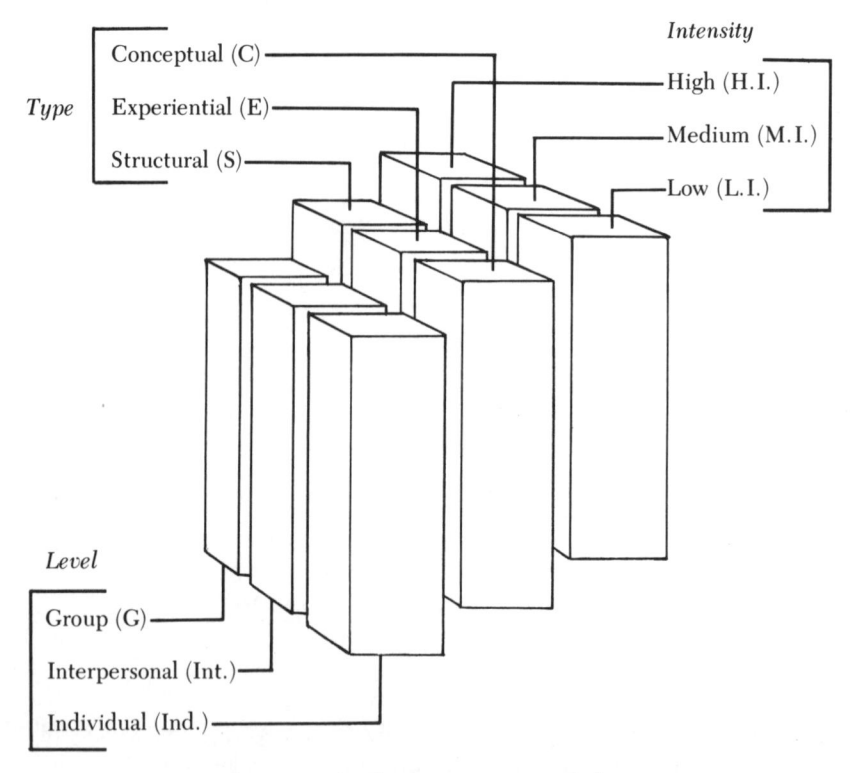

Figure 3.1. The Intervention Cube

LEVEL OF INTERVENTION

The group leader may choose to focus his intervention on the group as a whole, on an interpersonal relationship within the group, or on one member of the group. In order to demonstrate the wide applicability and generality of this dimension, several examples of various interventions follow.

> The silence was broken by one individual who said that he had not understood all the trainer had said and would he repeat himself. The trainer said he would be glad to and, using about the same phraseology but more briefly, said again that he

felt the group could learn from examining its own interactions and process and that he did not propose to serve as leader. (Bradford, Gibb, & Benne, 1964, p. 137)[1]

The important point to be noted is that, although the question came from one group member, the leader focused his response directly on the group as a whole. Hence, the level of intervention was the group.

The final moments approached, the session closed, and members started toward the door. As they reached it, Cy spoke out and said that he did not want to be the only one not to get help from the group, and would they come back and tell him their reactions to him. There was a stunned silence. A final closing session for the entire laboratory was to start immediately. The trainer turned back to the table. He told Cy, quietly and without hesitation, that he was sorry Cy had chosen this time to ask such a question because it made it extremely difficult for the group to respond. He felt that Cy did not really want help from the group or he would not have waited until the group ended. The trainer said he would be glad to talk with Cy immediately after the final closing session, which the trainer had to lead, but he did want Cy to recognize his behavior was difficult for the group to respond to at this point in time. (Bradford, Gibb, & Benne, 1964, p. 167)[2]

In this intervention, a consistently deviant group member made a request of the entire group. The group leader chose to intervene on a one-to-one individual level and respond to the person directly, thereby attempting to encapsulate the problem from the group.

During the discussion some rather direct statements were made to George concerning his motives in the whole affair. Was he trying to manipulate and control the group? Why had he encouraged the other two to carry out the act rather than doing it himself? (Bradford, Gibb, & Benne, 1964, p. 154)[3]

This last intervention, directed at three group members and their behavior, is on an interpersonal level because, while it does not pertain to the group as a whole, the force of the intervention is to examine the dynamics involved in the interrelationships of three members of the group.

It is important to keep in mind that any given intervention choice may contain elements of all three components, i.e., *individual, interpersonal,* and *group.* However, it is not the content of the intervention that leads to its classification level, but the focus of the response that is the determinant. For example, the group leader's intervention "I wonder what the group has been experiencing these past few moments," directed toward an individual member for response, occurs on the individual level. A slightly different statement, "What just occurred between George and Bill?," is an individual-, interpersonal-, or group-level response, depending on the specific focus.

---

[1]From L. P. Bradford, J. R. Gibb, & K. D. Benne (Eds.), *T-Group Theory and Laboratory Method: Innovation in Re-education.* New York: John Wiley, 1964. Reprinted by permission.
[2]See Footnote 1.
[3]See Footnote 1.

Although the Intervention Cube pays attention to the content of the statement as well as its focus, the focus of a statement is much more easily described than the content.

In the previously cited examples, the content of the interventions contain elements from the group, interpersonal, and individual levels. Frequently it is difficult, if not impossible, to decide whether a given statement of content with its nuances of emotional expression belongs predominantly to one specific level. The same statement, with the same content, delivered with different facial expressions and different tones of voice, may involve different levels of intervention. There is seldom any difficulty in determining the focus of an intervention. The Intervention Cube uses the focus or intended recipient of the intervention as the basis of classification.

The effective group leader is one who is able to combine or contrast more than one level of intervention response. The intervention statement "I wonder what you're feeling now, Bill? And I also wonder if this isn't the same feeling all of us are having right now, because of what just occurred?" combines a direct intervention on the individual level with a subsequent shift to a group-level intervention that blends personal concerns with group applicability. When combining levels, the direction or flow of any given intervention is primarily one of individual judgment. However, interventions should move from general, surface kinds of statements to statements dealing with specific individual issues. Once the group has progressed to the point where it is able to deal effectively with meaningful personal disclosures, another style of intervention is required. At this point it is generally appropriate to begin with the individual level and subsequently move to the group level. This style encourages dealing with group process instead of concentrating exclusively on personalities.

There are occasions when the experienced group leader may wish to begin with the group level and shift downward to the interpersonal or individual level. This intervention style usually results in (1) applying powerful pressure on the last focus point, i.e., the individual level, and (2) increasing the probability of one-to-one emotional encounters. An example illustrates this point:

Group Leader (after a lengthy silence): "I feel pretty uncomfortable at this point and somewhat depressed. I seem to sense the rest of the group is feeling this way, too. Maybe even a little angry. Is that it—what everyone feels?" (Seeking consensus at the group level.) "I wonder if it has anything to do with you, Bill, and what you said to Jane a few moments ago?" (Movement down to interpersonal level.) "Bill, would you share with us what's going on right now?" (A final focus at the individual level; note that this direction seems to carry more impact than if the procedure were reversed.)

According to our specific orientation, an increase in critical incidents of a personal and emotional nature could be expected following this type of intervention. In a similar manner, if one or more group members attempt to deal prematurely with intense emotional issues, an appropriate intervention strategy might be to begin briefly at the individual level, but move rapidly to a more abstract and emotionally distant group conceptual level. The following example makes this clear.

Group Leader (having observed [1] that some group members are attempting to pressure a reluctant group member to reveal problems of an intensely personal nature, [2] that this is occurring early in the group before any firm guidelines have been established to offer support for such exposure, and [3] that it is beyond the ability of the group to handle such information should it come out): "Bill, I notice that you and George have been making some observations about Sally, trying to draw her out, in an attempt to be of some help." (Intervening on the intrapersonal level to define the target of concern for everyone.) "I think, in general, that this sets a very good tone for the group in that you both are interested and involved enough to want to share your observations, and I hope that this sort of concern and interest will continue in the future." (The intervention now moves to the interpersonal level, identifying and supporting the intention, if not the means, of these two individuals.) "I have a couple of observations that might help increase our skills at being able to do this. It seems to me that in order for observations to be effective, they should involve feedback that inquires as to the feelings of the person involved, gives support to those positive aspects of the receiver of the feedback, and shows that person, through what you say and do, that you have respect for this person's ability to share very real feelings and experiences. How do the rest of you feel about this point? What's the best way to handle such a situation?"

This final intervention has removed the pressure from the individual. Yet, at the same time, the positive aspects of the incident are retained for discussion at the group level. This procedure allows emotional distance to occur and prepares the group, through this experience, to handle future events of a similar nature more successfully.

TYPE OF INTERVENTION

The Intervention Cube allows the group leader to select from three major modes of response, or combinations of these, in which to express his intervention. Thus, the *conceptual type* is one in which the group leader attempts to abstract or conceptualize some significant idea or issue. It may or may not be a direct reflection of an ongoing process, i.e., it may be planned or spontaneous, lengthy or brief. The following statement by the group leader is an example of a conceptual type of intervention that attempts to pull together certain group issues: "We've had a number of ideas tonight, and all of them seem directly concerned with ways to reach agreement, to know when a decision has actually been reached."

The *experiential type* of intervention usually deals with a direct reflection of current ongoing behavior, a reporting of direct experience, as in "I'm feeling pretty tense and angry over what just occurred." The *structural type* of intervention is the deliberate use of planned structured activities, such as structured experiences. The focus of this type of intervention is on surface or underlying issues and the emotional involvement in those issues. This could briefly be illustrated by the following statement of the group leader.

"I think we've all been silent for the last few minutes because we're probably not too sure about how we feel about the issue brought up by Bill. I'd like to suggest that we take a moment to close our eyes and focus on how we feel. I'd like to try and have us identify those feelings, if we can, and then after about a minute, open our eyes and state our feelings. Afterwards we can discuss our statements. O.K.? Let's go."

Conceptual Type of Intervention

This type of intervention enables the group leader to summarize and abstract a pertinent ongoing process, idea, or issue. It is important to recognize two distinct categories of conceptual interventions: the *planned theory input* (PTI) and the *spontaneous theory input* (STI).

PLANNED THEORY INPUT (PTI)

The planned theory input may be carried out at any time in a group session. When carried out at the beginning, it usually serves two major functions. First, it provides a major bridge of continuity between sessions, enabling the group leader to shape at least the initial action of the group. This permits continuity of direction and allows major issues such as conflict and conflict resolution, leadership, decision making, and many other group phenomena to emerge and evolve. Second, it facilitates and enhances the mood when a particular climate is judged to be desirable. The following example illustrates these points.

Group Leader (addressing the group at the beginning of a session): "I recall that near the end of our last session Bill was attempting to describe the split we have noticed in our group between those who want to discuss feelings and those who want to discuss other, nonemotional issues. Up to that point, we seemed to be at a loss to know what to do. Moreover, we seemed to be pretty depressed. When Bill summed up the problem, it seemed like we all became pretty optimistic about resolving it. I still sense that same mood of optimism today. Is that how we feel? Could you give me some feedback on this?"

This relatively brief PTI by the group leader points out the major issues that had been a source of concern during one or more preceding sessions. It allows the group the option of continuing with this line of discussion in order to facilitate its resolution. This would be particularly true if the issue (such as the one dealt with in the above PTI) is one that threatens to block the group from further progress.

Finally, the PTI ends by attempting to establish an atmosphere or mood conducive to further discussion. It should be noted that some group leaders might prefer not to deliver such a PTI even though it might be necessary: they might prefer that the topic be raised by a member of the group. This approach is certainly to be desired, although the group is not always aware of the areas of investigation that would lead to the greatest growth.

A good guideline for design strategy would seem to be to wait and allow the group to pick up on a specific issue; if this does not occur, then the leader should consider intervening with a PTI. A group is able to select those issues most important and relevant and to function effectively in direct proportion to its growth and level of maturity.

In the initial stages more guidance will be needed, since group members cannot work with each other with full-fledged effectiveness, particularly in trying to cope with important, specific problems. As the group progresses and as an awareness of what is occurring in the group becomes identifiable to the members, there will be less necessity for leadership intervention.

When a PTI is utilized at the end of a group session, its purpose is to provide a framework for the events that have transpired, to show regularity among groups by comparing and contrasting, and to direct thinking toward important future issues. An example of a PTI at the end of a session follows.

Group Leader: "I'd like to offer a few of my observations before we adjourn. Some of the concerns we've been discussing tonight—cognitive versus emotional or thinking versus feeling, as a way to operate—are the same concepts that man, and groups of men, have always struggled with in attempting to create a livable world; they are the same ones we're struggling with to create our own community, our own world. In essence, we are in here attempting to identify, handle, and resolve many of the same issues that plague us in the outside world. This issue has not been resolved, but it has been identified; its impact on the group can be pointed out. Hopefully, we will reach the point of being so aware of what is going on in this group that we can deal with it before it deals with us."

This intervention serves to draw the group's attention to the pervasive and recurrent issues in the group, whether explicit or implicit. Most importantly it attempts to combine a conceptual framework as an explanatory device for an ongoing group process. The words and the concepts employed are not considered to be the crucial aspect of a PTI. Rather, it is the attention paid to the underlying process involved in the group's growth that is significant. In order to illustrate this point, consider the following PTI, given at the end of a session from a neo-analytic group.

Group Leader: "We have been struggling tonight with those parts of our superego that society demands from us, as contrasted to what we want to do and feel—the emotional side of our ego. Perhaps, in future sessions, some solution will be found as we continue to discuss ways of walking that thin line between our two harsh masters. I'm referring, of course, to something we discussed all through this session, the id and superego."

This PTI differs in the conceptual phrases used to describe the same underlying process. A nondirective group, a T-group, a Gestalt group may approach the phenomenon of group process with concepts unique to its orientation. The nature of a conceptual system depends largely on the basic issues and values emphasized. It is important to note that all major orientations with their respective intervention styles may be described in terms of the Intervention Cube.

Representative examples from a variety of theoretical approaches as they would be described in the Intervention Cube in terms of level, type, and intensity are covered in Chapter 4. Each unique style of intervention assumes a specific position on the Intervention Cube and may be described graphically. The effective group leader should be able to combine any conceptual type of intervention with the ongoing behavior in the group for maximum impact, regardless of the specific nature of the concepts involved. Some caution must be exercised, however, in that an excessive number of PTI's used during the closing periods of a group may cause premature closure on issues still needing examination. The leader may thus acquire the role of a professional summarizer. At its worst, this paternalism would give group members the feeling that the group leader starts them and stops them and that all the group needs to do is to move in some active way. In this situation, independent choice and responsibility would be hindered.

A Formal PTI

Occasions may arise where the group leader feels the need to introduce and explain some concept or theory in a more formal manner—a mini-lecture. This kind of formal PTI should be well prepared before the session begins. It is offered to the group as a tool to help handle a current group concern. The nature of a PTI may vary from group to group; e.g., T-groups might utilize PTI's centering about knowledge, skills, and values; Gestalt groups might best use a PTI involving the interaction between what is felt in body awareness and in cognition; nondirective groups might choose to explore self-growth and actualization theory. Regardless of the approach, the procedural steps in conducting a formal PTI are as follows:

1. An introductory statement is given to establish an appropriate mood or climate.

2. A brief statement relating certain expected group happenings to an explanatory theory or framework is given to establish the purposes of the PTI.

3. The PTI theory is explained directly and simply, with actual examples from the group whenever possible.
4. Questions are answered concerning any points that remain unclear.
5. Finally, the group members are asked to evaluate the relevance of this PTI for themselves. Does the theory relate to what has been happening here and now? In this last step, the group is encouraged to handle the PTI in a descriptive and prescriptive manner. Descriptively, the PTI should provide a means of recognizing the phenomenon referred to when it arises in the group. Prescriptively, the PTI should suggest possible options available so that the group will be able to deal effectively with this issue for future growth.

The following example illustrates each of the previous steps in a formal PTI and points out the difficulties inherent in trying to establish close relationships. The background of this group is one in which relationships between individuals have been marked by suspicion and blindness: suspicion that one must not reveal feelings because of the danger of being hurt, of being found out; blindness because very obvious life styles of the group members were not being discussed. At the beginning of this session the group leader has decided to present a formal PTI as a way of better understanding the relationships between people and as a means of facilitating discussion of the issues.

Group Leader: "I'd like to offer a few observations at this point, if I may. For the last several sessions I've noticed that we seem to be particularly stuck in trying to describe our relationships with each other. Some of you are closed off, others are wide open. We don't really have a good grasp on how to discuss these things. I'd like to present some ideas that I think might help us in trying to grasp much of what we have been struggling with. The main concept is called the Johari Window (Luft, 1963)[4] and it seems to be a useful way of graphically visualizing the relationship between individuals. It's simply a window with four quadrants. The four quadrants represent the whole person in relation to others." (The group leader goes to the board and sketches Figure 3.2.)

"Quadrant 1 is behavior and motivation known to self and others. It shows the extent to which two or more persons can freely give and take, work and enjoy experiences together. The larger this area, the greater is the person's contact with reality and the more available are his abilities and needs to himself and to his associates. This can also be labeled the quadrant of openness, honesty, and frankness, but not naïveté. Remember when you told us how scared you were of showing your feelings, Frank? And you agreed, Bill? You both were in quadrant 1.

"Quadrant 2, the blind area, represents behavior and motivation not known to self but apparent to others. The simplest illustration of this quadrant

---

[4]The authors' description of the Johari Window is based on material from *Group Processes: An Introduction to Group Dynamics* (2nd ed.) by J. Luft and is used by permission of Mayfield Publishing Company, formerly National Press Books. Copyright © 1963, 1970, by Joseph Luft.

1. Free to self and others. On top of table.	2. Blind to self, seen by others.
3. Hidden agenda under the table.	4. Quadrant of the unknown.

Figure 3.2. The Johari Window

is a mannerism in speech or gesture of which the person is unaware but which is quite obvious to others. This can be in the form of a certain facial expression when a person is being defensive; or an individual may have an excessive tendency to dominate when in a committee meeting. This tendency to dominate may be perfectly obvious to everyone else but not in the least obvious to the man who is doing the dominating. Most people's quadrant 2 is larger than they think. This is evident particularly in group or committee types of situations where an individual's behavior is under the scrutiny of many people. I believe that the two group members who tried to force me to tell them what to do were not asking for information; they wanted to be dependent on me, and the group correctly pointed this out, especially you, Sally.

"Quadrant 3 is behavior and motivation that is open to self but concealed from other people. This quadrant is sometimes referred to as the 'hidden agenda.' For example, a man may want to get a particular assignment from his boss in order to make himself look good as a result of carrying out the assignment. He does not tell his boss why he wants the assignment, nor does he go about trying to get the assignment in an obvious way.

"Another illustration is the person who resents a remark made by an individual in a meeting, but keeps the resentment to himself. As an example, in our meeting a member focused attention on a particular project that he knew was embarrassing to one of the other members.

"A convenient way of differentiating quadrant 1 from quadrant 3 is to think of quadrant 1 as composed of those things that are on top of the table and quadrant 3 as behaviors that are motivated by the issues under the table.

"Quadrant 4 is the area of unknown activity, where behavior and motivation are known neither to the individual nor to others. We know this quadrant exists because both the individual and persons with whom he is associating occasionally discover new behaviors or new motives that were really there all along. An individual may surprise himself by taking over the group's direction during a critical period, or another person may discover that he has great ability in bringing together warring factions. He never saw himself as a peacemaker nor did anyone else, but the fact is that the potential for this activity and the actual behavior were there all the time. This occurred when Sally, who describes herself as shy and retiring, told Bill to shut up and really stood up to his criticism, a new and surprising behavior for her."

(The group leader displays Figure 3.3.) "Figure 3.3 illustrates how a person looks when he is in a new group situation or when he first meets another person. The area of open and shared activity represented in quadrant 1 is very small. People tend to behave in a relatively polite and superficial manner. Social convention provides a pattern for getting acquainted, and it is considered bad form to act too friendly too soon or to reveal too much. This same constricted picture may be typical of some persons who have difficulty in relating to other persons. An overly shy person may, for example, have difficulty in developing a large quadrant 1 even after spending much time with a group or with another individual. Sometimes an individual hides behind a flurry of work or words, but very little of him becomes known or available to other individuals.

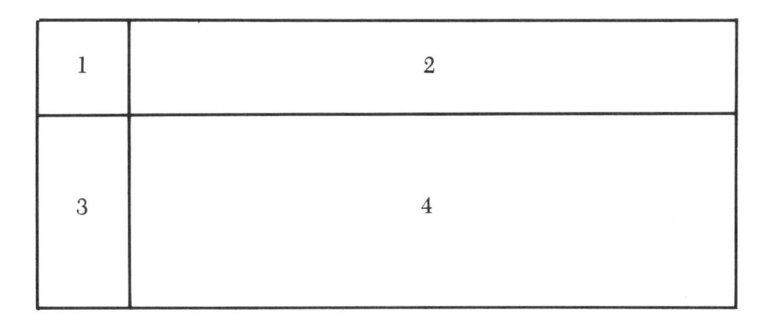

1	2
3	4

Figure 3.3. Attitude of Distrust

"Figure 3.4 shows how it takes energy or psychological resources to wall off quadrants 2, 3, and 4. The larger the first quadrant, the closer to self-realization is the individual. He is meeting his needs and utilizing his abilities and interests at the same time that he is making himself available to others. It would be a mistake, however, to think of a large quadrant 1 as mere extroversion, gregariousness, or sociability. Rather the emphasis is on personal freedom and the capability of working with others and enjoying experiences with others according to one's needs and work requirements. The attitude of persons toward the individual illustrated in Figure 3.3 is often one of suspicion and distrust. On the other hand, the attitude toward the individual represented in Figure 3.4 is often one of acceptance and understanding.

1	2
3	4

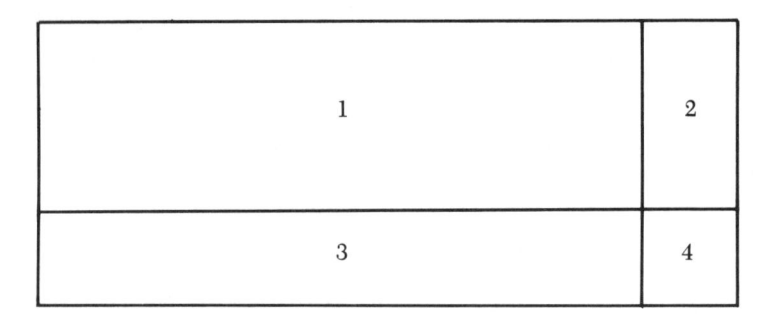

Figure 3.4. Attitude of Awareness and Openness

"Whether between peers, superior and subordinate, or divisions or departments of the company, the relationships that conform to Figure 3.4 result in greater understanding, cooperation, and freedom of activity. Those relationships that follow the Figure 3.3 pattern are characterized by suspicion, distrust, tension, anxiety, and backbiting. These conditions result in lower work output and the thwarting of individual as well as organizational growth. Individuals who have been used to operating with a small quadrant 1 find it somewhat painful to enlarge this quadrant.

"However, the enlargement of quadrant 1 does result in a better and more productive relationship. This can be illustrated by individuals who have had an argument that resulted in a dramatically improved subsequent relationship. It can also be illustrated by the cohesive bond of those who have been through a crisis together. Under great tension and stress we tend to reveal more of ourselves to those who are experiencing the same stress and tension.

"Now, are there any questions concerning this model, or is it pretty clear? Are there any points that need to be cleared up? If not, let's discuss your feelings and ideas concerning what we have just covered. What relevance do you feel it has for what we have just been through in our group, and, most importantly, what relevance does it have for you personally?"

The previous example illustrates the steps involved in carrying out a formal PTI. The discussion that follows this PTI should serve to facilitate further group growth and development. The principles are applicable to a variety of groups and organizations as well as to individual relationships.

SPONTANEOUS THEORY INPUT (STI)

Often referred to as an "on the spot" theory, an STI is a reaction to immediate ongoing events in the group. It is generally quite short in duration since any intervention that becomes extensive tends to stop the action of the group and may temporarily immobilize it. An STI usually consists of two basic elements: a brief descriptive observation concerning ongoing events and a brief tie-in between the observation and theory.

The STI is effective in a number of areas:

1. It communicates an awareness and involvement on the part of the group leader toward the group;

2. It sharpens and defines the role of the trainer as a capable resource;

3. It puts the current problem into focus and/or points the way to a larger question to which the group may need to be sensitized.

In briefer form, the STI may involve any of the topics identified under PTI. For example, a few sessions after introducing a formal PTI involving the Johari Window, the group leader may make the following STI.

"Tonight, I notice everyone seems to be encouraging everyone else to be open and to share. I feel good about our getting to this point. It seems we, as a group, are rapidly moving into quadrant 1 of the Johari Window, and I think we like the view."

Another STI might be as follows:

"I notice Bill just made a suggestion for the group which was completely ignored; it's as if he tossed his idea out into the middle of us, and it sort of dropped like a rock. We may notice this phenomenon occurring again in the group, from time to time, and it's something I call a plop-flop. I think this occurs, not because we're insensitive, but because we are still searching for some direction, and we don't quite know how to use our resources." This STI should facilitate further identification and discussion of important ongoing group processes as they occur.

Both a PTI and an STI are conceptual-type interventions. They allow verbal input, which, although it may be focused on one or more levels and may involve different intensities, is always classified as a conceptual type of intervention in the Intervention Cube.

Experiential Type of Intervention

Since it deals with a straightforward expression of feelings concerning ongoing behavior, the *experiential type* of intervention may be one of the most difficult skills for the beginning group leader to acquire. Experiential intervention responses invite disclosure, intimacy, and sharing responses from others and, as such, are potential sources of movement in the group. However, a group may be moving too quickly and not pausing long enough to absorb and consolidate its learnings. In this instance the group leader may wish to consider switching to a conceptual type of intervention to slow the experiential rate of the group.

Experiential interventions also provide a model for the group whereby members learn to explore such areas as sharing, trust, and disclosure through imitation of the group leader. A PTI on sharing and disclosure, for example, might well be followed by a series of experiential-type intervention responses.

The primary function of the experiential intervention is to focus on the here-and-now of group life instead of the more abstract there-and-then. An example of an experiential type of intervention follows.

> One of the trainers asked how people had felt when they first saw the change in name cards. Some said they felt pleased. Others said momentary resentment was quickly washed away. The trainer persisted. He asked if anyone felt pushed around by the incident . . . the other trainer said that he also felt pushed around . . . others strongly criticized the trainer for feeling pushed around. (Bradford, Gibb, & Benne, 1964, p. 153)[5]

This experiential type of response intervention leads not only to more sharing of feelings among members, but also to an increased probability that the leader will be confronted by the group members. This is a realistic expectation with this type of intervention, and the group leader should be prepared for it.

Structural Type of Intervention

The generic term *structural intervention* indicates a range of activities from highly verbal, conceptual, and task-oriented activities to highly nonverbal, basically non-concept-oriented activities. A structural intervention must be distinguished from one of its components, a structured experience. All structured experiences are structural interventions but not all structural interventions are structured experiences.

A structured experience is a procedure that attempts to focus learning or attention on emotions and feelings within an individual, between two or more individuals, or in the group as a whole. The verbal involvement is either quite low or is specifically directed toward a direct reflection of feelings rather than thoughts, concepts, or abstract tasks. Thus, structured experiences are distinct types of structural interventions.

The framework in this book allows for a wide variety of structural interventions, ranging from those that are highly conceptual and task oriented to those that are specifically nonverbal and highly emotional activities, depending on the immediate needs of the group.

The straightforward presentation of a structural intervention designed to be completely or primarily conceptual, task oriented, and nonemotional is not always received as such by the group. Sometimes a simple task-solving activity becomes a heated debate between individual members or subgroups. This is certainly to be expected from time to time and does not invalidate our

---

[5]See Footnote 1.

model. The leader chooses the focus of the structural intervention as being primarily concerned with task or with the reflection of emotions. It is possible, but less probable, that the leader may introduce a highly emotionally charged structured experience, attempting to focus on feelings, only to have the group engage in a discussion of its abstract, conceptual characteristics. Once again, the focus is on the functional intentions of the structural intervention.

THE SHARING PROGRESSION

An example of a structured experience that has as its focus a "mix" of both task-oriented activities and emotional components follows.

During a one- or two-week workshop, people are arranged in dyads early in the week and asked to meet together for about an hour each day. It is essential that they continue to meet no matter how difficult the relationship becomes. They are given the following instructions:

"You are to describe the tasks or problems in the group that cause you the greatest difficulty. Each of you must help the other in exploring the emotional aspects that may prevent effective functioning in the group. In other words, you should try to express your feelings about each other and the group as well as attempt to conceptualize the problem in a meaningful way. Each of you is to act as a resource to the other."

This situation places group members in a position rarely seen in everyday life, where withdrawal is a common reaction to stress and pressure. Remaining together usually evokes new modes of dealing with the solution on a more productive level. Furthermore, exploration of typical behavior and feelings teaches perseverance in interpersonal and group relationships. This example is a modification of a typical experience utilized by Schutz (1967) and is fairly representative of the attempt to use a structural intervention for task and maintenance purposes.

SLAPPING CONVERSATION

The final example of a structured experience is one that is designed to enhance and focus on the expression of feelings and emotions. It is taken directly from the work of Bernard Gunther (1968) and represents his specific approach to group leadership.

Partners face each other. The area to be slapped is over the entire arms and shoulders, including the backs of the hands and fingers. *Without verbalizing*, one partner starts the conversation by slapping (with both hands simultaneously). The other partner answers. This goes back and forth like ordinary conversation. *Don't try to be logical.* Try to say different things by changes in tempo. Don't hog the conversation. Talk to one area; other times talk to the whole area. Don't talk (slap) too loudly or too softly. Have a slapping argument (not too wild). Gradually make up. Slap something tender. Say something funny in slap talk. Slap each other "so long." Close your eyes and feel the effects of this type of conversation. (Gunther, 1968, p. 156)[6]

It is important to note that in this structured experience no attempt is made to employ logical, abstract, or cognitive components. In fact, the participants are urged not to be logical; there is no verbalizing.

Structured experiences are important and potent tools in the group leader's armamentarium. They appear to work because they tend to by-pass the majority of cognitive components and work directly on the emotions. If these emotional components are tied to concepts, theories, or frameworks for looking at behavior in the real world, there is a better chance of initiating and maintaining a real and significant change in an individual. Groups that utilize a noncognitive, encounter approach and focus almost exclusively on feelings and emotions in order to enhance some desired "peak" experience may also profit from a systematic approach. If structured experiences are arranged along a continuum of intimacy, potency, or other relevant dimension, there is less chance of their haphazard administration. The group leader would tend not to use an otherwise good structured experience if its effect might be negated by using a later experience inappropriately or by using one of lower potency. Such an occurrence would certainly delay the achievement of any "peak" experience, if that is indeed the purpose of the group meeting.

INTENSITY OF INTERVENTION

Intensity is the extent to which the underlying theme of behavior (interaction style) is exposed, interpreted, and directly communicated to an individual, subgroup, or the group as a whole to achieve an awareness of the underlying dynamic of the behavior.

Intensity is a continuous variable, but for purposes of its applicability in the Intervention Cube, it is treated as discrete and categorized as *low*, *medium*, or *high*. The impact of an intervention of a particular degree of intensity will vary depending on the stage and climate of the group and the readiness of members to accept and usefully incorporate clarification that may be painful. The force of the intervention also depends on the type and level characteristics with which it is used.

In this regard, intensity is defined as the *intended* impact (not the actual), the degree to which the intervention is aimed at increasing the awareness of an individual, subgroup, or group as a whole, regardless of the particular dynamic underlying the behavior. The degree of intensity would be inversely related to the extent to which an intervention is diffused, that is, not limited to

---

[6]Reprinted with permission of Collier Books, Macmillan Publishing Co., Inc., from *Sense Relaxation Below Your Mind*, by Bernard Gunther. Copyright © 1968 by Bernard Gunther.

the appropriate focal point of the problem. To gauge the appropriate intensity of an intervention, the group leader also takes into account other variables and runs the data through his personal intervention computer.

Different degrees of intensity can be applied to group, interpersonal, and individual levels. For example, directing the intervention at the group level does not mean that it is intrinsically of low intensity; this is not the meaning of diffusion. Intensity is determined, instead, by the degree of intended confrontation, regardless of level, even though high intensity is more often associated with one-to-one interventions.

In Figure 3.5, the innermost circle is the region of high intensity; it represents the core or center of the particular psychological dynamic that is involved at the time of an intervention. It represents direct confrontation between the leader and one or more members or the group as a whole. It deals with affect, diagnosis, and/or interpretation regarding the hitherto unexpressed meanings underlying a person's or group's behavior. Medium-intensity and low-intensity regions represent respectively less direct confrontation by the leader regarding the affect, diagnosis, or interpretation of previously unexpressed meanings underlying the behavior.

In the following examples, a group member is judged by the leader/trainer to have problems dealing with authority; he has frequently responded with hostility to the leader's intervention. By utilizing the Critical-Incident Model,[7] the three different degrees of intensity are illustrated in conjunction with variations in type and level, the other two dimensions of the Intervention Cube.

1. *Context:* This is the seventh session of a thirty-session program. The group has been struggling with questions of intimacy, disclosure, and risk. In particular, long silences usually began the sessions, followed by out-of-field discussions dealing with generalities about life and people.

After a silence of about ten minutes the group started to discuss outside topics superficially and in generalities. The leader intervened by calling the group's attention to such behavior. This halted the group's discussion and was followed by a brief but uncomfortable silence which was broken by Dan's comment to the leader.

The group leader and Dan, then, are involved in the critical incident. Dan has frequently followed the leader's interventions with criticism of him, in apparent defense either of another person or of the group. At different times, Dan has criticized the leader for too much direction, too little direction, and for producing too much frustration by his interruptions. Dan has also expressed feelings about the leader's apparent chastisement of the group.

---

[7]The reader should refer to Chapter 4, "The Critical-Incident Model: Its Use and Application" for a detailed examination of the model.

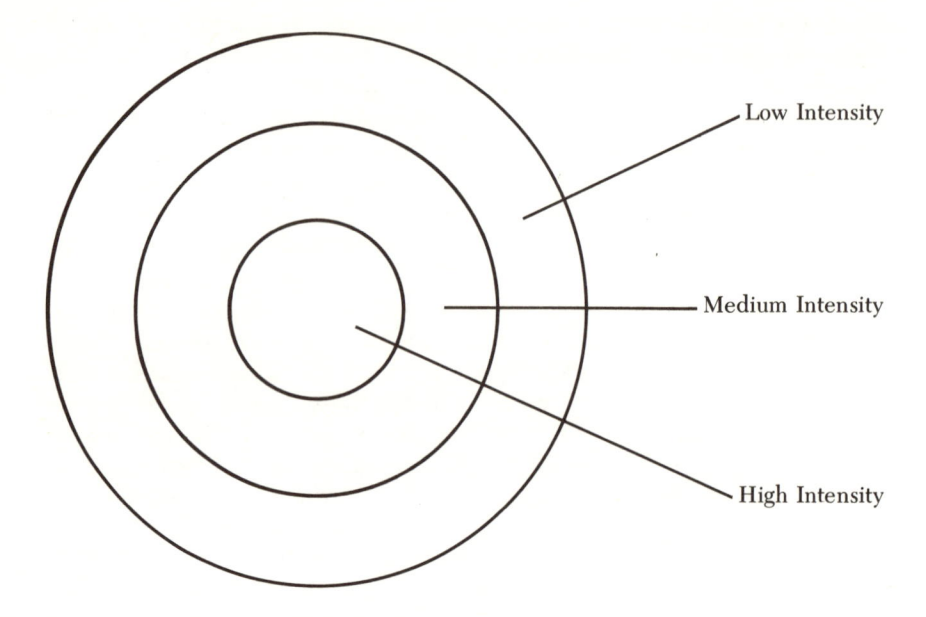

Figure 3.5. Concentric Circles

2. *Event preceding choice point:* Following the leader's intervention, Dan turned to the leader and said, "Dammit, there you go again, stopping us and criticizing us. If we don't talk we're punished. If we do talk, you stop us and tell us that we're saying and doing the wrong things."

3. *Choice point:* The surface issue is one of power and control and the effectiveness of the leader vis à vis the group. The underlying issue is Dan's problem with authority.

4. *Suggested intervention:* The intensity of intervention can be designated as low, medium, or high.

Low Intensity (Group Level, Conceptual Type)

Group Leader: "Part of the problem of adjustment that every group faces has to do with feelings that group members have about power and authority — their own and others'. Our group is no exception. This seems to be what is occurring now as we search for our own individual places in the group and as our group builds its own character."

In this intervention, Dan's authority problem is not discussed directly. His authority problem is diffused to those of the group as a whole and is discussed at the conceptual level.

Medium Intensity (Interpersonal and Group Level, Experiential and Conceptual Type)

Group Leader: "Dan, I'd like to relate your last remark to some things I've observed in our group." (Addressing the group.) "Dan's remarks, and those of others like Bill, who earlier in this session wondered out loud if the group wouldn't be 'looser and better today' if I weren't here, led me to think that as a group we are facing the problem of how to deal with authority, with me. In this situation of uncertainty, how each of us tries to cope with his feelings of dependency (wanting to lean on authority) or counterdependency (wanting to resist or attack authority) is quite important."

High Intensity (Individual Level, Conceptual and Experiential Type)

Group Leader: "Dan, let me add some thoughts that I have. They may help you explore and understand some of the things with which you may be struggling in relation to the group and perhaps to me, in particular.

"One way of looking at the kinds of responses that you've been making to me, as I have already indicated, is in terms of my authority or the lack of it. If there's a consistency in the type of response to me, i.e., criticism or hostility, then this gives us a clue as to what to explore in thinking about how you might be feeling underneath, and I need to test this out with you. One way of trying to understand an underlying dynamic is to bring in a model, and there are many we could use.

"One such model that we have already talked about is the one of the Parent, Adult, and Child. One of the handouts you've read has to do with this model, so let me not review it except to say that I think what's going on is that your Angry Child is responding to me as a Critical Parent. I've noticed on other occasions that your responses have been characterized by a certain degree of provocativeness.

"Now, I have some choices. If it is your Angry Child that is responding to me and I respond as the Critical Parent, then you and I would be colluding to reinforce your feelings and behaviors. That would certainly justify and be complementary to your Angry Child. I don't want to do that, however. I'd like to respond to you in the Adult mode, which says: 'Dan, what's troubling you? What are you angry about? What do you see me doing that makes you feel like a relatively helpless child who is somewhat errant and uncertain and may be likely to encounter some form of criticism or punishment?' I'd like to explore that with you because the extent to which you respond to me, either with uncritical acceptance (which is not the case) or with relatively uncritical rejection of me (which is the case)—to that extent are we unable to explore these dimensions in the Adult frame and facilitate insight and growth."

Two major aspects of intensity are illustrated in the previous example: (1) focus, i.e., whether the intervention really deals with the source of behavior or is diffused, and (2) whether the intervention attempts to explain the behavior, clarify it, and communicate it. The same illustration holds whether the intervention is on the group, interpersonal, or individual level.

These examples of low, medium, and high intensity can be ordered (or rated) according to the degree to which Dan's problem is dealt with directly. In the low-intensity intervention, the pressure is taken off Dan and diffused over the whole group (group level) within the framework of a combined experiential-conceptual type of intervention.

In the medium-intensity example, another member, Bill, is mentioned in order to indicate that the problem is not only Dan's. The diffusion is less than in the low-intensity example. Authority issues (dependency and counterdependency) are more sharply defined conceptually and directed at group members with some importance given to the problem.

In the high-intensity example, the experiential and conceptual aspects of the intervention are very sharply defined in terms of the underlying dynamics of the behavior. Confrontation is direct. There is no diffusion by addressing the group, nor is there a diffusion of the concept focus by a more abstract and less person-centered conceptualization of the problem.

Low, Medium, High Intensity (Interpersonal Level)

Examples of low-, medium-, and high-intensity interventions on the interpersonal level dealing with the issue of authority follow.

LOW INTENSITY

Group Leader: "Let me share some observations I have about what I sense has been going on during the past few sessions. John, you and Sidney, and you too, Mike, have on numerous occasions become angry with each other. As I have tried to intervene, you have ignored me or criticized me for interfering. It seems as if you are competing with each other and want me to leave you alone."

MEDIUM INTENSITY

The intensity of the above intervention would be increased if the group leader added the following: "While, on the surface, the issues you three seem to be disagreeing about seem to be intellectual, that is, dealing with different points of view regarding the nature of man, I believe that underneath there is a leadership struggle going on among you. The underlying question you seem to be wrestling with is who will be highest in the leadership 'pecking order' of our group."

HIGH INTENSITY

The following addition to the intervention would further increase the intensity. "What makes your interactions especially significant for all of us is that they probably symbolize deeper personal meanings regarding sex and aggression which are far from the easiest subjects to deal with directly. Questions such as 'Am I potent?,' 'Will I be subordinated to a more powerful person who will control the expression of my impulses, my passions?' These questions are pretty deep and pervasive in here as well as outside our group."

Low, Medium, High Intensity (Group Level)

On the group level (experiential type), the intensity of the intervention could be raised from low to medium to high in the following way.

LOW INTENSITY

Group Leader: "I want to share some thoughts about what has been going on. You, as a group, spent the past thirty minutes trying to decide what kind of group you want and even proposed to turn tomorrow's session into a party. I'll admit the prospect of turning this into a party is very attractive; however, I do want to point out that you have made all these decisions without regard to me, as if I didn't exist. Sometimes, people deal with authority by not dealing with it at all, by ignoring it. I think this has been happening with us."

MEDIUM INTENSITY

Additional comments to focus on underlying dynamics: "I am pointing to an issue now that would have surfaced even more so a little later; that is, our group is being divided into two parts: you and me. Sooner or later you will have to deal with me, since, if I am not involved in making decisions, I will not feel a commitment to go along with them. Then the situation could become an even more blatant power struggle in which the rights of my leadership and your membership would have to be faced squarely."

HIGH INTENSITY

To increase the intensity further, the leader could add: "What we are facing may be like the phenomenon described in myths and legends about primordial man and even in recent folk-hero sagas. In the animal world the young males compete with each other for a position in the 'pecking order,' ignoring the leader except to obey, out of fear, when commanded. Then, if and when the time is right, the leader is challenged by another or others supported by enough of the group, and he is eventually beaten, driven off, or killed."

These interventions have been given to illustrate the sharpening of focus by adding higher-intensity comments. This is not the only way to intervene with high intensity, although generally high-intensity interventions are associated with clarification of issues in greater depth. The following is one example of a short high-intensity intervention dealing with authority in the situation described in the previous interventions.

"John, and you, Mike, and you, too, Sidney, have been talking with each other as if I have already been displaced as leader. I am a reality to be dealt with."

To follow an already identified behavior, another intervention could be: "You're doing it again." This very short intervention can have a sharply focused impact that dramatizes the issues to be handled.

Additional Comments

Intensity has primary and secondary qualities. Primary characteristics have already been discussed; secondary characteristics and other variables relating to the choice of the intensity of intervention are discussed in the following pages.

The intensity of an intervention by the group leader serves several functions:

1. The establishment and maintenance of the appropriate group climate. The group leader, for example, may start a group by relating a serious topic or issue that encourages a sober, serious discussion between group members. Conversely, he may lighten the depression or frustration of a group by adapting the tone and content of his intervention to a light-hearted mode. This is largely a matter of individual judgment on the part of a group leader. As a general guideline there should be a healthy mix of intensities of interventions depending on the specific needs of the group at any given moment.

2. The enhancement of any given intervention statement by increasing its potency and impact on the group. The same statement, delivered in different tones of voice, with different inflections and facial expressions, can have quite opposite effects on the group. The group leader should be aware of his leadership style and its impact on the group and be open to corrective feedback. For example, if the group leader considers himself to be delivering a PTI or an STI in an objective manner while the group members report him as coming across in a critical or skeptical manner, it may be the high intensity of the intervention that is overriding the intended effects. In other words, for any given content, the degree of intensity, in conjunction with other variables, may produce different kinds of consequences in the group.

3. The modification of ongoing behavior on the part of a group member, via the appropriate intervention intensity by the group leader. For example,

the group leader may observe an ongoing interaction among two or more group members, in which their facial expressions, tones of voice, and body postures reveal either high-, medium-, or low-intensity responses. This differs from the primary quality of intensity as *intended* impact on the part of the leader. The group leader is now faced with a choice of three different intensities (low, medium, high), and he may choose to intervene with the same measure of intensity or a different measure of intensity from that which is evidenced by the behavior of the members.

In speculating on the consequences of each of these two alternatives (responding with the same or a different degree of intensity), the group leader must consider that tempers have been flaring and that interactions have been of a heated nature. He would have to take into account the high intensity of the current emotional forces. If the leader responded with a different intensity of intervention, there would be two probable reactions on the part of the group: first, a low-intensity intervention might soften and de-escalate the immediate tensions and lead to a general "cooling off" process. On the other hand, a low-intensity intervention might either sustain the group at its present level or escalate tensions even higher, especially if the group members reject the leader's intervention because they feel that their degree of involvement is not being met by an equal involvement of the leader. Intensity may be manipulated according to the theoretical orientation of the group leader and the specific needs of the group.

If, on the other hand, a low-tension interaction has been occurring for some time among the group members and the leader now chooses to intervene, the same relevant options are available. He may intervene at the same degree of intensity, i.e., low intensity, or he may choose a medium- or high-intensity intervention.

If the leader responds with low intensity, this may perpetuate and prolong the existing mood. If the leader responds with a medium- or high-intensity intervention, it may successfully move the group into a more productive atmosphere, or it may be seen as "out of phase" with the existing needs of the group and as an overreaction that reflects the personal needs and anxieties of the leader. This may lead to emotionally depressed responses by the group.

It would be extremely valuable to observe and record a group leader's patterns of intervention intensity and the consequences of these on the group. Using the Intervention Cube, the group leader would soon be able to anticipate, with increased success, the results of specific intensities of interventions on group members.

Cutts (1972) has established that the intensity, level, and type of intervention can be judged with a high degree of reliability regardless of the orientation of the group. Intensity may be manipulated as an important factor in attempts to achieve individual, interpersonal, and group growth.

OTHER VARIABLES THAT AFFECT CHOICE OF INTENSITY

In conjunction with the type and level of intervention, other important variables must also be considered: the stage of the group, its readiness to accept and incorporate clarifications that may be painful, and the climate of the group.

Stage and Readiness of the Group

If a stage or evolutionary model of group growth and development is accepted, then it can be assumed that the group as a whole, as well as its members, grows and changes over time. Following the same logic, it can be assumed that parts of the group and the group as a whole are able, at different times, to accept and integrate different degrees of intensity. This readiness has two primary, substantive aspects: an intellectual component and an affective component. The intellectual component involves conceptual readiness: that is, the extent to which members have been exposed to terms, concepts, and principles relating to their experiences up to a particular point. Consequently, when a given intervention is made, new insights via additional concepts and inputs can be validly assimilated.

The second dimension, phenomenological-experiential, is the extent to which the members have experienced enough of the phenomena to which clarification is directed so that the intervention refers to material that is "point-at-able" and familiar.

Even with conceptual and phenomenological-experiential readiness, members may not be ready psychologically to "hear" certain degrees of clarification of problems with which they are dealing. For example, in the early life of a group, authority issues may be expressed in certain ways, e.g., excessive dependency, that is, reaching out to the leader for direction; or counter-dependency, that is, rejection of the leader as a resource.

These reactions will vary according to the personalities of members and their own openness to exploration. Members may not be ready to hear interpretive interventions regarding the feelings that cause them consistently to behave in certain ways, e.g., feelings regarding the group leader and his authority. At the beginning of group life, the inclination would be to refrain from deep interpretive statements regarding individual members of the group. The rationale for this is that individual members are ready neither conceptually nor phenomenologically-experientially. In addition, in the early life of a group, members probably do not have enough trust and security in the group as a whole or in their relationships with other members to utilize such interventions.

Climate

There are several aspects of climate that affect the choice of intensity of intervention in combination with the stage of the group. One is the extent to which members are dealing with problems at an intellectual level. If members are fixed on an intellectual level when dealing with certain issues, one of two things may be indicated: they have not really come to grips with the experiential qualities of the issue because of the early stage of their life, or the issues are so provocative and produce so much anxiety that the members cannot deal with them other than by means of intellectualization.

In the first case, an intervention of fairly low to medium intensity that has experiential as well as conceptual components would be more appropriate since it would be aimed at getting members to refrain from intellectualizing. In the latter case, where issues are very provocative, a relatively high-intensity intervention might be useful, providing the members involved are judged to be capable of internalizing the clarification.

If the issue is extremely potent, a high-intensity intervention could produce even greater alienation—a flight into intellectualization and denial. However, if group members have had experiences in the group in dealing with other fairly potent issues and have managed them somewhat successfully, then a high-intensity intervention would be helpful in shifting the focus of the group from intellectualization and abstraction to personal, experiential exploration and understanding.

The Plop-Flop

One phenomenon related to intensity is the "plop-flop." This phenomenon occurs when an intervention by the leader or another member is responded to with apparent nonacceptance, that is, when the members continue with what they have been doing and seem to ignore the intervention. This may be due to one of several things:

1. The intervention itself may have been inadequately couched or communicated; i.e., there were no "handles" for the members to grab and use.

2. Members have been so intensely involved in the interactions that they regard the intervention as an interruption and therefore do not deal with it.

3. The intervention is so disturbing in terms of the dynamic toward which it is directed that members cannot deal with it overtly; hence they appear to ignore it. The following example illustrates these factors.

Group Leader: "I notice that a number of the group, Jane, Sally, Joe, and Ted, have been looking at the floor, moving about in your seats, and generally looking pretty uncomfortable as Marilyn has been telling us about her feelings of despair related to her affair with John. I wonder if it could be that we seem to feel that she is revealing a great deal and we don't really know what to do with this information. At the same time, I'm wondering if we are not also saying something like 'I wonder if this is what is expected of us, whether we are all going to open up too much.'"

The level of this intervention is group, and the type experiential. The intensity would be medium, since the focus is neither diffuse (as in a low-intensity intervention) nor very interpretive at a deeper level (as would be true in a high-intensity intervention). If the group accepts this intervention, discussion of legitimate norms could ensue. If the group does not accept it, the intervention would be labeled a "plop-flop" and might be followed by another intervention aimed at testing which of the three factors described previously might be operating in the group, leading to the plop-flop.

Group Leader: "A little while ago, I commented on what I felt were signs of considerable discomfort on our part as Marilyn was talking. I speculated that maybe her self-disclosure was threatening to us. My observations were not dealt with. Is this because I was off target, or because you didn't know what to do with them, or possibly because I was pushing you too far and making you feel anxious, as Marilyn's disclosure may have been doing, leading you not to respond to my comments?"

If members respond directly to this second intervention, their response would probably be to affirm that the leader was off target or to seek additional clarification on what to do with the first observations, thus signifying a search for handles. If this occurs, the third factor that could have accounted for the plop-flop would have been rejected. If, on the other hand, the group still does not deal directly with the intervention, the third factor was probably operating as a deterrent to discussion.

Another way of handling the critical incident alluded to in this intervention would be for the leader to label Marilyn's intervention as a plop-flop and then deal with the dynamics and feelings leading to the apparently uncomfortable avoidance responses on the part of the other members.

An intervention is usually not given in isolation; instead, a chain of interventions usually ensues in "piggyback" fashion. This does not necessarily denote an increase in intensity. Actually, movement could occur inversely to the number of interventions following some kind of intense affective response. This response may be due to an earlier intervention that may be getting in the way of members utilizing the clarification. Subsequent interventions by the trainer could de-escalate dysfunctional tension and redirect the group's energy toward the more realistic management of the dilemmas that are facing its members.

As a general rule of thumb, high-intensity interventions should be avoided if the individual is likely to be so threatened by the intervention that he would be forced to deny in his own mind the dynamic that is clarified and hence withdraw from further involvement. The intervention should be avoided if there is the possibility that the person feels so exposed that some serious decompensation might occur; that is, the ego controls of the individual would be so jarred that he could not deal with the dynamic in a way that would not cause him to break down and exhibit great stress and dysfunctional behavior.

In the context of our model of group growth and development and of the traditional laboratory approach, the interventions in the beginning life of a group would be at the group level, of a conceptual type (with a smaller proportion of experiential type), and of low to medium intensity. The projected progression would be from this combination of intervention characteristics to interpersonal and personal levels, with increased frequency of interventions of the experiential type, in addition to the continuation of the conceptual characteristics of the earlier stages. As the group evolves and matures, higher-intensity interventions tend to become more appropriate.

The framework consisting of level, type, and intensity is useful in investigating and categorizing the different styles of leadership interventions; e.g., the inexperienced group leader might prefer to make interventions consisting of a conceptual input at the group level in the form of a PTI while avoiding direct experiential confrontation with individual members. Further research might reveal that this hypothetical group leader would emphasize the cognitive elements of group growth and development, as revealed in a progressive step pattern of conceptual-group, conceptual-intrapersonal, conceptual-interpersonal, with only a few growth- or encounter-group interventions. On the other hand, an experienced group leader might reveal a pattern that blends several different levels, with a distinct form emerging as the group moves through different phases. Awareness of an intervention style may lead the group leader to adopt a more healthy mix of interventions as well as allow him to experiment with new styles and chart his progress.

CHAPTER 4

The Critical-Incident Model: Its Use and Application

A critical incident is defined as the confrontation of a group leader by one or more members, in which an explicit or implicit opinion, decision, or action is demanded of him. It may also be an observed conversation, a confrontation among members, an event taking place, or a period of silence in which an expectation or demand is made of the leader. The essential property of a critical incident is that it is judged important enough for a group leader to consciously and explicitly consider whether to act in a specific way that is assumed to have an important impact on the group.

Whatever form the critical incident takes, the group leader is faced with a number of "choice points" or alternatives in the content and style of his possible responses. If the final choice of response is appropriate and effective, individual and group growth and development are facilitated. On the other hand, if the choice of response is inappropriate or ineffectual, the group may be unable to perform or may move into nonproductive areas. With each response the group leader uses, he simultaneously constructs alternate universes, opens new branches of group movement while inhibiting others, and blocks still other pathways.

The selection of a particular intervention response has implications regarding the future direction of group movement. One implication is that certain types of interventions usually result in a lowered probability of receiving a certain class of responses from the group. During the middle phases of group life, for example, when dealing with an aggressive and hostile group member, an intervention on the individual level increases the probability of future expressions of feelings and decreases the probability of an abstract response to the event. An intervention on the individual level delivered during the early stages of a group may increase the probability of abstract, conceptual statements while decreasing the probability of personal, revealing statements. This result occurs because the beginning group feels threatened by material of a personal nature. Thus, the same intervention, delivered at different times in the group life, is likely to influence group responses differently. (See Chapter 3.)

The Critical-Incident Model: Its Use and Application 115

An even finer distinction can be made. If a given leader intervention is perceived as a threat by a member, this member may increase the frequency of his conceptual responses. This may not be true of the group as a whole. Therefore, the group leader must be prepared to understand and estimate both the individual and the group reactions when choosing an intervention.

An intervention choice may open a continuing series of critical incidents, each related to the first intervention in a "piggyback" fashion. An example:

Margaret: "Could you tell us just exactly what it is that you want us to do—what are we supposed to do?"

The group leader responds with an intervention to return the responsibility to the group for making its own decisions.

Tony: "You still haven't answered her question! Isn't it your job to tell us what to do?"

The group leader responds in essentially the same manner, relaying, in different words, the same message as before.

Will: "You know, I think he has everything we do planned in advance."

Walt: "Yeah, but shouldn't we know—be let in on it—if it's happening?" (To group leader.) "Are you planning everything we do?"

This initial critical incident involves a request for direction and guidance from the group. The group leader intervened in a manner he judged to be most appropriate. The process did not stop but continued to carry implications of freedom, control, and dominance. In piggyback fashion, a series of responses finally evolved into a critical incident reflecting the trust issue.

It is a moot point whether a different response by the group leader would have prevented or merely delayed the emergence of this final critical incident involving trust. The group leader should be prepared to handle either an isolated event or a series of chained critical incidents. It is obviously impossible to cover all contingencies. The critical incidents explored here usually involve a single set of intervention responses that are judged to have the widest generality. In this approach many of the significant issues in the major group phases can be pointed out and a technological framework presented to understand the process as it is occurring. The fact that certain effects are highly likely to occur after each choice should motivate an attempt to systematize intervention decisions and study their consequences.

The critical-incident concept evolved with the observation that certain critical situations emerge and repeat themselves time and again in different groups and at various developmental stages. The wording of the question or statement might vary; the person involved might be female or male; the tone of voice and the timing of the statement might be different; yet, the basic issues—the nature of the observed confrontation or process—are the same.

A basic knowledge of the critical-incident concept coupled with a number of appropriate intervention alternatives adequately prepares the beginning group leader and offers him the security and freedom to develop his own group leadership style. The advanced group leader is offered a technology and a model of interventions that may be applied to all groups regardless of their nature or purpose. Examples given point out the wide applicability of the Critical-Incident Model to different groups. (See the *Manual* for details on sixty-one critical incidents.)

The critical incidents chosen were selected from specific situations judged to meet the definition of a critical incident and were collected from two years of direct group observation and recording, especially tapes. These critical incidents were then examined to determine the most general and relevant situations faced by the group leader, particularly the beginning group leader. Following group sessions, each group leader was interviewed according to a format that fit the Critical-Incident Model.

These critical incidents are thus embedded in a framework that specifies such parameters as the *climate of the group, the number of sessions or phases the group has experienced, specific events that led up to and preceded the group leader's response,* and the *level* (group, interpersonal, individual), *type* (conceptual, experiential, structural), and *intensity* (high, medium, low) of the intervention. This model suggests certain intervention responses to the critical incidents as well as certain probable results of those interventions.

All these critical incidents were checked for the frequency of their occurrence as well as the frequency with which certain specific critical incidents clustered together.

The group leader stimulates growth and development through appropriate responses to certain vital situations. This is a field-dynamic view in which the leader is seen as the center of a high potential in a social field at a particular, critical period of time. At some point during the development or culmination of an idea, the group leader is faced with critical situations or incidents and has to choose a method of responding. Some of the incidents may be trivial; others are crucial to the development of group solidarity, productivity, and direction of movement. The productive group leader must have at his fingertips an effective means of dealing with these critical incidents and must choose a good intervention response. This prescription applies to both task-oriented and process-oriented groups.

Many investigators dealing with the issue of trainer interventions assume that maximum group progress is somehow a function of consistency in the trainer's behavior and attitude (Lieberman, Yalom, & Miles, 1973; Rogers, 1958, 1967) or a function of "sensitivity" judgment (Bach, 1966; Berzon & Solomon, 1966; Solomon & Berzon, 1972). There are books that offer many intelligent and well-thought-out conceptualizations about the small group, but few are of much help in the concrete here-and-now, give-and-take of group interaction. It is important to know, for example, that "maintenance and building problems, as they emerge, exercise a prepotent demand on the energies of the T-group" (Bradford, Gibb, & Benne, 1964, p. 226); it is of equal importance to know how to respond concretely at a particular point to a hostile, confused, or otherwise involved group member.

BACKGROUND RESEARCH

Research studies relating group experiences to the behavior of T-group leaders were given a firm base by Bradford, Gibb, and Benne (1964). They discuss

> crucial situations which test the trainer's diagnostic skill, his ability to integrate his own actions into the group process, the extent to which his own personality presents problems to the group, his ability to make intervention decisions, the consistency of his behavior, and its congruence with his beliefs. (pp. 136-137)[1]

They then present six episodes that reveal a number of "crucial situations" to which the group leader replies and for which he notes the effect of the situations on the group. These six episodes are very useful, but would be even more instructive to the beginning group leader if they were embedded in a systematic technological approach to leader intervention, with a focus on specific outcomes and the probabilities of certain desired outcomes, and if leader responses were more specifically related to one another, with discussions and evaluations of the alternatives.

A related approach is the leaderless or instrumented T-group described by Berzon and Solomon (1966). In their studies, each intervention is programmed for introduction at an appropriate moment and, most importantly, the effects of that intervention on the group are evaluated. Another researcher (M. B. Miles, 1960) has defined the problem areas as "action skills: the ability to intervene effectively in ongoing situations in such a way as to maximize personal and group effectiveness and satisfactions" (p. 303).

Other studies (French, Sherwood, & Bradford, 1966) have mentioned such important findings as the fact that

> a person's self-identity is influenced by the opinions that others have of him which they communicate to him and the more that is communicated, the more change there is in self-identity. (p. 218)[2]

This last study is representative of literature in the group area in which feedback and leader interventions are considered important. However, there is no systematic presentation of what feedback specifically entails. In a critical situation, the leader needs to know how to deal with a maintenance issue or a counterdependency problem.

Although other very good reviews of the literature on small-group work have appeared (Buchanan, 1965; House, 1967; Stock, 1964; C. L. Cooper, 1971), the work by Campbell and Dunnette (1968) has special relevance to this chapter. In their comprehensive review, they point out:

---

[1]From L. P. Bradford, J. R. Gibb, & K. D. Benne (Eds.), *T-Group Theory and Laboratory Method: Innovation in Re-education.* New York: John Wiley, 1964. Reprinted by permission.

[2]Reproduced by special permission from *Journal of Applied Behavioral Science*, "Change in Self-Identity in a Management Training Conference," J. R. P. French, J. J. Sherwood, & D. L. Bradford, 210-218, 1966, NTL Institute.

Research concerning the relative contributions of specific technological features of the T-group is also sparse. For example, there are no systematic studies examining the influences of differences in trainer personality and/or style on the outcomes achieved by participants. Case reports and anecdotal evidence are all that exist. (p. 97)[3]

In advocating needed research approaches, these authors point out seven major research deficits. One is especially relevant:

It is imperative that the relative contributions of various technological elements in the T-group method be more fully understood. It is surprising indeed that essentially no research has been done on the differential effects of changes in the trainer role in spite of frequent allusions in the literature to the crucial role played in a T-group by the trainer's behavior. Questions concerning the optimal procedures for giving feedback, for enhancing feelings of psychological safety, and for stimulating individuals to try new behavior should also be investigated. (p. 100)[4]

Among more current group research is the comprehensive work done by Lieberman, Yalom, and Miles (1973). The research design included evaluation in five major areas over a period of time with eighteen different types of groups, along with a control group. Follow-up studies were also done to assess the degree of change. Extensive narrative accounts of what happens in a T-group are given in Klaw (1961), Weschler and Reisel (1959), and Kuriloff and Atkins (1966). The important point is that there are certain basic problems or issues common to all such groups. Even though each group is unique, it shares with others recurrent and consistent critical situations.

Therefore, a conceptual model of group growth and development, with descriptive and prescriptive properties and based on the evolution of critical incidents, is needed. Descriptively, the model provides a framework for recognizing the salient features of an ongoing group process and places important events in an ordered perspective. Prescriptively, it presents a systematic approach to effective group leadership through appropriate and effective interventions. The utilization of this model would seem to lead a step nearer to the prediction and control of behavior toward a desired group goal.

If the assumption is valid that the majority of groups have to deal at one time or another with certain basic common problems, i.e., critical incidents, then an attempt should be made to systematize and deal with those issues to promote effective group development. Within each of these critical situations, a number of alternative responses should be available to the group leader. His decision to utilize one particular response or not to respond at all is then based on his leadership style and the needs of the group.

---

[3]From J. D. Campbell & M. D. Dunnette, "Effectiveness of T-Group Experiences in Managerial Training and Development," *Psychological Bulletin*, 1968, 70(2), 73-104. Copyright © 1968 by the American Psychological Association. Reprinted by permission.

[4]See Footnote 3.

The Use of the Critical-Incident Concept

The words *critical incident* probably communicate a common meaning to a great many people. These words are used frequently in everyday speech. One would expect them to have occurred quite often in psychological literature, particularly in those situations where selective observations were involved. A greater breadth and depth of usage would also be expected in those fields in which there is a growing tendency to base theoretical descriptions and prescriptions on empirical data, e.g., applied group work. In reviewing likely sources of the use of the term *critical incident* or a similar phrase, however, it became clear that this concept has appeared only in spotty and undistinguishable ways and has not had a systematic history nor been tied very systematically to theory or model building in the applied behavioral sciences. There is certainly no direct history of the critical-incident approach as used in this book. The only systematic use of the critical-incident technique was developed by John C. Flanagan and first reported in the *Psychological Bulletin* (1954). The summary and conclusions from his review article follow.

> This review has described the development of a method of studying activity requirements called the critical incident technique. The technique grew out of studies carried out in the Aviation Psychology Program of the Army Air Force in World War II. The success of the method in analysing such activities as combat leadership and disorientation in pilots resulted in its extension and further development after the war. This developmental work has been carried out primarily at the American Institute for Research and the University of Pittsburgh. The reports of this work are previewed briefly.
>
> The five steps included in the critical incident procedure as most commonly used at the present time are discussed. These are as follows:
> a) Determination of the general aim of the activity. This general aim should be a brief statement obtained from the authorities in the field which expresses in simple terms those objectives to which most people would agree.
> b) Development of plans and specifications for collecting factual incidents regarding the activity. The instructions to the persons who are to report their observations need to be specific as possible with respect to the standards to be used in evaluating and classifying the behavior observed.
> c) Collection of the data. The incident may be reported in an interview or written up by the observer himself. In either case it is essential that the reporting be objective and include all relevant details.
> d) Analysis of the data. The purpose of this analysis is to summarize and describe the data in an efficient manner so that it can be effectively used for various practical purposes. It is not usually possible to obtain as much objectivity in this step as in the preceding one.
> e) Interpretation and reporting of the statement of the requirements of the activity. The possible biases and implications of decisions and procedures made in each of the four previous steps should be clearly reported. The research worker is responsible for pointing out not only the limitations but also the degree of credibility and the value of the final results obtained.

It should be noted that the critical incident technique is very flexible and the principles underlying it have many types of applications. Its two basic principles may be summarized as follows:
a) reporting of facts regarding behavior is preferable to the collection of interpretations, ratings, and opinions based on general impressions;
b) reporting should be limited to those behaviors which, according to competent observers, make a significant contribution to the activity.

It should be emphasized that critical incidents represent only raw data and do not automatically provide solutions to problems. However, a procedure which assists in collecting representative samples of data that are directly relevant to important problems such as establishing standards, determining requirements, or evaluating results should have wide applicability.

The applications of the critical incident technique which have been made to date are discussed under the following nine headings: a) measures of typical performance (criteria); b) measures of proficiency (standard samples); c) training; d) selection and classification; e) job design and purification; f) operating procedures; g) equipment design; h) motivation and leadership (attitudes); i) counseling and psychotherapy.

In summary, the critical incident technique, rather than collecting opinions, hunches, and estimates, obtains a record of specific behaviors from those in the best position to make the necessary observations and evaluations. The collection and tabulation of these observations make it possible to formulate the critical requirements of an activity. A list of critical behaviors provides a sound basis for making inferences as to requirements in terms of aptitudes, training, and other characteristics. It is believed that progress has been made in the development of procedures for determining activity requirements with objectivity and precision in terms of well defined and general psychological categories. Much remains to be done. It is hoped that the critical incident technique and related developments will provide a stable foundation for procedures in many areas of psychology. (pp. 354-355)[5]

Since 1954, no additional review has been made of the critical-incident technique as Flanagan developed it. Its use has been primarily in military-related studies.

Even though there has been a significant increase in proposals for models of group growth and development and in systematic prescriptions for leadership interventions in groups, the concept of the critical incident has not been widely employed as a tool for data collection, the study of leadership styles, or the evaluation of group growth and development. The following are some examples of the use of the concept of the critical incident.

N. E. Miller (1947) carried out his studies of the critical incident by examining the proceedings of the elimination boards. These proceedings contained the reasons each board member gave for eliminating a given pilot

---

[5] From J. C. Flanagan, "The Critical Incident Technique," *Psychological Bulletin*, 1954, *51*(4) 327-358. Copyright © 1954 by the American Psychological Association. Reprinted by permission.

during World War II. Most of the reasons were tied to specific behaviors. Flanagan (1947a) did a study in which he collected reasons for the failures of bombing missions as reported in the Group Mission Reports, and here again, many of the reasons for failure were related to specific behaviors. Wickert (1947) conducted a study

> to gather specific incidents of effective or ineffective behavior with respect to a designated activity. The instructions asked the combat veterans to report incidents observed by them that involved behavior which was especially helpful or inadequate in accomplishing the assigned mission. The statement finished with the request, 'Describe the officer's action. What did he do?' Several thousand incidents were collected in this way and analyzed to provide a relatively objective and factual definition of effective combat leadership. The resulting set of descriptive categories were called the 'critical requirements' of combat leadership. . . . Flanders reports. . . . The aim of this organization is the systematic study of human behavior through a coordinated program of scientific research that follows the same general principles developed in the Aviation Psychology Program. (Flanagan, 1954, pp. 328-329)[6]

Included in this research are studies by Preston (1948), Gordon (1947, 1949), and Nagay (1949a, 1949b). Preston (1948) developed a procedure to determine the critical requirements for the work and evaluation of officers in the United States Air Force. Gordon's (1947, 1949) studies identified the critical requirements of a commercial airline pilot. The study by Nagay dealt with determining the critical requirements of the air route traffic controller's job.

In several master's theses dealing with the critical-incident technique in relation to psychotherapy (Goldfarb, 1952; Mellett, 1952; Speth, 1952), incidents were collected about patients who had shown improvement. These incidents consisted of replies to the following question.

> "What did the patient do that was indicative of improvement?" Although these studies were primarily exploratory in nature, the tentative finding that different therapists stress different criteria of improvement and nonimprovement suggests that the critical incident approach may be of use not only in developing objective measures of improvement but also in experimental studies of the types of improvement resulting from the therapists' use of specific procedures. (Flanagan, 1954, p. 354)[7]

Pigors and Pigors (1965) developed the Incident Process, a five-step method for the purpose of improving decision making and leadership skills in industrial relations.

The five steps—or phases—are: 1) Studying an Incident; 2) Getting Information About Facts; 3) Stating the Immediate Issue—or hub of a problem; 4) Deciding

---

[6]See Footnote. 5.

[7]See Footnote 5.

this Issue; and, 5) Thinking about the case as a whole, to answer the practical question: What Can We Learn From It? (pp. 2-3)[8]

One of the main features of this process is that it provides four different leadership skills: director, team leader, observer-reporter, and discussion member. This process has been used since 1950 at the Massachusetts Institute of Technology.

In time-sampling studies pertaining to longitudinal child studies that pinpoint identifying characteristics in behavior at specific times, the following examples were noted. M. E. Smith (1952) made a comparison of personality traits as rated in the same individuals in childhood and fifty years later. The behavioral dimensions discussed in the survey were initially pinpointed by the mothers of six children. These behavioral dimensions were then observed at different times for a period of fifty years. Dimensions such as ambitious, happy (contented), jealous, etc., were recorded and scored on a scale from 0 to 4, with 0 meaning an absence of a given dimension, and 4 meaning a great deal of a given dimension.

The data on critical incidents in the area of controlled observational measures come from analyses of present behavior. A situation or person to be observed is selected; the dimensions of behavior to be observed in this setting are operationally defined. Even though the particular behavior is measured at only one point in time, measures can be compared to other individuals and settings. Controlled observational measures are used in every area of study from physics to speech.

B. Cooper (1963) discusses the critical requirements for effective school principals as measured by other principals, teachers, pupils, instructional supervisors, visiting teachers, school board members, and college instructors. Many child psychologists use two-way mirrors to get data on children who are allowed to play in playrooms (Axline, 1964). Counselors and psychologists frequently record anecdotal comments as part of the data when writing their case studies and case reports.

THE CRITICAL INCIDENT IN INTERVENTIONS

The concept of the critical incident has been utilized only peripherally in the literature dealing with interventions by group leaders. By and large the concept has been used implicitly (rather than explicitly) by those such as Bach (1954) who have tried to articulate the desired functions and characteristics of group leadership. Bach views therapy-group leadership as serving three different functions: procedural, catalytic, and interpretive. These functions should be directed selectively at human-change targets at appropriate and critical times. For further study of these functions in this sense, the works

---

[8]Reprinted by permission from The Pigors Incident Process Case Studies for Management Development published by BNA Incorporated, Copyright 1965.

of Fiebert (1968), Berzon and Solomon (1966), Miles (1953, 1960, 1965), and Campbell and Dunnette (1968) should be consulted.

Fiebert (1968) proposes that during the course of a group's life the trainer should vary the focus, quality, and intensity of his interventions. Fiebert provides a general outline concerning the nature of the changing role of the trainer as catalyst, orchestrator, and participant.

In the studies of Berzon and Solomon (1966; Solomon & Berzon, 1972), a "leaderless" or instrumented setting exists wherein each intervention is programmed to be introduced at an appropriate moment, and, most importantly, the effects of the intervention on the group are evaluated.

M. B. Miles (1960) labels his method of intervening as

action skills: the ability to intervene effectively in ongoing situations in such a way as to maximize personal and group effectiveness and satisfaction. (p. 301)

In all cases, the desired result is that the intervener use the process to facilitate personal or group growth. However, group leaders continue to face the dilemma of when and how to intervene most effectively. Campbell and Dunnette (1968) comment:

Questions concerning the optimal procedures for giving feedback, for enhancing feelings of psychological safety, and for stimulating individuals to try new behaviors should also be investigated. (p. 100)[9]

The Critical-Incident Model has potential use in the evaluation of proposed models of group growth and development and in the generation of new and more valid models. If the hypothesized stages or phases in a given model are appropriate, then a frequency count of the critical incidents during specific periods of a group's life should reveal the characteristics of that particular phase. In this way not only can specific models be evaluated, but additional and perhaps more integrating and incorporating ones can be constructed. There are almost as many distinct models of group growth and development as there are people studying group process. Some models involve two phases, others three or four, and some more than four phases. The amount of attention paid to certain phenomena and time periods also varies widely.

THE CRITICAL-INCIDENT MODEL

The proposed Critical-Incident Model is a way of arranging events in sequence, beginning with those that led up to and immediately preceded a critical incident to those that specify the consequences of certain interventions. The model is an attempt to identify and understand the important influence of each of these phases on the growth and development of the group. In essence,

---

[9]See Footnote 3.

the group leader is asked to organize his perceptual framework concerning the group around a model that observes events now occurring and to evaluate and decide on one or more specific interventions. Thus, group movement becomes a series of critical-incident sequences and not isolated or unrelated occurrences. From a careful analysis of the nature and frequency of certain critical incidents, it is theoretically possible to determine the specific phase as well as the direction of group movement. For example, if the lack of movement in one group was due to low-intensity interventions of a highly abstract, conceptual nature directed exclusively at the group level, a shift in intervention choice could then be prescribed to bring about more effective group movement. Research on group growth and development would be facilitated by the use of the critical-incident approach and the model could serve as a counterbalance to either rigid or unplanned approaches to leadership interventions.

The Critical-Incident Model should be viewed as an attempt to study ongoing group processes. This is accomplished by selecting a representative sample of behavior, breaking it down into its component parts, and suggesting certain responses to be made by the group leader.

Outline of the Critical-Incident Model

I. SPECIFY THE CONTEXT WITHIN WHICH THE CRITICAL INCIDENT OCCURRED (CONTEXT OF INCIDENT)

1. The approximate phase of the group is indicated (beginning, middle, or end) and the session number specified.

2. The climate or mood of the group as it relates to the critical incident is specified (dependent, counterdependent, unified, silent, hostile, depressed, etc.).

3. A brief description of the person(s) involved with each other and/or the group leader is given, including both past and current behaviors.

II. SPECIFY THE BEHAVIOR AND/OR CONVERSATION THAT LED UP TO AND IMMEDIATELY PRECEDED THE CHOICE POINT (EVENT PRECEDING CHOICE POINT)

Tom (to group leader): "I think you should answer me."
 Joyce: "I agree, and furthermore . . ."

III. DESCRIBE THE CRITICAL-INCIDENT CHOICE-POINT SITUATION AS YOU PERCEIVE IT: SPECIFY BOTH THE "SURFACE ISSUE(S)" AND THE "UNDERLYING ISSUE(S)" (CHOICE POINT)

Both surface issues and underlying issues are identified and detailed.

IV. SPECIFY THE LEVEL, TYPE, AND INTENSITY OF THE INTERVENTION RESPONSE (SUGGESTED INTERVENTION)

The chosen intervention is classified according to (1) *level of intervention* (group, interpersonal, individual), (2) *type of intervention* (conceptual, experiential, structural), and (3) *intensity of intervention* (low, medium, high).

V. SPECIFY THE RESULTS OF THE INTERVENTION ON THE GROUP (INTERVENTION OUTCOME)

The results of the intervention include the intended directional movement of the group and the actual group response to the intervention (silence, agreement, hostility, further developing critical incidents, etc.).

Context of Incident

The first section of the model specifies a complete description of the context within which the critical incident occurs.

GROUP PHASE AND SESSION NUMBER

The context is especially important when one considers that the same critical incident, emerging at different periods in the group's life, may be treated quite differently. For example, thinly disguised anger directed toward the group leader or another person in the early stages of group life demands a certain set of responses from the leader. It is conceivable that he might choose to ignore the anger until the group feels the freedom to engage in personal confrontation. On the other hand, should this same critical incident occur during the later stages of group life, the group leader might respond on a more direct, personal level.

This generalization regarding directionality would seem to be true regardless of theoretical orientation. An encounter-group leader, for example, might begin by encouraging direct, personal confrontation as a means of facilitating personal growth and as a means of providing a model for future contacts. Nevertheless, he would handle the same critical-incident encounter differently, depending on whether it emerged in the beginning, middle, or end phase of the group's life. The first encounter, for example, might involve helping the individual label his feelings as he attempts to communicate. Later in the group life the same critical incident might be used to explore all the personal ramifications of the relationship. Consequently, for purposes of research and clarification, the group leader should always record the session number in which any critical incident occurs. Doing so will permit the ebb and flow of critical incidents to be charted over the entire life of the group. In this manner, a precise frequency count of those critical incidents most likely

—and least likely—to occur may be recorded, within any theoretical orientation. This is especially valuable in a training and research capacity.

GROUP CLIMATE

The climate or mood of the group during the occurrence of the critical incident is important and intimately connected to the approximate stage of the group. Almost every group will be somewhat dependent on the group leader during the first few sessions. This is true even if the leader consciously refuses to fulfill a traditional leadership role and makes public his intentions. In such situations the group consciously or unconsciously attends to the behavior of the group leader and often attempts to use him directly as a leader. The mantle of leadership is not easily renounced. Consequently, the early stages of group life are usually marked by a climate of dependency and even a mood of passive expectancy. In later sessions, the climate or mood of the group may develop into depression, enthusiasm, or hostility. A specific critical incident, emerging during different group climates, may require a different intervention response from the leader. When the mood of the group is one of enthusiasm, a critical incident involving a request for direction and guidance may require a different response from that required when the group's mood is one of distrust and anger. An appropriate intervention, therefore, is achieved by carefully evaluating the preceding steps in the critical incident.

The group leader may also wish deliberately to establish a specific mood or climate in the group in order to facilitate the emergence of certain productive issues. These issues may involve such areas as intimacy, sharing, open communication, expression of values and norms, etc. This mood may be accomplished in a number of ways, but perhaps most relevantly by a personal reference, a literary passage, or a brief introductory talk by the group leader. The general approach of the group leader should be one that encourages the sharing of feelings. Any artificial and premature attempt to impose a specific climate on the group usually has several undesirable effects.

1. It may "freeze" or "short circuit" the ongoing group behavior to the extent that it is either temporarily delayed or never productively resolved, e.g., the group leader who attempts to impose a climate of trust and sharing on a group that is deeply involved in the direct expression of conflict and anger. Such an attempt might cause a group to delay the resolution of personal issues or, worse, might induce feelings of guilt in group members for their expression of anger.

2. If the transition or attempted shift in group mood is performed too quickly, the group leader must usually deal with the residues of the previous group mood. If, for example, the previous group mood has been one of depression and dependency, an attempt at a swift transition to a mood of independence and optimism may be met with resistance or the emergence of insistent dependency questions as well as long periods of silence.

3. Even if the transition to a new climate or mood is accomplished, the overall intention or impact of the mood may be diluted by the effects of a preceding (perhaps antagonistic) group atmosphere.

With the preceding cautions carefully kept in mind, the group leader has the ability to enhance the prevailing mood of the group, to facilitate movement into productive group discussions, and even to help bring about peak experiences in the group. It must be stressed, however, that this is a gradual process to be introduced appropriately, with discriminating judgment and discretion on the part of the group leader. Furthermore, establishing an appropriate mood or climate is not a substitution for active group work; it simply provides the setting in which group process may develop more adequately.

For example, a certain group has been gradually moving toward more open and free expression of feelings; however, several people have been resistant and have complained that to open up is to be hurt. Furthermore, they assert, opening up means running the risk of being ugly, of others not liking what they see. In the judgment of the group leader, the discussion of these feelings has been beneficial and productive; however, the group seems to be slowing to a crawl and making little progress.

This is a time-limited series of group meetings, and the goal of the leader is to try to move the group in the intended direction. It is at this point that the group leader should consider the deliberate attempt to evoke a mood of increased sharing and trust. The attempt should involve some indication that the hesitations of the group members are acknowledged and answered. While a number of different approaches—ranging from an intensely personal experience to a short literary passage or poem—may lead to establishing this mood, it is nevertheless vital to convey the importance of the mood to the group. Consequently, the group leader might begin as follows:

Group Leader: "I would like to begin the group today by discussing a few of my observations. Many of the problems of sharing, openness, and fear of pain I have felt and struggled with in groups where I was a member. But it doesn't seem to stop there. I don't really believe that the concerns we are voicing are limited just to this group, to this place and this time. It seems I have heard these same concerns of love and fear time and again. I would like to share a sort of story or parable with you, one that has been important to me and one I hope will have some importance for you. It goes something like this:

What is real, asked the
Rabbit one day
When they were lying side by side
Does it mean having things that
buzz inside you?
Real isn't how you're made
said the skin horse

It's a thing that happens to you
When a child loves you for a
long long time
Not to just play with, but really
loves you
Then you become real
Does it hurt? Asked the rabbit
Sometimes, said the skin horse for
he was always truthful.
When you are real you don't mind
being hurt
Does it happen all at once, like being
wound up or bit by bit?
It doesn't happen all at once,
you become
It takes a long time. That's why it
doesn't happen often to people who
break easily, or have sharp
edges, or have to be carefully kept.
Generally, by the time you are
real, most of your hair has been loved
off, and your eyes drop out and you get loose at the
joints and very shabby.
But these things don't matter
at all because once you are
real you can't be ugly, except
to people who don't understand.
Inside you're different
and you won't ever be
the same again. Not ever. (Williams, 1958)[10]

There are no guarantees that the attempt to establish a desired mood will be successful. However, it is better to plan for the deliberate evocation of a group climate through various techniques and resources than to permit a haphazard development of the group into areas that are not beneficial. Those group leaders who feel that such an approach lacks sincerity and is artificially technical must remember that sincerity and genuine concern transcend any technique; they must not be confused with the technique itself.

PERSONS INVOLVED

It is important to emphasize that the decision by the group leader to respond with a particular level, type, and intensity of intervention is largely deter-

---

[10] Paraphrased from "The Dialogue Between the Skin Horse and the Rabbit About Being Real," in *The Velveteen Rabbit or How Toys Become Real*, by M. Williams. New York: Doubleday, 1958. Reprinted by permission.

mined by the person or persons involved. A group member who has a history of being reserved and quiet and who has finally developed the courage to confront the group leader with anger might well be handled with encouragement and support. On the other hand, another group member, who apparently seeks out intense encounters, might be handled by interpreting his life style, by involving him on a very deep and intense level, or by directing his anger back to the group for discussion.

The life style of any given individual in the group largely determines whether his responses will be encouraged or inhibited, whether his behavior is productive for himself and/or the group, and whether certain interventions will be more effective than others. Group work has not been refined to the point that the life style of a certain group member always demands a specific intervention response. At present, there are too many contributing, but unknown, variables to establish any such relationships. An effective group leader thus bases the level, type, and intensity of his response on these three factors: the phase of the group, the climate of the group, and the persons involved. Obviously these factors interrelate and overlap; any one may be manipulated to affect the others. For example, a desired climate may be deliberately established by focusing on the key group members who can help provide the proper group direction or by extending the length of group sessions so as to accelerate movement into a different group phase.

Instead of providing definite answers, the Critical-Incident Model offers guidelines and a method by which the guidelines may be refined. Leadership strategy varies among groups and among leaders; e.g., where one group leader might interpret group hostility as productive and encourage its expression, another group leader would see it as threatening and nonproductive and seek to extinguish those responses by the group. Which approach is most effective is an empirical question best approached by a model that evaluates the effects on the group over a period of time.

Event Preceding Choice Point

The second section of the Critical-Incident Model requires that the group leader specify the behavior and/or conversation that led to and immediately preceded the choice point. This section attempts to provide specific behavioral cues to which the group leader can respond. More importantly, it allows these cues to be utilized as an index of group movement, since different concerns are voiced at different times. The effective group leader will be alert not only to what is being said, but also to the manner in which it is expressed.

Certain key group members may be described as "barometric"; i.e., they may, through expression of feelings and attitudes, accurately register the group climate and stage. On the other hand, every group has members who may express feelings that are personal, idiosyncratic, and opposite from the direction of most of the group. Therefore, the group leader must be prepared to evaluate the group needs and personal needs of the members before deciding on a specific evaluation.

The actual behavior or conversation to be recorded should follow logically from the preceding events. The following quotations serve as examples of actual conversations leading to the choice point, where a response is required. The first quotation drawn from the first session of an ongoing T-group illustrates the basic concern. The second quotation directs this concern toward the group leader.

> After a few seconds of silence someone very mildly suggested that perhaps they might introduce themselves, adding that this seemed customary in groups of his experience. . . .
>
> "When we did accomplish something, even though it was only introducing ourselves, you've indicated you didn't like what we did. If you don't like what we do, tell us what to do; otherwise you have no right to criticize us." (Bradford, 1964, pp. 138-139)[11]

It is important to note that although the manner of expression may vary, the basic intent of the critical incident remains the same, i.e., to structure the group so as to provide superficial personal information with a minimum of personal involvement. The group leader is then faced with the need to consider and integrate the context within which the event occurred, as well as the concrete behaviors involved in a specific affect-loaded statement.

Choice Point

A decision to respond to the content of a statement, the affect involved in that statement, or a combination of these two factors largely depends on the leader's basic assumptions concerning group growth and development. The third section of the Critical-Incident Model, therefore, attempts to take these factors into consideration in its discussion of both surface and underlying issues. It is not assumed that surface and underlying issues are always different or opposed. There are many occasions when both the surface issue and the underlying issue are the same, when the expressed concern is the real concern. More frequently, however, the surface issue or the issues under consideration may be masking other more important underlying issues. The following example illustrates this point.

Mark: "I wonder what the other groups are doing, I mean, whether they have something planned?"

---

[11]From L. P. Bradford, "Trainer Intervention: Case Episodes," in L. P. Bradford, J. R. Gibb, & K. D. Benne (Eds.), *T-Group Theory and Laboratory Method: Innovation in Re-education.* New York: John Wiley, 1964. Reprinted by permission.

The Critical-Incident Model: Its Use and Application   131

Patricia: "I understand they have some leaders who are certified in this area and are really sharp."

Tony: "How is it that we can't get started? What is it we're supposed to do?"

In the interaction, several factors stand out as being important. *On the surface level*, one member appears to be wondering what other groups are doing. A second member makes a statement concerning the training and competency of other group leaders. A third member, apparently irrelevantly, asks a question concerning the direction. These statements seem unimportant, casual, or even irrelevant when viewed from a surface or content level. However, what a group is saying on a content level often reflects its unnoticed struggles about issues at an *underlying* process level. In the example, the *underlying issues* appear to be (1) a concern over the lack of an agenda and a direction for the group, which increases the members' frustration and hostility; (2) a concern with the degree of leadership ability of the present group leader, stated as an oblique comparison; and (3) the issue of dependency and seeking for the "right thing to be done."

An attempt to specify underlying issues and concerns can modify the leader's response. In addition, investigation of surface issues as a reflection of underlying processes may yield more understanding concerning group growth and development. This is especially true when the content of a given statement does not match the affect associated with it. In the example, the statement by Patricia, delivered in a sarcastic, hostile tone, makes the discrepancy between the surface issue and underlying issue even more obvious.

Another example might be an intellectual disagreement between a male and a female group member regarding man's rationality. On the surface or content level, this appears to be a philosophical exercise. On a deeper, process level, the underlying issues may be a struggle for power and possibly an acting out of sexual fantasies.

It is difficult to specify the exact, underlying issues involved in any given critical incident, since they vary with the assumptions of the group leader. The psychoanalytic group leader, for example, tends to make certain assumptions concerning the basic underlying group issues that are different from those of a nondirective group leader. What is important is to recognize the importance of both group content and the underlying group process. This subject is discussed later in the chapter.

Suggested Intervention

The *level*, *type*, and *intensity* of the intervention response to any given critical incident is considered in the fourth section of the model. The level of intervention (group, interpersonal, individual), the type of intervention (conceptual, experiential, structural), and the intensity of intervention (low, medium, high) are utilized in order to determine the focus of a given intervention. All interventions, regardless of the group leader's theoretical orientation, may be described by these three components of the Intervention Cube. An example of the wide applicability of this technique is revealed in the following quotations from several group leaders, each one representing a different theoretical orientation.

A young woman chimes in, 'How do we communicate better with each other?' There is a long pause. No one responds. I ask myself, 'What now?' Shall we talk about the topic or communication? No, let's act instead. 'Are you game to experiment a bit?', I ask. There are a few tentative nods from some of the students. 'O.K., push the chairs aside, mill around the room and pick out a person you don't know but would like to know better. This may sound a little crazy, but sit on the floor back-to-back with your partner and carry on a conversation for a few minutes!' After a short period of time I ask the pairs to turn around face-to-face and share their feelings. Next, the pairs face each other. (Thomas, 1969, p. 70)[12]

The preceding intervention is an example of a leader's response common in encounter groups. It may be descriptively analyzed by means of the Intervention Cube as follows:

"Are you game to experiment a bit? . . . O.K., push the chairs aside, mill around. . . ." This intervention is aimed at the entire group (level: group). Furthermore, the group leader has decided not to focus on talking or conceptualizing, but to focus on structuring an activity (type: structural). Finally, this intervention is delivered in the early stages of the group, in a calm, straightforward, descriptive manner that does not try to expose underlying dynamics in depth (intensity: low). If the emphasis is on the activity as a means to an end, as illustrated in the example given, then the type of intervention is classified as structural. On the other hand, the activity might be designed to elicit direct awareness of feelings, in which case the intervention is emotional in focus (type: experiential). An example of this latter type of intervention:

"Now, I want each of you to close your eyes and verbally express the feelings inside of you. Do this right now!" This intervention would be classified as an intervention aimed at the group level (level: group), directed toward immediate expression of emotions (type: experiential), and with little intended direct clarification of underlying dynamics (intensity: low).

A different theoretical orientation is reflected in the directive psychotherapeutic approach. This is characterized by the group leader's attempt to uncover the patient's underlying conflicts, to interpret to the patient what is

---

[12]From H. F. Thomas, "Encounter: The Game of No Game," in A. Burton (Ed.), *Encounter: Theory and Practice of Encounter Groups*. San Francisco: Jossey-Bass, 1969. Reprinted by permission.

revealed, and to guide him toward positive actions designed to effect personality changes. An example of the directive approach in the group is as follows:

> Patient: "I am strangling my own feelings of a great desire for sexual intercourse with her."
> Leader: "So the girl stands for your desire which you are so afraid of, just as the devil stood for it. In this fantasy of strangling the girl you are dramatizing the struggle that is within your own mind. (Berg, 1948, p. 81)[13]

This intervention by the group leader is focused on the individual (level: individual). It attempts to conceptualize the conflicts involved (type: conceptual) and to make an effort at some interpretation and clarification of the underlying dynamic (intensity: medium).

Another theoretical approach is the nondirective orientation, revealed in the following brief excerpt.

> Patient: "I am afraid I am falling in love with her . . . and I can't study or do anything when I don't see her . . . and yet I know she would not be faithful to me . . . I just don't know which way to turn."
> Leader: "You want to continue seeing Frances but you are afraid you will be hurt. . . ." (Coleman, 1964, p. 568)[14]

In contrast to the preceding interventions, this one is directed at the individual (level: individual). There is no attempt, however, to conceptualize or theorize about the critical event at a deeper level. There is, instead, a simple summation and reflection of the feelings that were involved (type: experiential; intensity: low).

Intervention Outcome

The final section of the Critical-Incident Model requires that the specific results of the intervention on the group be recorded and reveals the underlying orientation of a specific approach. Without knowing the impact that a particular intervention has on a group, a group leader cannot determine the types of interventions that are most effective. In order to do this, he must judge the extent to which an intervention moved the group in the desired direction. The group leader is forced to specify the intended direction and, hence, the goals of the group.

It is immediately obvious that the intended direction of group movement is not always the actual direction a group takes. An intervention designed to encourage members to engage in personal feelings and self-exploration

---

[13]From C. Berg, *The Casebook of a Medical Psychologist*. London: George Allen & Unwin, 1948. Reprinted by permission.

[14]From J. C. Coleman, *Abnormal Psychology and Modern Life*. Glenview, Ill.: Scott, Foresman, 1964. Reprinted by permission.

may be met by silence, hostility, or minimum cooperation. The verbal and nonverbal responses of the group members following a specific intervention must be recorded to calculate its impact.

An intervention is not necessarily wrong or incorrect if there is no immediate group response. The intervention may have been introduced prematurely, during an intense emotional period, or during the early stages of group life when the members were not ready to apply it. The following quotation, taken from an early stage in group life, illustrates this point. In response to an intervention by the group leader,

> the group had difficulty hearing the intervention, not to mention understanding its implications, partly because of anxiety about what the trainers thought of them and partly because of irritation that the movement of the group—any movement—had been stopped. (Bradford, 1964, p. 138)[15]

Interventions may have a number of effects on the group. Often the group leader will give an intervention that is apparently ignored, only to see it surface later in the group as a spontaneous idea by one or more members. Certain well-timed interventions may offer key concepts or explanations that are referred to by members time and again. Other interventions are not only ignored but are faced with anger and hostility. Until the group leader records the effects of a particular intervention style on the group, there can be little basis for making comparisons and improving intervention quality.

THE APPLICABILITY OF THE CRITICAL-INCIDENT CONCEPT TO DIFFERENT GROUPS

If the Critical-Incident Model is to fulfill its function as a teaching, training, and research tool, it must be flexible enough to describe any ongoing group. Several representative examples follow, selected from the group literature of groups in process and incorporated into the framework of the Critical-Incident Model. In order to preserve the uniqueness and theoretical orientation of these widely divergent groups, actual quotations have been incorporated wherever possible. Although representative, these examples do not exhaust the number of approaches within any given orientation. Each group example represents a major approach for the group leader and for the specific orientation. Although certain exceptions may be found, this selection is a valid guide to major similarities and distinctions among the various groups.

Incorporating each unique group-process example into the Critical-Incident Model permits two major advantages: the systematic exploration of

---

[15]See Footnote 11.

The Critical-Incident Model: Its Use and Application   135

intervention style within a given discipline or orientation and the systematic comparison of basic issues and of the effectiveness of intervention styles among groups.

Within each critical-incident example presented, the characteristic response style of a number of orientations clearly defines itself. Since each style of intervention, i.e., level, type, and intensity, has its own unique configuration when viewed within the Intervention Cube, four figures (4.1, 4.2, 4.3, and 4.4) have been designed to represent the typical style of intervention for each specific approach. A fifth figure (4.5) presents all the intervention cubes side by side for comparison of group leader styles. In this manner, a quick reference to the position of a specific set of leader interventions on the Intervention Cube yields information concerning possible therapeutic orientations, areas not dealt with, experienced versus beginning group leaders, etc.

The overt, behavioral process of group growth and development is relatively easy to describe; however, problems of meaning, definition, and understanding arise when an attempt is made to explain qualitative, subjective, or dynamic aspects. These are phenomena that go beyond the verbal. To attempt to communicate the nonverbal in purely verbal terms means that the possibilities for misunderstanding will be multiplied. What seems to be straightforward and logical when read on paper may need to be modified by emotional or intuitive cues specific to time and place. There is no substitute for the reasoned and mature judgment of the group leader.

A Nondirective Critical Incident: 1

In the first example, the Critical-Incident Model is applied to an individual-therapy session and a group-therapy session. The Rogerian nondirective intervention style of responses is consistent throughout both examples.

CONTEXT OF INCIDENT

> Miss Gil, a young woman who has, in a number of therapeutic interviews, been quite hopeless about herself, has spent the major part of an hour discussing her feelings of inadequacy and lack of personal worth. Part of the time she has been aimlessly using the finger paints. She has just finished expressing her feelings of wanting to get away from everyone—to have nothing to do with people. After a long pause comes the following. (Rogers, 1951, p. 46)[16]

EVENT PRECEDING CHOICE POINT

> Client: "I've never said this before to anyone—but I've thought for such a long time—this is a terrible thing to say, but if I could just—well," (short, bitter

---

[16]From C. R. Rogers, *Client-Centered Therapy.* Boston: Houghton Mifflin, 1951. Reprinted by permission.

laugh; pause) "if I could just find some glorious cause that I could give my life for I would be happy. I cannot be the kind of person I want to be. I guess maybe I haven't the guts—or the strength—to kill myself—and if someone else would relieve me of the responsibility—or I would be in an accident—I—I just don't want to live." (p. 46)[17]

CHOICE POINT

Rogers (1951) has described, at great length, the process known as client-centered therapy. Essentially, it is based on a warm and supportive relationship of mutual liking and respect, at times described variously as unconditional regard for a person's self-worth. In the nondirective approach, the client begins with a somewhat intellectual discussion of his problems but quickly moves toward a more personal exploration of self. As the client permits more of these actual experiences to enter his awareness, his picture of himself keeps changing and enlarging to include these newly discovered aspects of himself.

Translating this orientation into the Critical-Incident Model demonstrates a general nondirective flow or process. The client tends to begin on an individual level. He is concerned with a conceptual approach to his problems which is reflected in low-intensity statements.

In turn, the client-centered reflections of the therapist oriented along a one-to-one experiential level of low intensity gradually encourage the client to move from a conceptual to an experiential focus. As the client does so, the intensity of his statements typically moves from medium to high.

> Therapist: "At the present time, things look so black to you that you can't see much point in living . . ." (p. 46)

This is an intervention on the individual level, of an experiential type, of low intensity.

> Client: "Yes—I wish I'd never started this therapy. I was happy when I was living in my dream world . . . and I suppose that if I accepted the fact that I am worthless, then I could go away someplace—and get a little room someplace—get a mechanical job someplace—and retreat clear back to the security of my dream world where I could do things, have clever friends, be a pretty wonderful sort of person . . ."

> Therapist: "It's really a rough struggle—digging into this like you are—and at times the shelter of your dream world looks more attractive and comfortable." (p. 46)

The therapist clarifies and summarizes the client's statement: individual level, experiential type, low to medium intensity.

> Client: "My dream world or suicide."

> Therapist: "Your dream world or something more permanent than dreams . . ." (p. 46)

---

[17]See Footnote 16 for this and following extracts from Rogers.

This statement is on the individual level, of an experiential type, of low to medium intensity.

These excerpts reveal a typical style or pattern that is consistent throughout the majority of nondirective sessions: interventions are almost always directed toward the individual level, with little in the way of interpersonal sharing in the usual sense. The basic approach is almost invariably experiential with no structural interventions. It is a moot question as to the presence of a conceptual basis, since an attempt is made to pull together and summarize feelings; however, little attempt is made to conceptualize dynamics, interpretations, or symbols as in the Freudian sense of conceptualization.

The intensity of interventions on the part of the nondirective therapist generally begins low and typically remains at this level throughout the period of therapy. This low-intensity feedback allows the client to experiment and feel free to open himself to expression at levels of intensity ranging from low to high. Thus, there is a distinct intervention pattern that not only represents one therapeutic orientation, but also reveals the changes in level, type, and intensity of client responses that are directed toward the therapist and evolve over time.

A Nondirective Critical Incident: 2

In the following example, a Rogerian critical incident in a group-therapy setting, it is important to note that the plea for guidance, dependency, and direction arises in a modified form. It is handled basically the same way with the same consistent style of intervention. This intervention style is to be contrasted with the intervention style of psychoanalytic groups and T-groups, both of which deal with similar problems.

CONTEXT OF INCIDENT

> Here is a verbatim transcript of part of a first hour of group-centered therapy with six university students, all preparing for jobs in schools or colleges. (Hobbs, 1949, pp. 114-115)[18]

EVENT PRECEDING CHOICE POINT

> Jane: "One thing I might say is my particular feeling that I want to work on a problem of the concept of dependence and independence in marriage. I've been married about a year and married to—he's a law student—who is primarily an unemotional person, and I would say there's a good deal of lack of understanding

---

[18]From N. Hobbs, Nondirective Group Counseling. *Journal of the National Association of Deans of Women, 12*(3), March 1949, 114-115. Reprinted by permission of the National Association for Women Deans, Administrators, and Counselors and the author.

between us. The conflict was mainly one of my desire to be independent and not being independent, in the marriage relationship, and the marriage not being a fifty-fifty relationship."

Therapist: "It's not wholly satisfactory to you now." (pp. 114-115)[19]

This intervention is at the individual level, of an experiential type, of low intensity.

Jane: "No, it is not a satisfactory relationship, but I do think there's a good deal of possibility of its being a satisfactory relationship."

Betty: (Pause) "I think most of my trouble is not having enough confidence in myself to assert myself when I am with others. I feel confidence in being able to do things, but when I'm in a social group or in a classroom, I more or less withdraw and let everybody else do the talking and thinking . . . Now, I suppose that feeling carries over into other relationships, too, a feeling of not being—of not having a great deal of personal worth or value."

Therapist: "You feel rather confident of your ability, privately or as an individual, yet when you work with people, you tend to devaluate yourself."

Betty: "That's right. I tend to evade issues or withdraw—instead of meeting them face on."

Therapist: "Yes." (pp. 114-115)[20]

(A continuation and elaboration of the same problem and related problems continues.)

CHOICE POINT

The issues involved in this nondirective critical incident are best explained by Hobbs (in the chapter "Group-Centered Psychotherapy," Rogers, 1951):

> With the above excerpt providing concrete material for consideration, we may gain in understanding of the subtle and complex process of group therapy by making comparisons with the more familiar process of individual client-centered therapy . . . they bring to the situation a freight of anxiety, a product of their unsuccessful efforts to relate themselves effectively to other people, and this anxiety is usually heightened by the indeterminate nature of the impending experience in therapy . . . he must find in the group situation increasingly less need for the defenses against anxiety which render him so ineffectual in living with others and so unhappy in living with himself . . . even in the first session quoted above we find members very open with each other, sensing somehow the support that was even then present, and that would grow as the meetings continue." (p. 286)[21]

SUGGESTED INTERVENTION

The previous intervention choice was on the individual level, of an experiential type, of low intensity. This intervention mode is consistent with the series of chained critical incidents as revealed in the pattern of responses.

---

[19]See Footnote 18.
[20]See Footnote 18.
[21]See Footnote 16.

INTERVENTION OUTCOME

The results of this critical incident are not clearly specified, but it is suggested that individual self-awareness and growth on the part of group members would be the expected outcome.

In both the individual and group critical incidents, there is a consistent intervention response style that allows a graphic representation on the Intervention Cube. (See Figure 4.1.) The shaded areas illustrate the matrix of specific intervention responses that characterizes a Rogerian nondirective approach. The unshaded areas dramatically reveal the intervention responses that are never used in this approach and considered of little consequence in group growth and development. In the examples given, the Rogerian leader may begin with the individual level and, as the situation demands, progress to the interpersonal and finally the group level. The heaviest emphasis is on the individual and interpersonal level.

Type
- Conceptual (C)
- Experiential (E)
- Structural (S)

Intensity
- High (H.I.)
- Medium (M.I.)
- Low (L.I.)

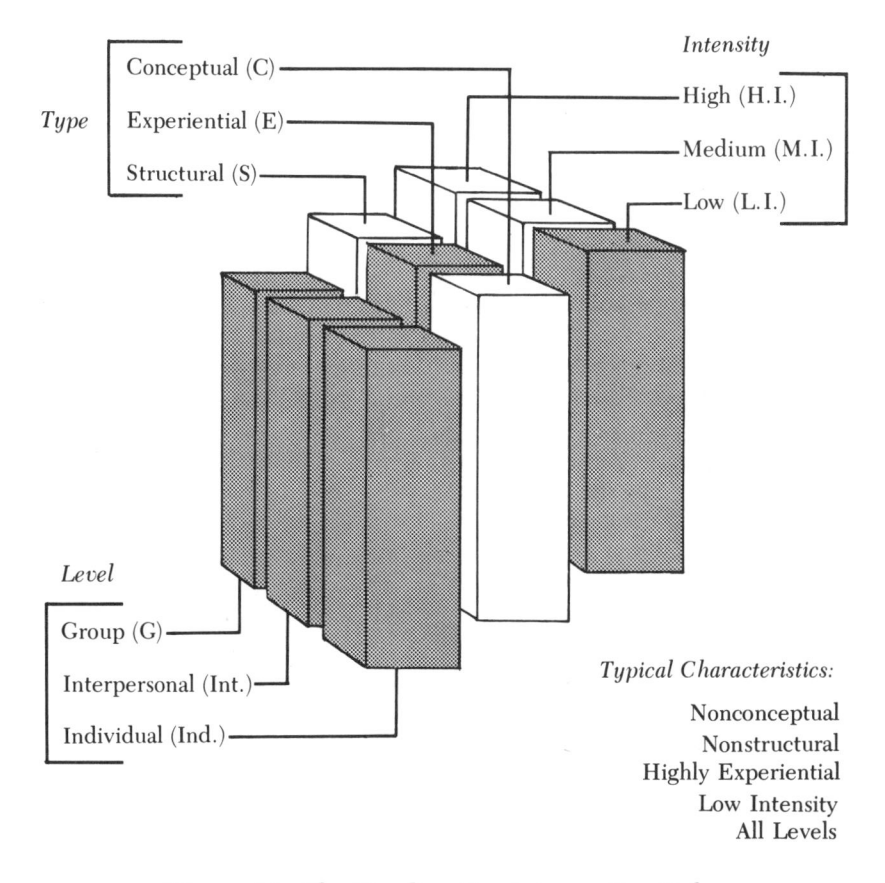

Level
- Group (G)
- Interpersonal (Int.)
- Individual (Ind.)

Typical Characteristics:
Nonconceptual
Nonstructural
Highly Experiential
Low Intensity
All Levels

Figure 4.1. The Nondirective Intervention Cube

In essence, the Intervention Cube reflects a style that is nondirective, nonconceptual, and nonstructural, with experiential-type, low-intensity encounters, usually on an individual level.

A Psychoanalytic-Group Critical Incident: 1

The second intervention style to be considered is group psychoanalysis as reported by Cohn (1972) and Durkin (1964). The basic orientation of group analysis is the application of appropriate fundamental psychoanalytic principles to individuals in a group setting. The approach is summarized by N. M. Locke (1961):

> The therapist can do specific things, take specific action, employ specific techniques, to further the process of psychotherapy. Group psychotherapy does not employ the so-called group dynamics. Although these may be present in the psychoanalytic group, as in any group, they play no conscious or directed part in the therapy. Furthermore, it is the individual who is being treated, not the group. (p. vii, Introduction)[22]

Two representative examples of this approach are given. In the first example, Cohn (1972) relates an episode to which the analytic therapist could have responded with one of two specifiable alternatives. The episode has been incorporated into the framework of the Critical-Incident Model.

CONTEXT OF INCIDENT

This incident supposedly occurs during the initial sessions of analytically oriented group therapy. The author, Cohn (1972), creates a fairly typical group-therapy episode. In this episode, the author has hypothesized the thoughts of both patient and therapist within parentheses.

> Dina is the patient on whom I would like you to focus your attention. She is 35 years old, married and has one two-year-old child. She speaks in a barely audible voice without intonation whenever she talks about herself at any length. But she is capable of sounding vigorous and vivacious when speaking about others. Her facial expression, accordingly, is either masklike and dead or quite animated. (p. 85)[23]

EVENT PRECEDING CHOICE POINT

> Dina: I feel awful . . . just awful . . . I think Bob feels . . . you know . . . like Craig said. And it's my fault. If I were more cheerful . . . if I could smile

---

[22]Reprinted by permission of New York University Press from *Group Psychoanalysis: Theory and Technique*. By Norman Locke, © 1961 by New York University.

[23]Reprinted from THE PSYCHOANALYTIC REVIEW, Vol. 56, No. 3, 1969, through the courtesy of the Editors and the Publisher, National Psychological Association for Psychoanalysis, New York, N. Y.

like Jane . . . My little sister is that way, always smiling even when it hurts . . . And I can't and I know Bob hates it.
   Dr. Ashley: (Her conscious guilt acts as a defense against showing any aggression). You think it's all your fault?
   Dina: I know it is and I don't really feel like talking here because (because they'll jump on me) . . . Because I get on everyone's nerves.
   Dr. Ashley: (Maybe she does . . . she often gets on mine). Craig was the only one who said you get on his nerves. You seem to have a radar system for negative judgments . . . you always hear only the negative.
   Dina: (What is he saying? . . . Can't think . . . Speak somebody! . . . please . . . I can't talk). (p. 87)[24]

CHOICE POINT

The surface issue was a plea for guidance and direction from a group member who, for underlying reasons, was hearing only negative statements regarding her situation. The underlying issue was one of dependency and a
   recognition of her repressed hostility which manifested itself in her masochistic way of torturing Bob by her as-if-crying reproaches, and torturing the group and analyst by her manner of speech. (p. 88)

SUGGESTED INTERVENTION

   Dr. Ashley: (I guess she went blank . . . Heard me negatively, too . . . Maybe I can help her see where this defense comes from . . .) I wonder why you go blank now . . . What of your childhood comes to your mind with regard to "negative judgments"? (p. 87)

This intervention is conceptual in nature, of low intensity, and focuses on the individual level.
   Dina: (Nothing . . . nothing . . . They're going to bed next door . . . Mummy, Daddy . . . radar station for the negative . . .) No . . . Nothing . . . They . . . My parents . . . They just didn't pay any attention to me . . . I had to be quiet when Daddy came home . . . Except for when I had good report cards. I had to be quiet . . . Always . . . When my parents went to sleep, I had to whisper to my dolls so they wouldn't hear me . . . and I couldn't wake Sis up . . .
   Dr. Ashley: Perhaps if your dolls could speak, they would tell us how angry you were at your parents for having to be quiet, for having to give so much to your sister and to them. And how you lost your voice. (p. 87)

This final interpretation focuses on a deep analytic conceptual statement of high intensity, directed at the individual level.

INTERVENTION OUTCOME

The author of the above critical incident felt that the specified intervention by the group leader would probably result in the following effects:

---

[24]See Footnote 23 for this and following extracts from Cohn.

Although the analyst had promoted a process of insight into the dynamics of repressed hostility, Dina was emotionally preoccupied with the feeling that Dr. Ashley did not like her . . . Her awareness of her own hatred for Dr. Ashley's "disliking" her and preferring "other children" fused with the memory of her revealing her rage about her parents to her dolls and their successor, the husband, and the baby, Freddy. This heightened awareness deepened into the experience of a recognition, here manifested with an awakening sense of humor and an ability to communicate with Bob on a masochistic level. (p. 89)

This last statement may be entirely justifiable and reasonable on purely theoretical grounds, but our bias is that the final answer is an empirical one. This would seem, once again, to argue for a systematic exploration of intervention alternatives within the various therapeutic approaches, utilizing the framework of the Critical-Incident Model.

A Psychoanalytic-Group Critical Incident: 2

The second example of the Critical-Incident Model applied to group psychoanalysis deals with similar issues of dependency, hostility, and anxiety over confrontation. It is offered to illustrate the generality of certain recurrent group phenomena and the differences in intervention styles.

CONTEXT OF INCIDENT

This analytic group consisted of five members, all of whom had not quite reached the point of working together productively. The author, Durkin (1964), specifies the context:

Ned became more than ever restless under these conditions. But in spite of signalling his anxiety directly, he drew enough support from Cynthia to make clever sarcastic comments about Jack's manners, his speech, and his dress (example of hostility and humor used as a defense). His barbs did not hit the target at this time because Jack lived blissfully in a different social world . . . and Netta quickly took over a role that was to be characteristic of her. She made sympathetic and reassuring remarks to all and changed the subject. (pp. 177-178)[25]

EVENT PRECEDING CHOICE POINT

The group leader sets up the choice point:

I commented on how quickly they were all ready to use Netta's reassurance, and her attempt to change the subject, and wondered why. There was a moment of silence and then a variety of expressive questioning glances could be seen among

---

[25]From H. E. Durkin, *The Group in Depth*. New York: International Universities Press, 1964. Reprinted by permission.

the group. Netta was the only one to show open anxiety. Her facial expression was worried, almost tearful . . . She said rather poutingly that she knew she shouldn't have come because she always managed to do the wrong thing. (p. 178)[26]

CHOICE POINT

The author describes her choice point as follows:
> I had the choice of picking up her annoyance and tying it in with that of the other members, or exploring further the anxiety she had expressed and which was also present in all of them. I decided intuitively that anxiety about starting in a group was the more immediate concern. (pp. 178-179)

In this instance, the therapist chose to focus on the underlying issue of group anxiety rather than on the surface issue of the group's quickly changing direction.

SUGGESTED INTERVENTION

The following quote reveals the nature of the intervention:
> I said to Netta, therefore, that I thought she was not the only one who felt nervous in the group today. [Individual level, experiential type, low intensity.] Then I turned to the others and added "How about that? I had a feeling you are all a little tense in this new situation." (p. 179) [Group level, experiential type, low intensity.]

This shift from individual to group level allows generalization and emotional cohesiveness to build.

INTERVENTION OUTCOME

> Immediately they came closer to the important feeling they were trying to ignore, and at the same time closer to one another in the realization of their common experience. . . . But even on this level their relief at these admissions was obvious and permitted a degree of therapeutic movement. At least they now knew their fears were mutual. They had their first knowledge concerning hidden feelings, and experienced the group as a safe place to acknowledge them. (p. 179)

The psychoanalytic-group intervention style reveals the unique configuration specific to this orientation. The shaded areas of the Intervention Cube in Figure 4.2 reveal a basically directive approach: individual or interpersonal level, experiential type, low intensity. The unshaded areas of the intervention model reveal the areas considered unimportant or not particularly salient.

---

[26]See Footnote 25 for this and following extracts from Durkin.

144 The Critical Incident in Growth Groups

Type
- Conceptual (C)
- Experiential (E)
- Structural (S)

Intensity
- High (H.I.)
- Medium (M.I.)
- Low (L.I.)

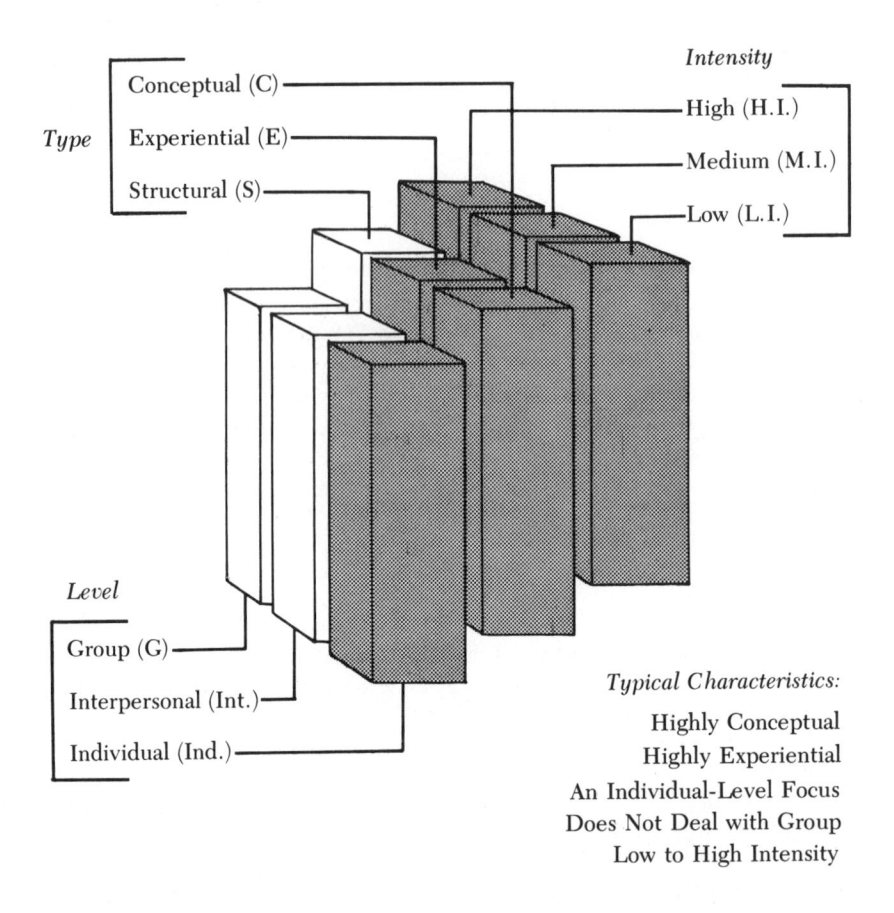

Level
- Group (G)
- Interpersonal (Int.)
- Individual (Ind.)

Typical Characteristics:
Highly Conceptual
Highly Experiential
An Individual-Level Focus
Does Not Deal with Group
Low to High Intensity

Figure 4.2. The Psychoanalytic Intervention Cube

A T-Group Critical Incident: 1

The following two critical incidents, taken directly from tapes of ongoing T-groups, represent the laboratory approach to training. While there are wide individual differences among leaders in intervention posture within any given T-group setting, the similarities in approach outweigh the differences. All training groups have certain shared goals and values: human relations, communications, and leadership skills. Every group member is encouraged to evaluate the effectiveness of his functioning and to actively explore new ways of achieving a desired goal. A concerted effort is made to enable each participant to integrate knowledge, skills, and values into self-awareness of the impact of his behavior on others.

The first critical incident involves the same recurrent phenomenon noted in the preceding psychoanalytic and nondirective groups. It is offered as a means of contrasting and comparing intervention styles.

CONTEXT OF INCIDENT

This is the second meeting of the group. The climate of the group has been shifting between dependency and veiled hostility directed at the group leader for not specifying exact directions. After a particularly heated exchange between group members over how to get started, one frustrated group member turns to the group leader and addresses him angrily.

EVENT PRECEDING CHOICE POINT

Alvin: "I'd just like you to spell out the exact goals of this group, and how we're supposed to reach them."

Group Leader: "That's a good question, Alvin, and one the group might consider."

Paula: "Why don't you answer Bill's question? He asked a concrete, factual question, and I haven't heard you give a good answer to him yet!"

SUGGESTED INTERVENTION

The intervention for this particular beginning phase is usually at the individual level, of an experiential type, and of low intensity, quickly moving to a group level and a conceptual type. A typical intervention might go as follows.

Group Leader: "I've heard you, Alvin, and I haven't ignored your question, which is an important one. I've noticed your anger and frustration." (A direct reply to the individual and a recognition of the feelings involved.) "I also sense that most of our group seem frustrated at this point and are asking for rules and to be told what to do and how to do it." (A quick movement to the group level and to a conceptual nature, which identifies the individual's question as one of general group concern regarding direction.) "I think one of the most important areas for us to work through is the development of meaningful goals, and this can only come about through the development of our own group life. Therefore, I can't legislate either your movement or your response since this is a growth process arising from the group.

"Another issue that I see emerging has to do with seeking to re-create an authority relationship, a relationship in which you depend on someone to provide some kind of structure and order. All of us struggle from time to time with some very crucial competitive issues." (A shift to the larger question of the importance of the authority problem, still at a group level, of a conceptual type.) "I wonder how the rest of you feel about this question?"

At this point, the group may pick up on the problem of group goals or the relationship of the group leader to the group. Selective responding on the group leader's part may lead the group to discuss one or more alternatives.

A T-Group Critical Incident: 2

The second representative T-group critical incident utilizes a structural intervention as a means of underlining and emphasizing group concerns. As in the preceding T-group example, this episode was also taken directly from an active ongoing group.

CONTEXT OF INCIDENT

This is the first group session. The general climate of the group is a mixture of awkwardness and anxiety. Members are unsure of their direction and unfamiliar with one another. A few dependency statements have been made to the group by particularly anxious members, but there has been little response.

EVENT PRECEDING CHOICE POINT

Tom: "Well, I think we should know something about ourselves. Let's go around the room and tell something about ourselves. You know, introduce ourselves and tell where we are from."

Bill: "That's a great idea; why don't you start?"

The group picks up on this idea and continues until everyone is finished. It is now the leader's turn, and everyone is watching him expectantly. What are the issues involved and the response alternatives available to him as a leader?

SUGGESTED INTERVENTION

Unless confronted by some particular individual, the leader almost always intervenes in this particular beginning phase at the group level. This kind of intervention provides the group leader with one or more alternatives. Experientially, the group leader may remain quiet, looking comfortably at the group. This frustrates their expectancies and allows anxiety to build within the group. It is probable, however, that this will result in a group member finally asking the leader to "Tell us a little bit about yourself, so we can get to know you." It may seem, from this example, that the selection of a certain choice alternative (in this instance, remaining silent) leads to a sequence of chained critical incidents, through which the future behavior of the group may be predicted from the nature of the response just made. Another response intervention involving the sharing of feelings might go as follows:

Group Leader: "I'd like to share some of my thoughts and feelings with you about how I feel right now. I'm feeling pretty boxed in and a little uncertain as to how I should reply." (A sharing of feelings and a modeling of behavior.)

"On one hand, I hear you asking for some straight information and I'm certainly willing to give that, but I also seem to hear each of us trying to feel each other out, to locate our personal boundaries and limitations, to categorize and pigeonhole. It seems to relieve the pressure and give us a direction." (A general, but superficial, interpretation of both content and group motivation.)

"I wonder if the rest of you feel that you really know each other that much better now? What sort of characteristics did we reveal about ourselves?" (A group-level intervention with movement from experiential type to conceptual type, encouraging sharing of ideas about the just-finished process.)

The degree of intensity is almost always very low during this particular interchange and during this stage of the group. The group leader has the option at this point of introducing a structural intervention that encourages familiarity and cohesion among group members. His decision to utilize this intervention will be determined by a knowledge of individual group members and their needs, the speed with which he would like to see the group consolidate its gains, and the importance he attaches to structural interventions. A typical and appropriate structural intervention is described in its entirety to illustrate the increased effectiveness of combining a variety of trainer approaches.

The Sharing Progression

When. This structural intervention may be used at any stage, but it is most useful in the group's beginning stages when members begin to build trust and break down resistances to knowing one another.

How. Since expression sometimes comes easier, or at least differently, when there is just one other person present, group members may be paired into dyads. These dyad meetings usually last from ten to fifteen minutes. Each member of the dyad is to take turns remaining quiet while one member speaks, and then the process is reversed. (A variation is to allow both members to speak and interchange comments at the same time.) The leader may explain the process: "I want both of you to get to know each other as fully as possible, to try to understand each other, to learn how to give and take from your partner and how to produce creatively with him. Tell each other what you feel is most important about yourself and about your partner."

The objective is to provide an opportunity for each participant to express himself and to receive the expression of another in such a way that a relationship can be built. The listening member of the pair should sit with his back to the speaking member. The listening member says nothing and concentrates on listening only. Then they reverse the procedure. This tends to promote individual disclosure and sharing.

Following the dyad meetings, it has been found productive to bring dyads together, forming groups of four each. They are given the same instructions as above. In this manner, groups of two become groups of four, then eight, etc., until the entire group is re-formed on a more trusting and freer interpersonal level.

The preceding T-group critical incidents reveal a pattern of responses utilizing all three factors of level, type, and intensity. As in the examples given, the T-group intervention style typically involves the conceptual, experiential, and structural types of response; ranges from low to high intensity, depending on the stage of the group; and focuses attention on all levels. While various trainers may differ in their specific emphases on the above three matrix factors, they generally adhere to a position that allows the utilization of all resources. Figure 4.3 illustrates the intervention approach of the typical T-group, along with its listed characteristics.

An Encounter-Group Critical Incident: 1

An encounter group is concerned almost exclusively with structural interventions aimed at experiential growth of the individual and the group. Generally, individuals and the group as a whole experience a series of planned activities in an attempt to achieve personal results of high intensity—"peak experiences." Schutz (1967) and Gunther (1968, 1969, 1971) may be considered as representatives of the rapidly growing area of encounter groups. Although Schutz advocates a more theoretical approach to conceptualizing group activity than does Gunther (e.g., his concepts of "inclusion, control, and affection"), an examination of his descriptions of ongoing groups rarely reveals much time devoted to sitting back and conceptually abstracting or theorizing about what is occurring. Indeed, his concrete, specific intervention style appears to be quite close to that of Gunther (1968), who does no theorizing. Schutz describes his encounter approach as "a term more in favor on the West Coast . . . [that] usually refers more specifically to groups oriented toward individual growth and development" (Schutz, 1967, p. 22).

The major difference between typical encounter groups and groups oriented around different goals is that encounter groups seem almost exclusively to utilize structural interventions, i.e., interventions that directly involve some planned exercise or movement activity with specific rules to be followed. In Schutz's terms

The Critical-Incident Model: Its Use and Application 149

Type — Conceptual (C), Experiential (E), Structural (S)

Intensity — High (H.I.), Medium (M.I.), Low (L.I.)

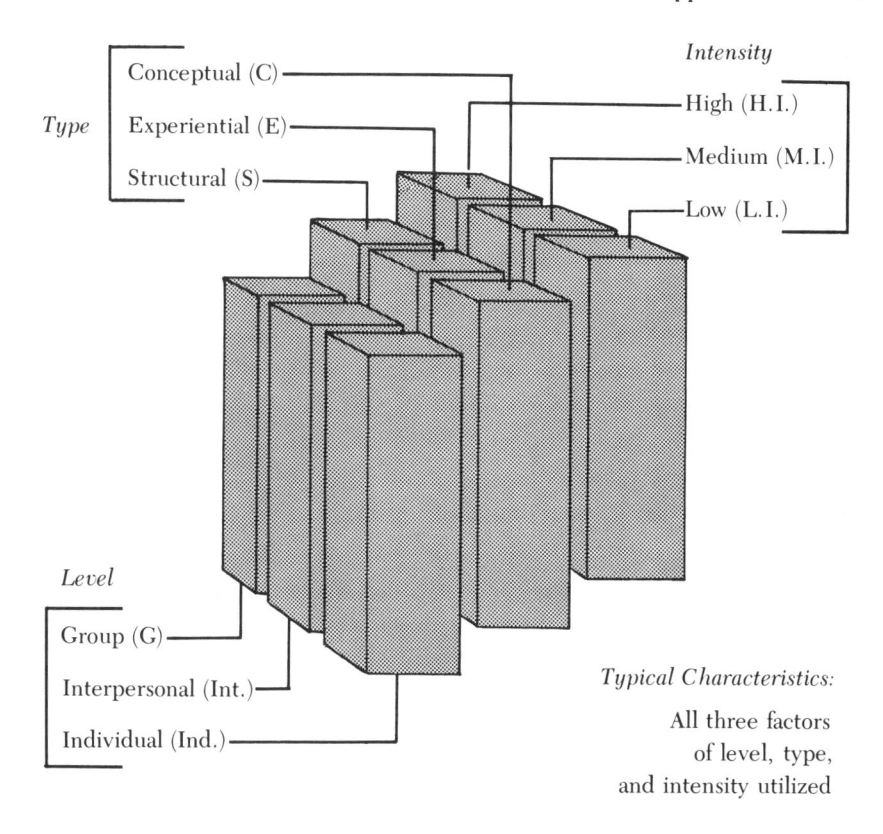

Level — Group (G), Interpersonal (Int.), Individual (Ind.)

Typical Characteristics:
All three factors of level, type, and intensity utilized

Figure 4.3. The T-Group Intervention Cube

the activity seems false and artificial to begin with, but if it is continued it usually becomes very real. It is important to continue despite the feeling of artificiality in order to experience the feelings. (Schutz, 1967, p. 44)[27]

The emphasis is on planned and spontaneous structural interventions aimed at individual, interpersonal, and group involvement. There is little conceptualization by the group members of an organizational or process nature and little time devoted to theories. A fairly typical encounter-group incident from Schutz (1967) follows.

---

[27]From W. C. Schutz, *Joy: Expanding Human Awareness*. New York: Grove, 1967. Reprinted by permission of Grove Press, Inc. Copyright © 1967 by William C. Schutz.

CONTEXT OF INCIDENT

This event might occur anywhere during the middle to end phases of group growth.

> For most people giving affection and receiving affection are very difficult matters. Many people feel that they are unlovable and that any gestures of affection or liking or admiration are extremely hard for them to accept. If a person "knows" he is unlovable, how can he believe it when someone professes love? For these situations there are methods to help the person experience fully the affection felt for him by others. At the same time the others have the opportunity to experience themselves giving, or being reluctant to give, affection . . . Suzy, a Chinese girl of seventeen, was a member of a mixed group of adults and teenagers. The group was a cross section of the school community, consisting of parents, teachers, and the superintendent, and several eleventh graders. (p. 178)[28]

EVENT PRECEDING CHOICE POINT

> Suzy felt oppressed by her strict, old country upbringing and her own inadequate self-concept to such an extent that she was totally incapable of trusting any remark of a positive nature made to her. However, if there were a hint of anything non-positive she would hear it clearly, believe it, exaggerate it, and use it to confirm her own picture of herself. Words couldn't help, although she actually engendered very warm feelings from virtually the whole group. (p. 178)

SUGGESTED INTERVENTION

> There are two approaches to this situation, verbal and non-verbal. The non-verbal is usually a more powerful experience but for the best results it should be used after the group has developed close feelings. The verbal method has been called 'strength bombardment.' The group members are asked to tell the person who is the focus of their attention all the positive feelings they have about him. He is just to listen. The intensity of the experience may be varied in a number of ways. Probably the simplest procedure is to have the focus leave the circle, put his back to the group and over-hear what is said. Or he can be kept in the group and talked to directly. A stronger impact occurs when each person stands in front of the focus, touches him, and looks him in the eye, and tells him directly. The non-verbal give-and-take requires the focus to stand in the center of a circle made up of the other members of the group. He is to shut his eyes and the other members are all to approach him and express their positive feelings non-verbally in whatever way they wish. This usually takes the form of hugging, stroking, massaging, lifting, or whatever each person feels. If the situation is timely, this procedure almost develops into tears for both the focus and for some group members. (p. 177)

This structural intervention was then applied to Suzy by the group leader.

---

[28]See Footnote 27 for this and following extracts from Schutz.

INTERVENTION OUTCOME

> The give and take affection exercise was suggested and she immediately began to cry as the first few people made contact with her. She broke down completely in the arms of one of the male teachers. Crying was very unusual for Suzy. Her 'cool' exterior had prevented anything to bring her to tears for years. The whole experience was so moving that several others began to cry. Suzy could not talk to anyone for an hour or so after. No one spoke, and the group gradually drifted off in pairs and trios to take walks and talk quietly. (p. 178)

This example shows the encounter group's tremendous emotional impact on the individual, when it is used skillfully and appropriately. A second encounter-group critical incident (Schutz, 1967) reveals another common approach.

An Encounter-Group Critical Incident: 2

CONTEXT OF INCIDENT

This event is likely to occur in the middle to end stages of group life.

> Nancy, a 24 year old girl, was trying to deal with her problem of being too tight and constricted. She spoke in a low and controlled voice, and was always very logical and organized. Her face was usually expressionless, her movements were stiff and graceless, and her relations with people lacked spontaneity and vitality. She had had an earlier fantasy in which she entered her body and found her father fastening down all the organs of her body with steel straps. This, together with her recollection of an early childhood, pointed to the central role of her father in her constriction. (p. 170)

EVENT PRECEDING CHOICE POINT

> These considerations led to a psychodrama in which she confronted her father, portrayed by another group member. Here she tried to express to him the feelings that she had never been able to articulate to him directly. When she attempted to declare her independence of him she weakened, her voice faltered, and she reverted to infantile behavior. At this point, something was required to give her the additional strength and confidence necessary for her psychodramatic confrontation with her father. (p. 170)

SUGGESTED INTERVENTION

The following intervention is aimed at relieving excessive internal, rather than external, control. It uses the group to externalize what is happening within a person. In this structural intervention,

> the group forms a tight circle, interlocking arms. If the group is very large, members form two concentric circles. One person stands in the middle of the inner circle and must break out in any way he can, over, under, or bursting through. Members of the circle try their utmost to contain him and not let him out. (p. 169)

Nancy was transferred from the psychodrama to the breaking-out situation. Her frustration led her to start out furiously, pounding fiercely at the people in the circle, but the group held fast and she fell to the floor exhausted and, characteristically, gave up. But the group wouldn't let her. They simply reminded her that she hadn't broken out, and they stood their ground around her. This unexpected reaction sparked her to get up and try again. Following a lengthy and combative exchange she finally smashed through. . . . She felt elated directly after the experience and her behavior changed markedly thereafter. She was lighter and gayer, became more feminine, her face brightened, and her relations became more informal. (pp. 170-171)

The preceding intervention is basically a structural intervention of high intensity. While primarily directed toward one individual, it was so structured that it cut across all three levels of the Intervention Cube: the group as an operating framework, the interpersonal level of Nancy's specific encounters in attempting to break out, and the primary focus on the individual level. This type of intervention is almost always action oriented and experiential; seldom is it highly conceptual and low in intensity.

The typical intervention style of an encounter-group leader is revealed in Figure 4.4. The shaded areas of the Intervention Cube reveal that the intervention characteristics tend to be highly experiential and structural but nonconceptual in type, to range from low to high intensity, and to involve all levels—individual, interpersonal, and group. The area of the Intervention Cube that is not stressed is unshaded.

SUMMARY AND OVERVIEW

In order to compare, in terms of intervention style, the distinctive characteristics of the various groups considered, Figure 4.5 presents an overview. In considering these figures, it should be remembered that the nondirective group, the psychoanalytic group, and the T-group were all faced with the same basic critical incident, i.e., the plea for guidance and direction. Yet, each group's response, as plotted on the Intervention Cube, was characteristically different from that of the other groups. A specific, identifiable intervention style seems to result for each group, reflecting the basic assumptions of a particular approach.

The intervention style the therapist employs in dealing with a group depends largely on the characteristics of his adopted design strategy. In turn, the utilization of a particular design strategy may accelerate or retard those group activities known as phases. Active, nonconceptual, highly experiential encounter-group leaders may immediately by-pass many of the initial stages of dependency and self-direction and begin to work directly on interpersonal issues leading to almost immediate emotional confrontation. On the other hand, a highly conceptual, nonexperiential group leader who remains cool, objective, and detached may significantly delay any group movement into emotional relationships.

Comparing the relative effectiveness of various interventions directed toward the same basic critical incident would be an interesting research problem. Another area of interest might be the development of a modification or a blend of two or more intervention Cube approaches, employing the Critical-Incident Model.

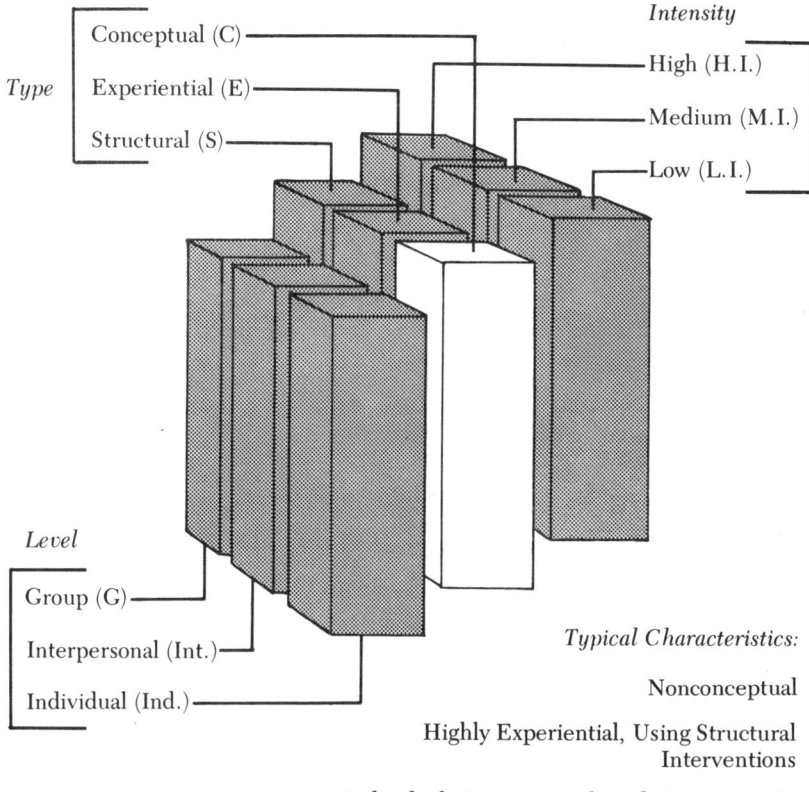

Figure 4.4. The Encounter-Group Intervention Cube

154   The Critical Incident in Growth Groups

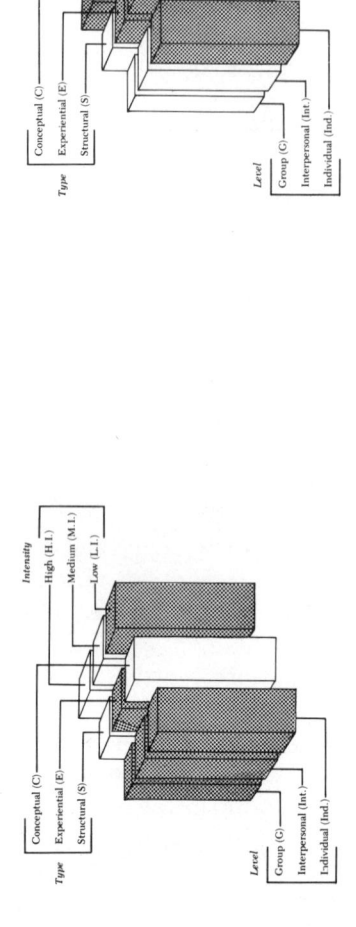

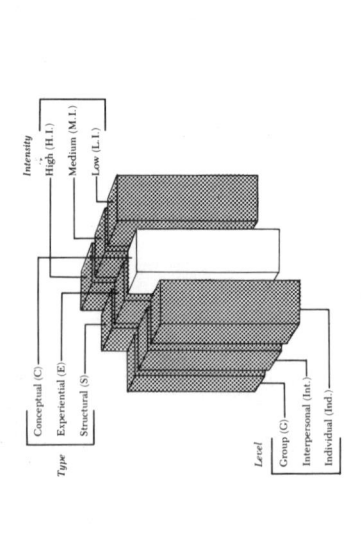

Figure 4.5. All Intervention Cubes

CHAPTER 5

A Theory of Group Growth and Development

Growth and development has been the subject of study in every major area of human concern. The assumption is that, in order to predict the future, it is important first to study and understand the significant events that have influenced the current state. Implicit in this study is the intent to control, to intervene, and to initiate change in the developmental pattern. This goal is shared by the economist, the biologist, and the military strategist, as well as the psychologist.

For centuries, historians have studied and recorded events as they occur. By tracing developmental trends—the important events influencing society—man is more likely to understand his current state and how he may act in the future. If one adheres to the popular view that history repeats itself, the past should provide a clue to the future. Or, if we can look back and identify those events that led to undesirable results, future mistakes can be avoided.

In the field of psychology, Freud was among the first to apply these principles to human development. He believed that the child passes through a series of dynamically different stages during the first five years of life. Subsequently, other prominent men in the field described developmental stages in life, and still later a new area of study appeared—developmental psychology.

With the proliferation of group approaches in recent years, more attention has been given to developmental processes. These group approaches offer a unique opportunity to study the developmental patterns of human relationships. Some of these groups can be viewed as a microcosm of the larger society. An understanding of their process development enables one more effectively to facilitate personal and group growth. The major goal of the helping professions is to make conscious, selected interventions to effect change in desired directions. In the case of groups, the leader or therapist may choose to

---

The authors are indebted to Dr. H. Ted Ballard for his work in the preparation of this chapter.

intervene in ways that enable the members to develop their own prescribed or desired directions.

Growth and development in a group is punctuated by a sequence of events, some more important than others. These events represent turning points in the life of the group and occur in an interrelated flow of processes. They take place in an orderly fashion. Each behavioral occurrence is a function of antecedent conditions and is also an indispensable contribution to events that follow.

A model of group growth and development is a charted flow of the behavioral events and processes during the life of the group. It provides contextual meaning to ongoing processes and serves as a reference against which a group's progress or deviations can be traced. A model of group growth and development provides a normative standard for comparison. It also aids in the hypothesizing of yet uncharted events or processes that might occur in the future. To the extent that a model can be predictive of group process relationships, it becomes a valuable theoretical conceptualization.

RATIONALE

Most experienced group leaders will agree that there are usually family resemblances among groups. Most leaders or therapists have observed the recurrence of certain similar processes and issues in various groups. They frequently hear nearly identical verbalizations or witness similar behavioral manifestations emitted by different people in different groups. From this repetition, it is not at all surprising that one should hypothesize the existence of lawful relationships governing behavior.

> It is assumed that the development of a functioning group out of the initial vacuum and the associated examination of interpersonal and group issues constitute the medium in which learning can occur. Thus, the question of how a T-group develops is of great practical and theoretical interest in understanding its character and potential as a setting for learning. In addition, the T-group offers a perhaps unique opportunity to study the general process of group development, since it begins without a prior history. (Stock, 1964, p. 397)[1]

However, a brief survey of the literature shows that very little work has been done in this area. It appears that the present state of knowledge concerning group growth and development is inadequate. Little attempt has been made to summarize or pool information in order to formulate a general foundation on which further work can be based. A few authors have attempted to

---

[1] From D. Stock, "A Survey of Research on T-Groups," in L. P. Bradford, J. R. Gibb, & K. D. Benne (Eds.), *T-Group Theory and Laboratory Method: Innovation in Re-education.* New York: John Wiley, 1964. Reprinted by permission.

deal with the complexities of tracing growth and development in groups; however, we have found only one author who has attempted to bridge one theorist with another in an effort to identify commonalities or trends in the development of a group (Tuckman, 1965). The need is to identify the commonalities among groups and to merge them into a useful, researchable, and theoretical framework.

In discussing the usefulness of group theories, Gibb (1964c, pp. 168-169) asserts that they are useful to at least four classes of people: (1) the theorist, (2) the researcher, (3) the trainer (practitioner), (4) the participant. Possibly one of the most deep-seated problems in the mind of the investigator or the potential theorist is the question "What is a good group?" On a normative level, one can establish the descriptive behavioral characteristics of a typical group process over time. At this point an investigator can begin to make inferences regarding the group character and to identify issues, either surface or underlying, confronting a group and its members. If a trainer adheres to an explicit model of group growth and development, he is in a position to make a more meaningful appraisal or diagnosis, and consequently some value judgments regarding the ongoing group process. He can determine whether his group is moving at an accelerated or decelerated pace and decide if this fits with his goals and the particular needs of the group.

A model that explicitly charts a flow of specific behaviors provides a meaningful context within which to cast specific behaviors. One can see how each event is specifically related to antecedent and consequent events. This increases one's understanding of ongoing events. Such a model better enables the researcher to study variations among groups and to trace the points of departure. It also allows the theorist to hypothesize about unobservable events or processes.

Using a model for comparison, the researcher or practitioner can plan his intervention strategy and readily see how group development may change. A significant gap in understanding group growth and development is the linking of a theory of interventions with a theory of growth and development so that the outcomes of interventions and the theories underlying them can be evaluated.

CRITERIA FOR A THEORY OF GROUP GROWTH AND DEVELOPMENT

Gibb (1964b) proposes three critical and central functions of theory related to groups: the selective, heuristic, and illuminative functions. The selective function is primarily the identification of a need area which then adequately fulfills this need. The heuristic function is met when constructs and relationships among variables are so defined as to lead to operational statements that are susceptible to empirical or experimental tests. The illuminative function provides a perspective for ideas, points of view, constructs, and fragmented theories. These functions should be useful to the theorist, the researcher, the trainer (practitioner), and the participant.

Hall and Lindzey (1957) give an extensive list of criteria for a good theory. It should be clear, explicit, functional, integrative, verifiable, and comprehensive; it should generate empirical research, incorporate known empirical research and findings, lead to systematic expansion of knowledge, and prevent the observer from being overcome by the complexity of events. They further state that a good theory should contain a cluster of relevant assumptions systematically related to each other and a set of empirical definitions (coordinating definitions that bring the theory at certain prescribed places into a definite contact with the observable data).

Using the work of these authors as a basis, a set of modified criteria has been extrapolated and tailored to a theory of group growth and development. These criteria could serve to set legitimate standards for any meaningful theory of group growth and development and help appraise various studies found in the literature. They could also serve as useful guidelines for the theorist who is building a model of group growth and development.

1. A model of group growth and development should provide both descriptive and prescriptive elements, with a clear distinction between the two.

2. A model of group growth and development should be specific in that it relates to the concrete group experience and avoids reification of concepts.

3. A model of group growth and development should be comprehensive, i.e., it should offer a sufficient number of descriptive statements to cover a wide range of behavioral occurrences found throughout the life of a group.

4. A model of group growth and development should be capable of being generalized to a variety of groups regardless of their theoretical orientations, i.e., within its descriptive framework it should be able to incorporate or subsume a variety of diverse groups.

5. A model of group growth and development should be easy to research: its components should be easy to relate to concrete group events.

6. A model of group growth and development should provide adequate methodology for its own evaluation as well as that of other models. It may accomplish this by virtue of its own component design.

7. A model of group growth and development should be heuristic.

8. A model of group growth and development should be useful to the practitioner and should serve as a means of training.

ASSUMPTIONS ABOUT GROUP GROWTH AND DEVELOPMENT

In order to hypothesize about group growth and development, a variety of assumptions must be made. Some assumptions are almost universally held; there is some disagreement on others. For example, an assumption that is widely agreed on is that psychology, as a science, is concerned with causal relationships and the prediction of behavioral events (Boring, 1950).

To discuss group growth and development, the existence of lawful relationships governing human behavior must be assumed. Stock (1964), in a survey of research on T-groups, suggests that there is strong support for the general assumption that as T-groups continue to meet, a definite structure emerges out of an undifferentiated state, and there also appear to be "lawful relationships among emerging total group characteristics such as cohesiveness and productivity" (p. 400). As early as 1879, however, Wundt not only held that the phenomenal mind is always in change, but that the changes are lawful. His fundamental principle of law was that of psychic causality, the principle of growth or development of the mind where lawful change is the natural process of an active mind.

"Psychic causality as a principle is merely an assertion that the course and pattern of the constantly flowing, conscious stream depend upon definite laws of sequence, that 'this' regularly follow 'that,' even though 'this' and 'that' are themselves processes and not fixed substantial things" (Boring, 1950, p. 335). Simply stated, historical antecedents are important for understanding the present and for predicting future events.

Another less widespread assumption related to group growth and development is that there are common developmental stages that cut across diverse groups, regardless of leadership style or theoretical orientation (Fiebert, 1968; Bugental, 1965a; Tuckman, 1965; Bradford, Gibb, & Benne, 1964; Bach, 1954). These writers believe that nearly all groups deal with about the same issues and go through about the same processes at approximately the same time during their lives. The underlying assumption is that the majority of groups have to deal at one time or another with certain basic, common problems in their developmental flow. Of course, variations due to special group characteristics such as setting, composition of the group, and length of time cause some alterations in the overall flow.

There is some disagreement among authors regarding the nature of the flow of group developmental processes. This flow is conceptualized in a variety of ways. Some authors view this process as being cyclical or as a recurring order of events in which there is a sequence of authentic interaction and personal growth (Clark, 1963). Bradford (1964) also adopts a cyclical view that is based on a process of recurrent learning in ever-increasing depth. Another cyclical model of learning and personality development proposed by Hampden-Turner (1966) is one based on a self-perpetuating cycle of accumulating experience. Bennis and Shepard (1956) also seem to be describing a recycling model in which events occur in a step-like fashion. Their model seems discontinuous in that the issues in each phase must be sufficiently resolved before the group can go on to the next phase.

The distinguishing features of a cyclical view of developmental process are somewhat analogous to the view that history repeats itself. This conceptualization of group interaction postulates that those issues processed in the past or experienced in the past will again surface and be recycled or re-encountered in the future. While the complexion of these issues may change to some extent, the underlying dynamics or processes remain much the same.

In contrast with the cyclical view, there are the proponents of a sequential, discontinuous conceptualization of developmental flow (Fiebert, 1968; Tuckman, 1965). These authors describe a flow of issues that are worked through in an orderly, sequential pattern that does allow for some overlap. However, this could be due to a prescriptive orientation, especially for Fiebert, as opposed to a pure description of events.

A sequential, discontinuous flow is one in which a chain of events or issues arises, is subsequently dealt with by the group in an orderly fashion, and is then set aside before the group progresses to the next set of issues or events. It is as if there is little overlap of issues. This conceptualization seems to imply that each set of issues must be resolved in order for the group to continue in its growth. Unresolved issues are blocking or paralyzing forces that can fixate a group at a particular state. This is analogous to the developmental stages of Freud (1921/1952) and Erikson (1950).

As opposed to a sequential-discontinuous orientation, Rogers (1970) proposes a continuous flow of development. He visualizes the flow as having threads that weave in and out of the pattern. Some of the trends or tendencies occur early and others occur late in the group. Rogers describes the interaction as being a "varied tapestry, differing from group to group, yet with certain kinds of trends evident in most of these intensive encounters and with certain patterns tending to precede and others to follow" (p. 15).

The concept of continuous flow implies a smoother flow or blending of one set of issues into another. There can be some overlap of issues that do not have to be necessarily processed and disposed of in order for the group to move forward. However, a general sequence or order of events is implied.

The Evolutionary Nature of This Model

The authors conceptualize group growth and development as a continuous interrelated process that is evolutionary in nature. Evolution in the group is "an unfolding; a process of opening out what is contained or implied in something; a development" (Webster's New Collegiate Dictionary, 1960). It also seems to imply a gradual, orderly change from one stage to the next. One assumption associated with an evolutionary approach is that development occurs in progressive states, each serving as a springboard from which new behaviors emerge.

Another assumption is that there is an implied improvement in group and individual effectiveness. Some of the essential features of this evolutionary concept: there is a variation through modification; more behaviors arise than can survive; and the fittest survive so that the most appropriate, compatible, adjustive behaviors remain. The survival concept of behaviors in groups is based on extinction and reinforcement. It occurs on two levels—personal and group.

The evolutionary model presented in this text assumes that all issues are current at all times throughout the life of the group. Among such issues are authority, control, and intimacy. However, only a few issues can be dealt with at any one time during the group—and during this time the issue is labeled as the dominant theme topic. It is immediately obvious that different issues may surface and be worked at different times while others remain below the threshold. At first glance, this sequential arrangement of the issues may appear to be a discontinuous process. It is, however, obvious that they cannot appear simultaneously. The sequential arrangement simply represents the surfacing of an underlying theme which, after being worked, returns to a subthreshold level of tension. These underlying themes appear to interact in such a way as to be best represented by an evolutionary scheme in which they are constantly being modified. This, then, is the idea of moving through prerequisite phases or stages, which are essentially tied in with the observation of dominant features and characteristics.

The group evolves because there are more behaviors (or critical incidents) born than survive; many behaviors terminate because they really do not fit with the overall flow that may be developing. There is a "stamping in" of certain behaviors and a "stamping out" of others. This extinction process is partly determined by the interventions of the leader, partly by the group, and partly by the time and phase of the sequence in which the idea emerges. There is, in a Darwinian sense, a "survival of the fittest." On the other hand, there are distinct periods where the critical incidents symbolize the opening or closing of an evolutionary gate.

Evolution, then, is the bringing together of what people know, what they do, and how they feel. There seems to be a movement into a life style of greater and greater individual expression, a greater sense of potency in terms of individual identity and worth. The personalities of the participants appear to go through various quantitative and qualitative changes, and the closer one gets to the end of this process, the more such human distinctiveness becomes an appreciable quality.

The Concept of Emerging Dominant Theme Topics

The concept of dominant theme topics gradually developed from:
   a) the collection and review of several hundred behavioral descriptions. These behavioral descriptions actually occurred in various stages of diverse groups. They were then factored out until there emerged a cluster of behaviors or categories designated as themes;
   b) a collection of critical incidents judged to be significant, which were classified according to the theme and phase in which they most frequently appeared;
   c) the construction of a theme-topic model, with which representative investigations in group theory might be compared. The result of these operations is a model consisting of ten dominant themes ranging from the initial theme of acquaintance to the final theme of termination. Within each theme topic, various group processes occur, rise, and submerge in a constant state of flux.

A dominant theme topic allows for the identification of molar events or categories. This in turn permits the capture of the changing essences of life in the group. Each dominant theme topic is much like the tip of an iceberg. A large amount of what occurs in the group is unobserved or unnoticed. The group leaders identify and deal with only a small but representative piece — the dominant theme topic. At different time points in the life of a group, the character of the group is acknowledged by identifying these peaks. This is accomplished by applying descriptive labels that sort out those special characteristics that are most critical, most dramatic, and most conclusive and that culminate in terms of where the group is at a given moment. Underlying issues and concerns surface at various times and coalesce or fuse into some classification of a body of notable events — the theme topic.

There may be a number of investigators in the group field who, because of a personal leadership style, a philosophical persuasion, or a predilection for a specific type of approach, feel that there are other theme topics that should be mentioned or emphasized; some investigators may choose to minimize or to ignore completely certain theme topics. Nevertheless, the ten theme topics chosen are inclusive and conceptually tied to specific research studies, thus permitting direct empirical verification of this model, which is based on a thorough review of the group literature and a classification of the studies of all the group investigators (forty-nine) that could be found and utilized as representative.

UNDERLYING GROUP PROCESSES

Experience in working with groups, as well as exploration of the group literature, leads to the hypothesis that a number of distinct underlying group processes precipitate the emergence of theme topics during all stages of group life. These underlying processes are outlined in Table 5.1. There are essentially five basic processes:

1. a motivating or instrumental process that reveals itself in various states of *anxiety* in the group, e.g., anxiety over intimacy and attempts at closeness revealed in theme topics of "acquaintance" and "goal ambiguity and diffuse anxiety";

2. a control process that surfaces in concerns over *power* and the establishment of norms, e.g., dependency or counterdependency and an attempt to establish defensive norms, possibly as an attempt to wrest control from the leader and elicit theme topics dealing with primary group transferences and countertransferences;

3. another control process, that of *normatization* —the attempt to establish norms for appropriate rules of behavior;

4. the intimacy process dealing with the degree of *interpersonalization*, i.e., the degree to which theme topics of acquaintance, empathy, etc., are expressed;

5. the *personalization* growth process, which parallels interpersonalization and indicates the degree of self-awareness, personal growth, and actual behavior change.

These underlying group processes are believed to be present throughout the life of the group and to elicit certain specific theme topics. A group's mounting anxiety over loss of defenses and possible disclosure (its underlying motivating process) may lead to the emergence of a series of critical incidents dealing with the theme topic of "sharpened affects and anxieties: increased defensiveness." Several underlying processes may be operating with varying degrees of strength at any one time in the group. This approach, however, clarifies the degree of importance these processes have in the functioning of a viable group.

The group process may be conceptualized as the underlying flow of dynamics that initiates or provokes the expression of a theme topic. This flow continues throughout the life of the group, whereas the theme topic is a focus of discussion that is more sequential in nature. The dominant theme topic, then, is a manifestation of this underlying flow.

The five basic underlying group processes—anxiety, power, normatization, interpersonalization, and personalization—are the main energy sources reflected in direct, observable group behaviors, which are summarized in packages termed theme topics. Each of these basic processes is present in the group, but each has a relative strength and weakness depending on the stage of development of the group; e.g., anxiety and power may be prepotent concerns relatively early in the initial stages of the group, but as the group progresses in its life, interpersonalization and personalization emerge as more salient concerns. Anxiety as a basic underlying group process is present in

Table 5.1. Basic Underlying Group Processes and Related Theme Topics

Theme Topic	Anxiety	Power	Normatization	Interpersonalization	Personalization
1. Acquaintance	Anxiety over intimacy and attempts at closeness	Dependency on leader or other strong members; initial attempts by dominant members to supply direction	Defensive and false consensus norms to protect members	Superficial acquaintance attempts	Reluctance to involve oneself
2. Goal Ambiguity and Diffuse Anxiety	Anxiety over ambiguity, lack of goals, and structure	Dependency on leader or other strong members; counterdependence on leader or strong members	Cleavage: disagreement on whether group should be structured or unstructured	Autistic, self-centered communication	Initiators becoming leaders
3. Members' Search for Position/Definition: Primary Group Transferences/Counter-transferences	Continuation of anxiety over ambiguity, lack of goals, structure; anxiety over anger/aggression, any intense affect	Generalized evaluation/testing of leader; power plays between dependence vs. counterdependence as to direction	Cleavage: personals vs. counterpersonals	Identification; handclasping	Hostility and/or deference toward leaders and members
4. Sharpened Affects and Anxieties: Increased Defensiveness	Anxiety over loss of defenses/disclosure	Cleavage: personals vs. counterpersonals; power used to attack and defend only	Discussion of norms centering around "hurting" and "disclosure"	The emergence of group game playing, e.g., "twenty questions," "psychoanalyst," etc.	Dealing with anger/affect directly; limited personal disclosure

Table 5.1. (cont.)

Theme Topic	Anxiety	Power	Normatization	Interpersonalization	Personalization
5. Sharpened Interactions: Growth-Identifying Activities and Reality Strengthening	Anxiety over personal needs, interpersonal conflicts, and hostility	Emergence of individual power and manipulation dynamics; attempts to reduce power of leader via seduction; dealing with perceptions of leader more openly and directly	Emergence, via effective feedback norms, of norms centering about exploring impact of members on each other	Continuation of group game playing, but with increasingly authentic and real interactions among members	Beginning to deal directly with others; evaluation of self
6. Norm Crystallization/ Enforcement-Defensification	Anxiety over group norms centering about authority, feedback, decision making, etc.; anxiety over deviance from group norms	Individual power and manipulation attempts; group beginning to exert power to establish and enforce rules and values of group	Articulation of norms concerning proper use of feedback, decision making, expression of affect, etc.	Beginning of members working/expressing personal problems in supportive atmosphere	Dealing with others' evaluation of personal, intimate problems

Table 5.1. (cont.)

Theme Topic	Anxiety	Power	Normatization	Interpersonalization	Personalization
7. Distributive Leadership	Continuation of anxiety over deviance from established group norms and anxiety over ability of group to solve all problems	Redistribution of power; leader becoming member; group recognition of members as having specific leadership resources to be used in services of group	Articulation of norms of "shared responsibility" and "shared leadership"	Continuation of working/expressing personal problems; verbalized empathy and intimacy among members	Members feeling equal but separate (integrated autonomy)
8. Decreased Defensiveness and Increased Experimentation	Anxiety over taking creative risks, trying out new behavior dealing with catastrophic fantasies, and trying out atypical behavior	Concerns over power and control almost nonexistent; power invested in group rather than in leader or individuals	Enforcement of group norms stressing "atypical" behavior; articulation of norms dealing with expression of intimacy, sex aggression, etc.; new behavior rewarded, old behavior suppressed	Members beginning to form strong emotional bonds during constructive resolution of interpersonal problems	Locus of evaluation shifting inward to self-evaluation

Table 5.1. (cont.)

Theme Topic	Anxiety	Power	Normatization	Interpersonalization	Personalization
9. Group Potency	Continuation of some anxiety over practicing and experimenting with new behaviors	Concerns over power and control typically not discussed; group secure in the use of power by group as a whole; group becoming an effective change agent	Group continuing to enforce norms of intimacy, closeness, potency of the group; possible encouragement of self-actualization norms and values	Periods of intense interpersonal affection, elation, and excitement with other members and group as a whole	Personal, satisfactory — perhaps peak experience about self
10. Termination	Anxiety over applying group learning to real world	Increased feelings of personal competence and inner-directed power; independence from external control	The attempt to apply some or all group norms to real world or to significant others; leaders stressing differences between group and world norms	Periods of sadness, withdrawing from involvement, and seeking closure	Self-preparation for real world; termination of involvement in group

many different forms. In the beginning stages, for example, anxiety over ambiguity, lack of goals, and structure is most evident. This underlying group process may be reflected in members' concern with the theme topic of "goal ambiguity and diffuse anxiety." As this theme topic is being worked through, members begin to express some anxiety over intimacy and attempts at closeness by others; this anxiety, in turn, may emerge in the theme topic of "acquaintance." Finally, toward the end of the group's life, there may be anxiety over separation from other group members—"termination." The basic group process of anxiety is present throughout the life of the group. It is conceptualized primarily as a motivating or instrumental process that may be utilized by the leader to promote exploration and group growth.

Power is a basic group process that also shifts its form from the beginning to the end of group life. In the early stages of the group, power or control concerns center around dependency or counterdependency toward the leader or other strong group members. This dynamic typically reveals its presence in the theme topic "members' search for position/definition: primary group transferences/countertransferences." By contrast, toward the end of the group, power as an underlying force tends to be invested in the group rather than in either the leader or other individuals and usually expresses itself in the theme topic "group potency."

Normatization is another basic control concern. It is a process of flux within the group that seeks to establish appropriate norms of behavior. In the beginning stages, for example, members attempt to establish defensive and false consensus norms in order quickly to form a measure of self-protection against disclosure. This might exhibit itself in members' attempts to define their position and tell how far they will go in revealing themselves or even in behaviors of increased defensiveness. Toward the end of the group, however, the normatization process reveals itself in the attempt to apply group norms to the real world in theme topics such as "termination."

Interpersonalization is essentially an intimacy process leading from a superficial acquaintance attempt, exhibited in the theme topic of "acquaintance," to withdrawing from involvement and seeking closure described in the final theme of "termination." It is a basic group process that underlies attempts between group members to become close to one another. It contributes directly to the empathy and support felt by group members in solving problems. This dynamic operates to reveal the basic life styles of individual members.

The final group process is personalization and is conceptualized as a personal growth process. As such, it begins with a reluctance to become involved or perhaps with hostility/deference toward leaders and members, expressed in the theme topic "members' search for position/definition: primary group transferences/countertransferences," and progresses to dealing with others' evaluation of self. This is expressed in the theme topic "decreased defensiveness and increased experimentation."

These five basic processes are considered to be an exhaustive framework—the model subsumes other possible theoretical processes. Sex and aggression processes, for example, would be translated into questions of intimacy, potency, power, etc. Although this is not the only possible system to be factored from all the group investigators considered, it is the system that appears to subsume other possible group variables across the span of group growth and development. Its power is determined not by the nature of the labels of the processes, but by its integration with the other theoretical systems of theme topics and critical incidents and by a review of the group literature. Several group processes may be operating at any given time in the group. Which process emerges as prepotent is a function of several interacting variables, e.g., the stage of the group, the leadership style, and the type of group.

A PROPOSED MODEL OF GROUP GROWTH AND DEVELOPMENT

The concept of emerging dominant theme topics permits the identification of ten basic phases of change. These offer a satisfactory model of group growth and development.

Each theme topic contains within it the seeds of many other theme topics. For example, the group leader who is faced with the group's topic of goal ambiguity and diffuse anxiety will also recognize the beginning minor theme characteristics of sharpened affects and anxieties: increased defensiveness. The theme to be discussed and explored is largely determined by the leader. If he selects for discussion a theme topic or group process that is marginally present, that theme topic may be elevated to a position of momentary dominance over another theme topic. But then again it may not, for groups may have to deal with, and partially resolve, certain basic issues and concerns before they can be manipulated into taking a short-cut or accelerating the group movement and growth. This is an empirical issue that is researchable.

The behavioral characteristics associated with each specific theme topic are summarized in the Appendix.

1. Acquaintance

In the beginning of group life, members become involved primarily in the process of getting to know one another, of categorizing and pigeonholing each other. During this procedure, outside roles and conditions tend to determine members' inside roles and positions. This is primarily accomplished through a superficial acquaintance process wherein members begin gathering insurance-type data—names, business, number of children. The underlying process during this period is a generalized anxiety over intimacy and closeness, which is characterized by superficial acquaintance attempts and a reluctance to involve oneself. The discussion also begins to include occasional references to attempts to establish norms to protect members, e.g., what they ought to be doing, how members should behave, and what to expect. The underlying group process at this point appears to be an attempt to establish defensive and false consensus norms for mutual protection.

Following closely on the heels of the acquaintance sequence is the observation that some members initiate covert appraisal and testing of others and the leader. Frequently, the leader is brought into the discussion through invitations for him to disclose something about himself. Other members attempt to handle their anxieties in this new situation by leading the ongoing discussion, seizing power and leadership, or attempting to establish a dependency on the leader and/or other strong group members.

2. Goal Ambiguity and Diffuse Anxiety

Overlapping considerably with the acquaintance process, goal ambiguity and diffuse anxiety frequently initiates continuing attempts at information sharing and acquaintance. The apparent lack of clearly defined common goals and values generates a great deal of diffuse anxiety. Members experience confusion, uncertainty, and difficulty in understanding the goals or purposes of the group. Attempts by members to define group aims, structure, and mode of function are largely unsuccessful. There is much fragmentation of direction, since the group tries and follows several issues at once. This general lack of productivity causes some members to avoid sustained work on issues and, consequently, to withdraw.

During this time, some members seek direction from the leader in a pronounced dependency approach. Others begin tentatively to express counterdependency statements. Still other group members avoid involving the leader and attempt to change the topic. There are also some members who act as passive observers, revealing a reluctance to involve themselves.

The inability of the group to decide on a goal and the group's desire for closeness, as well as its difficulty in understanding its purposes, lead to a variety of behaviors that are indicative of diffuse anxiety. Group members suggest topics and issues that range from the important to the trivial or irrelevant. As an issue is considered for discussion, it is common to find other members complaining that the group ought to be clear about what it is to do and how it is to go about doing it. In this phase, anxiety is diffuse and is expressed in concerns over the ambiguity of the situation and its unstructured nature. Due to this anxiety, certain group members begin to talk about the necessity of having some sort of structure imposed on the group. Others will be against any type of formalized structure. This is the first small indicator of cleavage, which grows as the group progresses.

During this stage, individual members feel very unsure. Some members may feel helpless to do anything and may become self-deprecating and express inadequacy. A few members may attempt to establish bonds with other members who seem to have similar problems, attitudes, and backgrounds. These attempts to form bonds represent defensive and security alliances. A few members may defend themselves by becoming hesitant to enter into interactions and by resisting all attempts to include them in the discussions.

The more assertive members may make broad intellectual statements and dogmatic assertions and propose encompassing theories. Not infrequently, these members may engage in autistic, self-centered communication monologues without really hearing or responding to what others have said. This occurs because the ambiguous group situation is a type of ambient Rorschach test in which the members' values and attitudes are in a state of flux before they begin to define their personalities in response to the setting. Their approach also avoids anxiety over intimacy and closeness by exhibiting caution, mistrust, and conformity.

3. Members' Search for Position/Definition: Primary Group Transferences/Countertransferences

Gradually, the goal ambiguity and anxiety increase. Against this "field," members begin to define and characterize themselves by their statements; there are attempts at leadership, or solving the problem, or establishing consensus norms. In general, members seek to establish a position or niche in the group. Power shifts rapidly during this phase as assertive members try to influence and/or control the group or engage in leadership struggles. Group members who take the initiative in interacting tend to become leaders.

The reaction to this process is varied among group members—some welcome attempts at leadership as meeting their own dependency needs, other members strongly resist attempts at influence. As previously noted, some members continue to engage in considerable intellectualization and generalization, being fearful of the group and of involvement.

Another form of fear is to keep the conversation going at all costs. At times during the conversation, one group member's statement may be related to another's, but his responses may not be in the context of the previous speaker. Group members may discuss an outside problem or intellectual concern that indirectly reflects issues in the group; e.g., a group with difficulties in resolving membership or attendance issues may discuss truancy in school children.

As group difficulties begin to arise, conflict and the projection of blame and responsibility on the leader and other members become more evident. As members begin to reveal themselves to others, anxiety over intimacy and attempts at closeness again continue to exhibit themselves as reactions to significant people and events in their past life.

This phenomenon may be understood in terms of the general family or primary group model in which transferences take place. For example, group members vie with one another for the approval of the leader by seeking to be closest to him and to please him the most. These group members are generally protective toward the leader and his image, defending him against any and all criticism and the possibility of being hurt. Some members continue to express their desire or expectation that the leader will tell them what to do and will assume all responsibility for what happens in the group.

On the other hand, other members become angry over the lack of direction and leadership and express this anger against the surroundings, the institution, or the leader himself. This is revealed by members engaging in resistance, delay, and disruption; i.e., group members may take negative attitudes, change the subject, or delay the actions of the group. Group members may be unwilling or unable to admit that they are experiencing negative feelings, even when the leader gives them clear evidence of their hostility. This break between the two opposing factions in the group is called dependence versus counterdependence.

There is yet another faction in the group. Some members remain independent of this cleavage and develop dependency relationships with their peers or siblings. This is exhibited in forming small partnerships for mutual support. Due to the cleavage and the development of mutually supportive but opposing factions, there is typically an increase in the occurrence of communication problems, misunderstandings, and outbursts of anger. The expression of intense affect arouses intense anxiety in some members, leading to their absences from the group or their reluctance to participate. There is frustration with the way the group is functioning: an inability to perform effectively on a task, to change its way of operating, or significantly to influence its own fate.

Increased hostility may be expressed toward the leader because of a number of complex factors. The leader is still an outsider and is viewed by members as not being a full member of the group; members become angry because of their perceived dependent or counterdependent relationship to him; still others are frightened of his real or imagined power.

Some of the group members may begin tentatively to test the strengths and limits of the leader in various ways by trying to provoke him, by seeing if they can shock him, by closely observing his reactions to everything in an effort to catch some fault or shortcoming. Other, more assertive, members may imply (sometimes quite directly) that the leader is incompetent and unnecessary, e.g., in statements or rhetorical questions about what would happen if the leader were to leave the meeting or not show up for a later one.

The emergence of intense affect among members causes relationships and feelings to fluctuate rapidly, ranging from intense but brief linkages to sharp reversals of feelings. In addition, some members engage in exhibitionism, striving to be the center of attention and willing to disclose themselves to the group to do so.

As a consequence of an ambiguous situation, members tend to communicate their own needs through their typical interpersonal life styles. The ambiguity of the situation may lead group members to respond to the leader (or other members) with feelings and behaviors learned earlier in family or primary group relationships. They tend to transfer these primary feelings and modes of relating.

At this stage in the life of the group, relatively little productive work has been done in building and reinforcing norms. Although implicit norms centering about cleavages have occurred, these are neither understood nor articulated by members. Norms that do seem to operate are frequently defensive, e.g., the procedural norm regarding the avoidance of silence.

There is also the noticeable emergence of a false consensus norm—in which members agree, implicitly and even explicitly, to reach and agree on decisions by some arbitrary method without really having dealt with covert and unexpressed underlying feelings. The underlying group processes tend to revolve around anxiety over anger, aggression, or any intense affect; a generalized evaluation and testing of the leader; more cleavages within the group; and the seeking of mutual support (handclasping).

4. Sharpened Affects and Anxieties: Increased Defensiveness

Following an intensification of behaviors previously described, sharpened affects of both a positive and negative nature tend to develop, but with a preponderance of negative affects, i.e., hostility, fighting, and more separations. Sometimes the males clash with one another while the females merely observe. Frequently there is a struggle among the males for leadership, while the females play more passive or maternal roles.

Hostilities and conflicts tend to become sharpened not only between individuals, but between subgroups; i.e., cleavages develop between people who are personal oriented and counterpersonal oriented, structured and unstructured, dependent and counterdependent. There is increasing anxiety over anger, aggression, and the potential loss of ego defenses on which members' self-esteem is built. Intense struggles develop over who will lead the group and in what direction. There are also anxieties and fears centering about belonging and acceptance.

During this time, members may try to avoid dealing with the aggressive impulses of other group members because of the intense, emotionally charged group atmosphere. Aggression is often exhibited in scapegoating, in which individual members of the group are singled out for hostility or ostracism. Concomitantly, there are indications of catharsis or the release of tension through anxiety-based jokes, laughter, and heavy sighs.

Some group members begin to vocalize the tensions they experience and the stress they feel as a result of subgroupings and cleavages and express a desire to move toward unity. False consensus and a reluctant tolerance of it tend to increase.

Members attempt to deal with the sharpened affects and anxieties described by sharpening their defenses. These sharpened defenses take many forms, ranging from regressive behavior to projection, displacement, and denial of affect.

Group members alternate between fight and flight, between sudden attacks and withdrawal or avoidance. They may defensively resist or ignore attempts by the leader to focus attention on immediate events in the group. They may also deny any charge of "misbehavior" or any need for them to examine or change their behavior in any way.

Defensiveness may also be observed by the focus on intellectual and content characteristics of a task; that is, group members attempt to limit their interactions to task-related activities of a conceptual nature. This is a form of escape into work utilizing intellectualism in the face of sharpened anxieties. For a few members, this threat leads to an observable increase in rigidity—a clinging to old values and attitudes in the face of apparent threats. False consensus norms and defensive norms are accepted as tacit collusion among members for protection and escape from the intense affective threat.

The basic underlying group processes center about the anxiety over loss of defenses/disclosure and the expression of norms dealing with avoidance of "hurt" and limits of "disclosure" of members.

Power is expressed in both cleavage formation and group "game" playing, e.g., "twenty questions," "psychoanalyst." Members, however, begin to deal with anger/affect more directly and engage in brief, limited personal disclosure to others.

5. Sharpened Interactions: Growth-Identifying Activities and Reality Strengthening

Following the increased anxieties and affects, clearly focused and articulated interactions develop between members as well as between members and the leader. When increased defensiveness is recognized as blocking interpersonal and group growth, greater energies become mobilized in the service of overcoming these defenses. Catalyst roles emerge as some members behave in ways that encourage the total involvement of members and precipitate group interaction. This behavior may involve direct verbal and nonverbal expression of feelings and deeper exploration of these feelings. As a consequence, group members take a vigorous part in the interactions. With the increase in activity, misunderstandings as well as insights occur more frequently as communication becomes sharpened. Group members share more of their significant personal experiences including early lives, dreams, and problems. Silent members are actively encouraged to interact with others.

These interactions have the characteristics of greater directness, threat-free relationships, and open confrontation in attempts to solve realistic problems as they occur. Once members have overcome, to some extent, their defensiveness, they are open to partial insights, self-exploration, investigations of their impact on others, and other growth-identifying activities.

During this phase, relationships between the leader and individual members become strengthened through a slow process of testing and evaluation. There are overt discussions of power and leadership: group members openly discuss their concerns about power and leadership in the group.

In addition to the behaviors exhibited in previous theme topics, group members attempt open confrontation with the group leader or attempt to reduce the leader's power by seducing him into membership. This latter behavior involves inviting the leader to be "just one of us" or "just a member." When these behaviors are confronted, reality testing between the leader and members is increased and strengthened. Members can test their perceptions and assumptions by verbalizing them to the leader.

Anxieties occur due to the loss of defenses and disclosure, although there is also anxiety associated with the development of group norms centering around authority, feedback, and decision making. The group may also involve itself with game playing. Finally, group members begin to deal with their own and others' anger and affect more openly. They actively begin to invite others' personal disclosure, listening closely to others' evaluations of themselves.

6. Norm Crystallization/Enforcement-Defensification

During this phase defenses begin to be lowered since members feel less threat and anxiety. There also emerges a solidification of norms wherein group members work on and evolve rules for behavior in the group. As a consequence, group attention stays on interactions and processes within the group and not on outside matters.

A norm of participation develops in which involvement of the total group becomes a group value. Various roles begin to develop within the group as revealed by the behavior of group members; i.e., certain members assume the role of gatekeepers, sanctioners, placators, disciplinarians. Group members give support to these emerging roles, and, consequently, daily, routine patterns of working and relating are established.

As more sophisticated norms of disclosure, decision making, and feedback emerge, these tend to become internalized within the members. In general, the members become more self-disciplined and self-regulated, which accelerates the rapid development of goals and values. There is more concern with working openly on conflicts of values and on reducing hidden agendas.

The group begins to form a unique culture that includes jargon, rites of passage, group roles, and differentiation from out-groups. Overt expressions of norms are offered, representing devaluation of outside ties, negative reactions to dissension in the group, and positive reinforcement for working and expressing personal problems in a supportive atmosphere. Psychological ties to outside relationships, even family ties, are weakened as members form attachments to the group. In fact, group members tend to view nonmember out-groups with suspicion, distrust, or hostility. As the members begin to exercise some influence over their fate and the group's direction, the crystallization of the group culture represents a sense of significant progress—a breakthrough. Those who dissent or refuse to cooperate with the group suffer temporary loss of status. These emerging norms and their enforcement lead to behaviors aimed at safeguarding the group's success and progress. They maintain a sense of unity and groupness—defensive unification.

In general, group members try to effect compromises between any remaining cleavages and factions to the extent of glossing over or ignoring some disputes among group members, thus preserving the illusion of greater unity. Members tend to concentrate on cooperating on simple tasks. They exhibit a willingness to work together on tasks and goals.

In addition, individual identities tend to be submerged in the group in the pursuit of group unity. At this stage, anxieties tend to be tied to concerns about deviance from group norms and its consequences for the unity and solidarity of the group, as well as to norms centering about authority, feedback, decision making, etc. Power is exerted as a means of enforcing these norms. Members also begin working/expressing personal problems in a supportive atmosphere, dealing with others' evaluation of personal, intimate problems.

7. Distributive Leadership

The final evolution of a group style of normatization and the dropping of many personal defenses encourage members to take individual responsibilities for their own problems and for what happens to them in the group. As a consequence, there is an increase in feelings of equality, with members accepting each other as equals. During this stage, anxieties over personal needs and dynamics tend to be fairly well articulated by individuals describing themselves introspectively.

The distinguishing feature of such public discussions and reflections is the deliberate search for the true reasons for behavior rather than superficial rationalizations. For example, it is not unusual to hear group members discuss relations with authority figures, e.g., parents, or with other significant figures in their lives. There emerges an integrated autonomy: group members assert individuality and independence without threatening group solidarity.

During this phase a more realistic view of the leader emerges. As the leader is seen less in terms of absolutes and more as a person with qualities that are helpful to the group, there is an increased willingness to use the leader as a resource. Group members now see him as one who can observe group processes and help them deal with emotional issues. This type of interaction differs considerably from earlier interactions, which were based on factors of fear, dependency, or competition. In general, members have acquired the ability to accept or reject the leader independently and maturely, rather than uncritically. In essence, the leader is seen as a person and as a member of the group.

The development of a more realistic view of the leader alters the primitive and artificial separations of the resource functions of the leader and of the members. Leadership becomes distributive as members become willing to assume functions and responsibilities typically accomplished only by the leader. They take individual responsibility for their own problems and for what happens to them in the group, thus becoming a collection of leaders.

The group begins to recognize its various group members as resource leaders, each of whom offers his own unique blend of talent, experience, and skill to help the group. This form of distributive leadership allows members to call on various members of their resource pool in order to solve problems.

Informality prevails when leadership and structure become functional to whatever the group is working on at the time; e.g., through informal rather than formal discussions of the issues involved, there may be an increase in decisions based on consensus. When conflict occurs during this stage, it is usually over substantive issues rather than hidden emotional issues, since members have become skilled at diagnosing the difference.

Finally, this stage is marked by an effective display of decision-making norms stressing maximally descriptive and minimally evaluative communication, which helps group members to deal more freely with other group members' evaluations of themselves. It also leads to the constructive working of interpersonal problems.

The basic underlying group processes exhibit a continuation of anxiety over deviance from established group norms and a redistribution of power, with norms of shared responsibility and shared leadership being articulated.

8. Decreased Defensiveness and Increased Experimentation

This stage of group growth and development is marked by individuals significantly relaxing their defenses in an atmosphere of trust and support and experimenting with atypical growth behaviors. Since the leader is no longer considered a threat and group members are seen as equals, masks and protective façades can now be dropped, resulting in increased freedom and insight into others. Generally, there is diminished aggression: members experience less anger and show less hostility. A more relaxed, informal state seems to characterize this phase, coupled with a freer flow of feelings, thoughts, and open expressions of physical feelings. There is an increase in the amount and appropriate application of feedback: members tell each other their reactions to and perceptions of one another, evaluating each other's group roles and interpersonal styles. There is an increase in empathy. Members understand the differences, feelings, and problems of one another without judging. They seem able to share and understand one another's personal and conceptual schemes regarding human behavior. There may be obvious symptom modification/relief.

There are more unbiased evaluations of the contributions of members — questions are evaluated with comparatively little regard for power or status in the group. Group members are also able to deal directly with emotional and maintenance issues.

It is typical of this phase that the focus of evaluation moves inward; i.e., group members begin to consider their self-evaluation more important than evaluation by the larger society. Concomitant with this development, there is a significant elimination of references to "real world" problems. Instead there is an increase in work on both personal and interpersonal problems. There is insight into others: group members perceive defenses, dysfunctional value systems, and underlying motivations. They discuss the problems that bother them inside and outside the group, and they share common experiences while focusing on a discussion of personal problems. As a result, self-awareness develops. Members become aware of their own personal involvement in the group and how it tends to affect their perceptions. They see their own biases and prejudices and are able to accept this and other aspects of the group process without alarm.

Finally, there is a significant increase in attempts to try new ways of behaving, new and atypical interpersonal styles, and new group functions.

The willingness to try out new behaviors toward others develops from the support, trust, and respect that members share with each other.

Members tend to exhibit increased self-reliance, self-worth, and self-confidence and have more realistic goals and better interpersonal skills. There is a noticeably improved perceptual reorganization as members develop new ambitions that utilize their potential, set realistic goals, and develop interpersonal skills. Since members are less fearful of intimacy, there is a greater willingness to compromise and make fewer defensive adjustments in the service of the growth needs of other members.

The basic group processes tend to be anxieties over taking creative risks, dealing with catastrophic fantasies, and trying out atypical behaviors. These lead directly to group norms stressing the enforcement of atypical behavior coupled with the norms of intimacy, sex, and agression.

Concerns over power and control become almost nonexistent. Power is invested in the group rather than in the leader or other individuals. As the locus of evaluation moves inward to self-evaluation, members begin to form strong emotional bonds during the constructive resolutions of their interpersonal problems.

9. Group Potency

Through an increase in experimentation and less defensive behavior, the group comes to be seen as a significant, if not the most significant, source of learning and growth: the group becomes potent and concretized. It accepts and supports individual members as well as rewards their positive changes. Members are better able to choose when it is appropriate to deal with something in the group, when to ignore it, or when to handle it with an outside resource, e.g., other members or the leader. The group's prevailing tone is one of dedication and committed purpose. These factors appear to make group members experience time as prolonged; they feel that they have been together and have been part of the group for a much longer psychological time than chronological time indicates. In some instances, there are longer spans of attention to interpersonal learning. The group is able to stay with complex and difficult issues longer and work more steadily on them.

There is an increased awareness of the need to work together as well as an increase in group members' loyalties and affections for one another; the group is integrated and cohesive. During this period the group might deal with highly intense, interpersonal interactions without becoming defensive or changing the subject. As a consequence, one or more members might have a peak experience with members experiencing intense joy and pleasure. Members accept and verbalize the group as a potent change agent for personal growth. Power is invested in the group rather than in the leader or other individuals, thus promoting rapid and effective personal growth.

In summary, there is a continuation of some anxiety over practicing and experimenting with new behavior. There are periods of intense interpersonal affection, elation, and excitement with other members and the group as a whole. There may also be peak experiences concerning self. The group continues to enforce norms of intimacy and closeness. As the group is seen as an effective change agent, concerns over power and control are not discussed.

10. Termination

The responses of individual members to the approaching termination of the group vary, but all members seem to have an intense reaction that reflects the previous phase of deep commitment to the group as a miniature society or community. There is a tendency to overestimate the group members' potential for resolving all their problems. In general, most members are individually and collectively optimistic about the future. However, some members might deny the impending termination by expressing disbelief and regret accompanied with a verbalized wish to extend the group sessions.

As a result of this separation anxiety, some members begin to withdraw their involvement in the group to seek some means of closure. Other members experience happiness over leaving, over going back to the outside world. They have a greater sense of identity and competence. Frequently, members experience the need to affirm that the group has been valuable to them, and they express these feelings in the form of testimonials.

There is a general reduction in the intensity of involvement in interpersonal feedback as members prepare to leave the group. There is also a growing sense of completion in that most members believe they have completed the task of the group and are now ready to move forward.

Many members begin to question the relevance of some group learning to the outside world, while others wish to explore the mechanics of transferring learnings to specific situations. Some members express apprehension over possible personality changes brought about in the group. The group leader and members must be prepared to spend sufficient time on the issue of the transfer of training to give group members a sense of productive closure.

The basic underlying group process during this final stage is concerned with anxiety over leaving the group and over applying the group experiences and learnings to the real world. Power concerns reveal themselves in increased independence from external control. Group norms and real-world norms are clearly differentiated as to transfer or carry-over. There are periods of sadness as group members seek closure in their termination of involvement in the group.[2]

THE APPLICATION OF THE MODEL TO THE GROUP LITERATURE

Despite the apparent need for a good theory or model of group growth and development, a comprehensive survey of the literature reveals a scarcity of work done in this area. Not only are laboratory studies of developmental phenomena rare, but the whole question of change in process over time has been relatively neglected (Tuckman, 1965).

After twenty-five years of the laboratory and T-group movement, only a few developmental models have been published. This scarcity may be the result of an avoidance of temporal change parameters (in order to simplify various research designs) by using short-term groups (Tuckman, 1965), the absence of a good methodology (Fiebert, 1968), and a change in research focus (Golembiewski & Blumberg, 1968). Other reasons seem to be a lack of understanding of a complex and confused field, its historical and philosophical underpinnings, and a tendency almost indiscriminately to intermingle or even confuse intervention theory with the theory of group growth and development.

There are certain, special characteristics of the field that militate against the development of theories of group growth and development: the multiplicity of schools of thought; the poor experimental methods utilized in research by many practitioners; and the humanistic-existential orientation of many of those working with groups. This orientation carries with it an emphasis on the uniqueness of each individual or group; a high valuing of the emotional, irrational side of man as opposed to the rational; and a concern for the experience of the immediate present, the "now" as opposed to a historical abstract view. All of these aspects of the existential-humanistic point of view tend to be barriers to theory building, which by its nature is an intellectual, abstract process that searches for commonalities among "unique" situations and that must concern itself with causality and history in addition to the immediate present.

In order to achieve some perspective of these difficulties and better understand some of the problems encountered in formulating a theory of group developmental sequence, one should consider historical and philosophical underpinnings: present historical-social trends, problems stemming from the adoption of a particular theoretical stance, and the characteristic

---

[2] For an independent, empirical evaluation of this model of group growth and development, see Ballard (1972).

nature of the field, which works against the development of systematic theories.

Industrial-technological societies tend to be present or future oriented while showing less concern or respect for the past (Clark, 1963). This de-emphasis of historical material is reflected in contemporary American psychology which is, for the most part, drifting from Freudian psychology toward the more recent orientations of Skinner and Perls. Both men de-emphasize historical material.

Today, man is living in an age of relativism that could hinder the construction of theories of group development. In a relativistic age, questions involving value judgments, e.g., "What is a good group?," "What is development?," tend to be avoided.

In the formulation of a theoretical position on developmental phases, several important issues must be noted: whether a group passes through cycles in which the same issues are dealt with over and over on progressive levels but in different ways (Clark, 1963; Hampden-Turner, 1966; Bradford, 1964); whether issues are dealt with and then set aside in a discontinuous fashion (Bennis & Shepard, 1956) or dealt with in a continuous or evolutionary manner; and whether, instead of a common pattern of group development, a number of underlying themes or subpatterns exist, which may or may not follow a set flow of events (Rogers, 1967).

Another related concern is the number and kind of developmental stages conceptualized in the life of a group. A brief survey of the literature quickly reveals authors who conceptualize two, three, four, or more than four stages of significant periods in the group's life. However, most writers hypothesize three or four stages. In most cases there are theoretically based reasons for the adoption of a given number of stages. This problem seems related to some of those previously discussed, such as what constitutes a flow of events that is continuous, discontinuous, cyclic, evolutionary, etc.

Two other questions stem from the adoption of a theoretical position: the molecular versus the molar view, i.e., what constitutes an "event," and the "great man" controversy, i.e., whether man causes historical change or is the product or instrument of an inevitable trend. In proposing, describing, or evaluating a trend, some decision must be made regarding the nature and scope of an "event."

The methodological problem is not only how but what to describe as an event in order to trace its development. The "great man" question is important in considering whether the theorist focuses on the individuals comprising the group, adds up their characteristics, and hypothesizes a flow; or whether the whole group is greater than the sum of its parts in determining flow.

In his review of the literature, Tuckman (1965) observes that the majority of research dealing with group development comes from the group-therapy setting and human relations training, neither of which is historically known for featuring strict experimental control or manipulation of independent variables. An example of this relatively poor quality of research is the fact that much of the work done in group therapy and training settings is based on the observation of a single group. It is often qualitative rather than quantitative and therefore subject to the bias of the experimenter. Control and systematic manipulation of independent variables is impossible when only a single group is the basis of inference.

In the absence of the manipulation of independent variables and the consequent discovery of their differential effects within studies, these effects can only be approximately discerned by comparing studies. However, many independent variables are likely to vary from study to study, for example, group composition, duration, and so forth, and little light will be shed on the effects of these variables on the developmental process. (Tuckman, 1965, p. 396)

Tuckman does not make any conclusions regarding the specific effects of these variables on the developmental process.

An appraisal of the literature makes it clear that there is not an equal representation of various theoretical orientations. Tuckman (1965) points out that therapy groups have been overrepresented while laboratory groups have been underrepresented.

In our survey, well over half the studies included were therapy groups; the remainder of studies were composed of work taken from a variety of growth-group settings. These groups included T-groups, laboratory groups, encounter groups, and task or discussion groups. Tuckman warns that inequality of setting representation necessitates caution in generalizing from this literature. He states that "generalization must, perforce, be limited to the fact that what has been presented is mainly research dealing with sequential development in therapy groups" (1965, p. 395). This precaution may not be necessary since our research findings indicate a relatively high degree of correspondence on developmental sequence among most groups, regardless of their theoretical orientation.

Tuckman (1965) presents a model offered as a conceptualization of changes in group behavior, in the social and task area. The model covers all group settings over time. His model, which is the first significant attempt at demonstrating commonalities across theoretical orientations, is based on his perceptions of trends in the studies he reviewed. This work showed that developmental studies could be linked together; however, it did not reveal the extent of commonalities.

An earlier and more cursory survey of the course of development in the T-group (Stock, 1964) did not attempt any link with other types of groups. It did point out resemblances and familial patterns in T-group growth and development over time, but indicated that these patterns may be greater regarding structural characteristics than regarding processes. However, the seeming existence of lawful relationships governing the emergence of some total group characteristics was suggested.

One characteristic of the many studies reported in the literature is that they seem indiscriminately to mix descriptive and prescriptive elements of group growth and development. Bennis and Shepard (1956) and Fiebert (1968) so thoroughly mix developmental sequence descriptions with proposed interventions that it is difficult to separate one from the other. In these cases the described growth and development is little more than a self-fulfilling prophecy.

Our model of group growth and development provides descriptive and prescriptive elements and clearly distinguishes between the two. Even though it is recognized that descriptive and prescriptive elements are integral and ultimately interrelated, the quality of a group can be prescribed and influenced to a large extent by the trainer or therapist. However, there must be a basis for comparison. This is achieved through the separation of how a group "is" from how it "should be." However, most authors who do propose an observed sequence in development, patterns of growth, or recurrent themes do so without ever really proposing a clear, separate developmental sequence integrated into a theory of group growth and development.

Some authors discuss developmental sequence by virtue of trainer intervention (Fiebert, 1968); others arrive at a description of group growth and development secondarily. Their primary focus may be group settings, selected target populations, or varied approaches. Since these foci are all reflected in the group process, the authors thereby engage in a discussion of sequential occurrences, i.e., group growth and development. Thus, in many of the studies reported, the growth and development of a group seems to be of subordinate concern. However, the very fact that process flow is necessary as an indicator of the effect of various group parameters is a testimony to its importance. Nevertheless, comparatively few works have group growth and development as a central focus.

Golembiewski and Blumberg (1970) suggest that there has been a shift in focus or emphasis in T-group research since its inception. This change in emphasis may have had some effect on the quantity and quality of productivity in the study of developmental or growth processes. They observe that the earliest research in T-groups focused on the processes of group development as they interacted with the characteristics of group members. Golembiewski and Blumberg's dominant focus was on isolating relations of various groups and individual properties such as the association of high cohesiveness with a high degree of agreement about norms.

The least dominant theme in early T-group research was the outcome or the payoff associated with specific internal group processes, e.g., attitudinal or behavioral change. However, the focus of attention has shifted so that the opposite emphasis in research is more common. For example, there is less concern with internal group dynamics than there is with the results of training, the diverse factors that affect these results, and the applications of the T-group model in various contexts.

Of the studies reported that describe a developmental sequence, the majority are severely limited in terms of what they accomplish. Furthermore, they have a narrow range of applicability. For example, the studies are of relevance only to those groups that fit into one specific theoretical framework. They have little usefulness for any other type of group.

These same studies usually reflect a strong author bias in issues or behaviors selected to be included in the espoused theory. For instance, most authors are predisposed to look for those aspects of a group process that fit their own predilections. Since few authors really attempt to include a broad range of behaviors, issues, dynamics, or processes, most work is limited by its narrow focus. While a narrow focus may facilitate research efforts, a theory of group growth and development should strive for comprehensiveness in order to characterize such a complex process as human interaction.

The Need for a Sound Methodology

One of the principal reasons given for the inadequacy of the literature of group growth and development is the lack of a good methodology. Group phenomena, especially the tracing of group development, are difficult to assess. It is difficult to analyze these phenomena and relate them to other research and theoretical attempts. However, our theory of group growth and development is based on specific behavioral descriptions, which provide a sound methodology for the evaluation and empirical validation of the model presented in this book as well as for the comparison of described developmental flows.

Procedural Explanation

By using the model in this book as a framework, it is possible to make comparisons and contrasts among studies, regarding major emphases, similarities and differences, and strengths and weaknesses. For this purpose, studies were selected that represent several different theoretical orientations. These studies include those that divide group life into two, three, four, or more than four stages. Of the approximately one hundred studies discussing a flow of events over time, we selected only forty-nine. *The main criterion for inclusion of a study was the description of events as occurring within a specific period of group life.* Other studies were concerned with group growth and development but were excluded because they did not describe discrete stages. For example, development may have been conceptualized as increased authenticity, intimacy, self-disclosure, or decreased defensiveness. If these group phenomena were not scaled on a time or sequential dimension, they could not be incorporated into or linked with a model that attempts to describe an orderly progression of events over time. Studies describing events or behaviors in group life in a nonsegmented narrative style were also excluded because phases or stages could only be inferred.

The studies selected include those based on laboratory groups, T-groups, encounter groups, task or discussion-oriented groups, therapy groups, and a variety of narrow-band groups. The term "narrow-band" is used to indicate those studies that seem to have a rather narrow or specific population focus. Examples of narrow-band groups are groups composed of retarded children or adults; deaf-mutes; discussion groups meeting bi-weekly; scientists on an Arctic expedition; or groups of cerebral-palsied children. A narrow-band group could represent any theoretical position such as therapy or encounter orientations. Of the forty-nine groups chosen, the growth or developmental phenomenon in groups was the primary focus of only thirteen studies.

After the selection of the studies, the specific behaviors described for each stage were equated or matched with the appropriate behavioral descriptions on which this model is based. (See Appendix.) In most cases, this procedure was expedited since all the behavioral descriptions comprising the model were drawn from many of the same studies.

In some cases there was difficulty in matching the behaviors described in a given study with those on which this model is constructed. Where such decisions were required, the best fit was made by judges well acquainted with the nuances of behavioral and issue descriptions but unfamiliar with the model and its described flow. To a large extent, this controlled experimenter bias, but there was no escape from the introduction of some bias, as all the behavioral descriptions could not be equated. However, this kind of bias was minimized since the descriptions comprising the model were drawn originally from the works of the same authors included in the literature comparison.

Explanation of Table Entries

Establishing a common denominator by matching behavioral descriptions allowed for flow comparisons to be made. All included studies were classified according to the number of stages of group life hypothesized. Four subdivisions resulted: those composed of studies describing two, three, four, or more than four stages of group life. The next step was to display a profile of each author's proposed flow so that it could be compared with our model for the degree of correspondence. Tables 5.2, 5.4, 5.6 and 5.8 show ten categories or phases corresponding to dominant theme topics described in the model. Each of these categories is comprised of a set of numbers corresponding to behavioral descriptions on which dominant theme topics are based. Consequently, it is a straightforward matter to match the behavioral descriptions of other models with those of our model.

The numerical entries listed across from each author's name correspond to the stage number in which that author has classified a specific behavior. The location of each numerical entry (under one of the ten phases of our model) indicates where we hypothesize that a particular behavior occurs in group life. In this way the profiles of behavioral flow for any authors can be compared; also, by looking at the flow charts the reader should be able to compare any author's described behavioral flow with the one presented in this text.

The number of numerical entries, corresponding to behavioral descriptions, gives some idea of the comprehensiveness of any model. If the entries for any model are evenly distributed, with the *1*'s preceding the *2*'s, which in turn precede the *3*'s, which in turn precede the *4*'s, etc., then it can be assumed that a basic agreement exists with the model in this text on the overall flow of events and the range of issues occurring during group life. However, if a behavioral description placed in our first phase is seen as occurring by another writer in his third stage, it is recorded in phase 1 and designated by the number *3*. This would indicate considerable disagreement as to when that particular behavior occurs in group life. This kind of disagreement is referred to as a "reversal."

As an example, in Table 5.2, Borenzweig and Dombey (1969) describe a behavior that occurs in their phase 1, but in phase 6 of our model. This is indicated by the figure *1* in column 6. Similarly, behaviors that they identify as occurring in their second phase occur in phases 8 and 10 of our model, indicated by the *2*'s in columns 8 and 10.

Two-Stage Models

There were nine studies in which the authors conceptualized two stages in the development of a group. Two of these studies were concerned primarily with the developmental process (Paterson, 1966; Bennis & Shepard, 1956). Only Bennis and Shepard attempted to advance a theory of group development.

Although most of these studies are narrow-band, T-groups and encounter and therapy groups are also represented. An average of approximately seventeen behavioral descriptions that arise in group life was described. Considering the wide range of possible behaviors that can occur in a group, this is a rather small number.

From Table 5.2 it is apparent that this average is boosted by the Bennis and Shepard study which describes fifty-six issues. If this study were not included in the calculation, the average would drop to twelve. In addition to being comprehensive, this study is somewhat atypical of other works in the two-stage grouping in that there is a relatively even distribution of behavioral descriptions across the group life. Furthermore, all categories but one are represented.

188 The Critical Incident in Growth Groups

Table 5.2. Behavioral Characteristics of Two-Stage Studies

Cohen-Smith Phases	1	2	3	4	5	6	7	8	9	10
Behavioral Characteristics	1-4	5-16	17-43	44-59	60-68	69-90	91-101	102-122	123-135	136-144
Studies										
Barrett, Hunt, and Jones (1967) N-B*		1,2	1							
Bennis and Shepard (1956)** T-Group	1	1,1,1	1,1,1,1 1,1,1,1 1,1,1,1 1,1,2,2,2 2,2,2	1,1,1,1 2,2,2	1,1	1,1,1,2 2	1,1,1,2	1,2,2,2,2	1,1,1,2 2,2	
Borenzweig and Dombey (1969) N-B*						1		2,2,2		2
Carter (1968) N-B* - Therapy		1					1,1	2,2	2	
Nadler (1968) Encounter - T-Group						2	1,2	1,1,1,1 2,2,2	1,1,1	

*N-B = narrow-band studies
**Studies with primary focus on group growth and development

Table 5.2. (cont.)

Cohen-Smith Phases	1	2	3	4	5	6	7	8	9	10
Behavioral Characteristics	1-4	5-16	17-43	44-59	60-68	69-90	91-101	102-122	123-135	136-144
Studies										
Paterson (1966)** N-B* - Task	1	1,1,1 1,2,2	1,1,1,2		1,2		2	2,2,2,2,2 2,2	2,2	2
Sarlin and Altshuler (1968) N-B* - Therapy			1,1,1,1,2	1,2				2,2,2	2,2,2	
Sikes and Cleveland (1968) T-Group		1	1,1,1	2				2,2,2,2 2,2,2,2 2	2,2	2
W. M. Smith (1966) N-B*			1,1,2,2	1,1,1		1,2,2,2			2	

*N-B = narrow-band studies
**Studies with primary focus on group growth and development

In looking at other study profiles in Table 5.2 it is apparent that there are many gaps in behavioral representations and that most are unequally distributed. This may be due to a number of factors: if an author describes as few as five or six behaviors, distributional gaps occur, since there are more categories than described behaviors. Descriptions of only a few behaviors occur when the author is concerned with a few specific behaviors, e.g., the writer whose interest is not in developmental phenomena. Another possibility is that the writer visualizes only two stages of development and does not feel required to describe as many behaviors.

Gaps in the sequential flow could also reflect author bias, research limitations, the nature and composition of the groups, trainer or therapist style, unintentional omission, or a different understanding of group development.

Table 5.2 shows that there is a relatively good agreement on the sequential ordering of behaviors. This can be observed by noting the trend in each author's profile—the number *1*'s ordinarily preceding the *2*'s. Although there are a few reversals, there is surprisingly good agreement on the sequential trend. This is unusual considering the diversity of the studies represented.

An analysis of the reversals and skewed distributions reveals special conditions that logically predispose a group toward a slightly altered sequencing of events without posing a serious flaw in the model. Two examples of this are noted in the works of Borenzweig and Dombey (1969) and Nadler (1968). The distribution of behavioral descriptions for these two studies is skewed toward events occurring in the latter stages of our model. The reason for this kind of distribution as well as the reversals in Nadler's study is that the group was composed of members of a civil rights organization who already knew each other, had an established commitment with relatively clear goals, and had probably experienced interpersonal encounter involving search for definition/position, sharpened anxieties, sharpened defenses, and sharpened interactions. This allowed the group to begin at a middle to later stage of development; issues such as trust and purposefulness occurred earlier than in most groups.

The Borenzweig and Dombey study was on discussion-activity groups of retarded teenagers. This group met for a period of two years and engaged in field trips, guest speakers, visual aids, and role playing, which enabled this group to circumvent many of the events that might ordinarily be confronted in therapy or growth groups. Perhaps this accounts for the absence of behavioral entries signifying early to middle group life. For example, there was no goal ambiguity since goals were well defined by the leader.

Another study by Carter (1968) is similar to the two just mentioned. The members were already acquainted, goals were structured, transferences had already been established, and sharpened interactions were curbed by the structure and character of the group. The profile for this group is also understandably loaded in the direction of the middle to end phases.

The profile of Barret, Hunt, and Jones (1967) has some rather striking reversals. These reversals could be due to circumstances that forced cerebral-palsied children to interact prior to the formation of the group. The study also seems narrow-band in that the focus is not so much on an interactive process as it is on a description of the formation of a group.

Reversals in the Paterson (1966) study center around anxiety over intimacy; identification or a bond with those having similar problems; and self-depreciation responses hinting at inadequacy. A plausible reason for the late occurrence of these behaviors is the hospital working climate of the psychiatric nurses who composed the group. The climate was one of competition and adequacy where many social and professional rewards hung in the balance. It might be expected, then, that decreased defensiveness would take longer.

Study characteristics also seem to explain why issues of leadership and subgrouping might come later in group life for W. M. Smith (1966) as compared with the model presented in this book. The subjects in the study were scientists on a polar expedition. Leadership and subgrouping were structurally assigned at the onset of the expedition; leadership issues would probably not be actively dealt with in group process until later. Well into the expedition the emergence of new leaders did occur in the group. However, the necessity of task performance delayed the emergence of new leaders and subgrouping based on supportive relationships. Some of the reversals in the flow of behavioral events as described by Bennis and Shepard (1956) do not seem as readily apparent. These disagreements could be due to procedural artifacts or to basic differences about when some behaviors appear.

Several characteristics of two-stage group theorists are revealed in Tables 5.2 and 5.3. First it can be seen that there is representation for all categories and that there is good agreement on the general flow or sequencing of events (Table 5.2) between our model and those in the literature. A frequency count of behavioral entries falling in each category from Table 5.3 reveals that more attention is given to certain behavioral events than to others. Most of the behavioral descriptions are subsumed under the members' search for position/definition: primary group transferences/countertransferences (category 3) in the early part of group life and under decreased defensiveness and increased experimentation (category 8) in the latter part of group life. It is also true that some categories are passed over lightly as indicated by the low frequency of behavioral descriptions discussed or attended to in the two-stage studies.

Three-Stage Models

There are twenty studies meeting the criterion for three-stage models. Seven of the studies focus primarily on developmental phenomena. Four of these seven studies are also classified as having a T-group orientation (Argyris, 1964; Miles, 1965; Theodorson, 1953; Whitman, 1964); one is classified as

Table 5.3. Two-Stage Studies—Frequency of Behavior-Description Entries

Cohen-Smith Phases	1	2	3	4	5	6	7	8	9	10	Total for all Categories
Behavioral Characteristics	1-4	5-16	17-43	44-59	60-68	69-90	91-101	102-122	123-135	136-144	
Studies											
Totals	2	13	40	13	4	11	9	40	18	3	153
Total 1st Stage	2	10	30	8	3	5	6	9	6		79
Total 2nd Stage	0	3	10	5	1	6	3	31	12	3	74

Number of Two-Stage Studies: 9
Mean Behavioral Descriptions: 17

A Theory of Group Growth and Development 193

an encounter group orientation (Schutz, 1958); one is classified as a therapy group (Osberg & Berliner, 1956); and one is classified as a narrow-band group (Bales & Strodtbeck, 1951).

Table 5.4 indicates that the studies focusing on group growth and development and those classified as T-group orientation agree on the flow of events. There is also fairly good agreement for encounter and therapy groups. Only the narrow-band group did not show good correspondence. The T-group-oriented studies displayed fairly even distributions across all categories with an average number of twenty-seven behavioral descriptions. (See Table 5.5.) The average number of behavioral descriptions for all three-stage studies was eighteen. The average number of behavioral descriptions for all studies focusing on sequential development was twenty-three, as compared with an average of fifteen for the remainder of the studies without a primary developmental focus. This indicates that those authors concerned primarily with a developmental flow tend to describe a greater breadth of behavioral events than those who are only secondarily interested in flow. It is also true that the studies with a T-group orientation and a developmental focus described the most behavioral events.

These findings fit our expectations that a study focusing on flow is concerned with events occurring in the group life. It is also expected that T-group work, with its emphasis on growth changes, would describe events in detail as they occur during the span of group existence. This expectation is valid because T-groups are more concerned with group dynamics, process, or interaction than other different theoretically oriented groups.

Of the twenty studies conceptualizing three stages of group life, five were T-group orientations, three were classified as having a growth group (other than T-group) orientation, ten were therapy group orientations, and two were narrow-band groups. It is clear from these figures that the greatest amount of work in three-stage studies has been done with therapy groups and the least with narrow-band groups. This finding can be contrasted with two-stage groups in which there was no study with a therapy orientation and in which most of the work was done with narrow-band groups.

Tables 5.2, 5.3, and Figure 5.1 suggest that the trend of agreement on behavioral events between the model in this text and those reported in the literature for two-stage studies is also true for three-stage studies. There is excellent agreement on behavioral events occurring in stages one and three, but there is less correspondence for second-stage behaviors. Many events that were predicted for the second stage in our model were not described by others as occurring during the middle of group life.

These results may reflect a common author bias. Indeed, many behavioral descriptions that can be categorized under the dominant theme topics of transferences/countertransferences and decreased defensiveness/increased experimentation seem to be popularized. These may have become catchall themes that are considered important in group life.

194   The Critical Incident in Growth Groups

Table 5.4. Behavioral Characteristics of Three-Stage Studies

Cohen-Smith Phases	1	2	3	4	5	6	7	8	9	10
Behavioral Characteristics	1-4	5-16	17-43	44-59	60-68	69-90	91-101	102-122	123-135	136-144
Studies										
Argyris (1964)** T-Group		1,2	1,1,1,2	2		2	2,3	2,2,2,2 3,3,3,3	3,3,3	3
Bales and Strodtbeck (1951)** N-B*- Task		3	1,1,3	3			3	2,2,2 3,3	1,3,3 3,3	
Berne (1961) Therapy		1,1	1				1,2	1,2,2,2 2,2,3,3 3		
(Cholden (1953) N-B* - Therapy		1	1,1,1,2			1	2	2,2,2,3 3		
Fiebert (1968) T-Group	1		1,2	1		3	2,3,3	2,3	3	
Grotjahn (1950) Therapy	1	1	1,2			3	3		3	
Herbert and Trist (1953) T-Group		1,1	1,1,1,1 1,1,1,1 1,1,2	1,1,1,1,1		1,1	1,2,2, 3,3		2,3	1,3
King (1959) Therapy		1,1	1,1	1,1,2,2		3		2,2,2 3,3,3	3	3,3

*N-B = narrow-band studies
**Studies with primary focus on group growth and development

Table 5.4. (cont.)

Cohen-Smith Phases	1	2	3	4	5	6	7	8	9	10
Behavioral Characteristics	1-4	5-16	17-43	44-59	60-68	69-90	91-101	102-122	123-135	136-144
Studies										
Landau (1968) N-B* - Therapy		1,3	2,2,2,2	1,2		3		3,3,3,3	3,3,3	
Martinson (1967) N-B*	1,1	1				1,1,2,2 2,3,3,3	3,3,3		2,3	
Miles (1953)** T-Group	1,1	1,1,2,2	2,2,2	2,2,3		1,2	3	2,2,2,2 2,3,3	2,2,3,3	3
Noyes and Kolb (1964) Therapy						1	2	3		
Osberg and Berliner (1956)** Therapy		1,1,1 1,2,3 3	1,1,1,1 1,1	1			3	2,3,3,3 3,3	3	3
Powdermaker and Frank (1948) Therapy		1	1,1,1,2,2	1,1	2	3,3		2,3,3,3,3	2,3,3,3 3,3	
Schutz (1958)** Encounter	1,2	1	1,1,1,2,3			2		3		

*N-B = narrow-band studies
**Studies with primary focus on group growth and development

Table 5.4. (cont.)

Cohen-Smith Phases	1	2	3	4	5	6	7	8	9	10
Behavioral Characteristics	1-4	5-16	17-43	44-59	60-68	69-90	91-101	102-122	123-135	136-144
Studies										
Stoller (1968a) Marathon Encounter		1,2				1,2	1	2,2,2,2 2,2,3	2,2,2,2 2,2	
Stoute (1950) Therapy		1,2	1,1,1,1 1,1	1	1,3	2,2		1,1,2,2 3,3,3,3	2,2	
Theodorson (1953)** Sensitivity Group Laboratory Training	1	1,1,1 1,1,2	1,1,2,2 2	2,2,3	2,3,3	1,1,1,2 2,2,2,2 2,3,3	3,3	2,2,3	2,3,3	
Wender (1936) Therapy			1,1,1	3				2,2,2,2 3,3,3,3,3	3,3	
Whitman (1964)** T-Group		1	1,1,1,1 1,2	1,1,1,2 2,2,2,2		1,1,2	2	2,3,3		3

*N-B = narrow-band studies
**Studies with primary focus on group growth and development

Table 5.5. Three-Stage Studies—Frequency of Behavior-Description Entries

Cohen-Smith Phases	1	2	3	4	5	6	7	8	9	10	Total Across Categories
Behavioral Characteristics	1-4	5-16	17-43	44-59	60-68	69-90	91-101	102-122	123-135	136-144	
Studies											
Totals	9	36	76	33	6	40	25	90	43	8	366
Total 1st Stage	8	26	54	16	1	13	3	3	1	1	126
Total 2nd Stage	1	6	20	13	2	16	8	41	14		121
Total 3rd Stage		4	2	4	3	11	14	46	28	7	119

Number of Three-Stage Studies: 20
Mean Behavioral Descriptions: 18

A Theory of Group Growth and Development   197

198   The Critical Incident in Growth Groups

Figure 5.1. Summary of All Studies—Frequency of Behavior-Description Entries

Cohen-Smith Phases	1	2	3	4	5	6	7	8	9	10
Behavioral Characteristics	1-4	5-16	17-43	44-59	60-68	69-90	91-101	102-122	123-135	136-144
Studies										

A Theory of Group Growth and Development 199

Therefore the experimenter, practitioner, or theorist may be predisposed to look for and deal with behaviors that are related to transference or defensiveness. This predisposition may be due in part to psychoanalytic heritage. Whatever the reason, some issues seem to be overworked. This is understandable. Since people working in the field have difficulty separating the many and complex facets of group life, only some of the more prominent issues will be discussed. A more-detailed examination of the finer nuances of group behavior will expand one's awareness to include a variety of other significant but underemphasized behaviors. However, only through a comprehensive approach to events occurring in group life can this be accomplished.

The narrow focus of attention to central issues or concepts has led to significant gaps in the developmental literature. To better understand what is central and what is not central, it is important to identify gaps and consider underemphasized events in group developmental process. A comparison of the literature with a comprehensive model such as the one proposed in this text should help to do so, since the model is based on significant behavioral descriptions drawn from the literature.

Table 5.5 indicates the same trends for three-stage studies as for two-stage studies. Based on the frequency of behavioral description for each of the ten categories, there is again a bimodal distribution. However, there is a greater weight on the later stages of group life.

Category 8 especially receives a great deal of attention from most authors. This category includes all those behavioral descriptions that fall under what is called decreased defensiveness and increased experimentation. One of the pervasive barometers of emotional health is the lack of defensiveness. Regardless of orientation, whether it be therapy or personal growth, one of the key dimensions concerning the practitioner is defenses. In recent years the proliferation of T-groups, laboratory groups, encounter groups, awareness groups, nonverbal groups, marathons, and many others has led to a focus on expanding consciousness, increasing openness, congruence, authenticity, intimacy, and other similar metagoals, all related to the concept of defenses. It is little wonder so much attention is given to this one category. To some extent it is a testimony to the validity of decreased defensiveness and increased experimentation and to the behaviors that have been subsumed under this theme.

The concerted attention given to decreased defensiveness raises some questions, such as whether it is really a key dimension of growth and whether the attention it gets is actually warranted. Although these problems are not easily resolved, one should be careful not to overlook or disregard other important aspects of group growth. For example, Table 5.5 shows that very little attention is given to those behaviors associated with the acquaintance process, sharpened interactions, and termination.

Table 5.4 presents apparent disagreements that are indicated by reversals. Bales and Strodtbeck (1951) describe cooperation and sharing of responsibility as coming at the beginning of a task group while the model in this text places it later in the group. Part of the difficulty lies in the translation of their description of behavior to the most fitting of our model's behavior descriptions. It is true, however, that for a task group, cooperation among members could occur early, even if on a superficial level. Another noteworthy reversal in this study is member tension that is described as coming late in the group. In our model, tension occurs early. This difference may be due to a translation problem in the conversion of behavioral descriptions; however, it is quite plausible that tension might occur much later in this group because it is structured and task oriented from the beginning.

In their first stage, Herbert and Trist (1953) described members' anxiety over termination, which would not ordinarily be expected until near the end of a group. However, this was a student training group in which members sometimes were unable to continue in the group. If the group was especially meaningful to them, anxiety about termination could occur early in the group. This is a case when structural characteristics are misleading with regard to process. There were one or two other less-striking reversals noted in this study, an example of which is the group's being able to work on a problem. In this case, disagreement on sequential placement seems less noteworthy. Herbert and Trist (1953) see this behavior for a single group occurring earlier than we would predict, based on observations of a large number of groups. However, there is a noticeable trend in this study that indicates the authors are primarily concerned with first-stage behaviors. They describe approximately twenty-eight behaviors in the first stage, four in the second, and four in the third. This could be due to a sufficiently large turnover that resulted from the group's never moving beyond first-stage issues.

In a narrow-band study of deaf retardates by Landau (1968), the lack of members' ability to think abstractly may have made it difficult for them to express their complex feelings. The discussion of concrete facts instead of feelings could be viewed as a form of defensiveness; however, in this case it may be due more to intellectual limitations, thus explaining the reversal. In terms of limitations, intellectual capacity may explain another reversal in perceiving common shared feelings or bonds growing out of a group process.

Suspicion and lack of trust were characteristic of a narrow-band group composed of prisoners in the Martinson (1967) study. This led to a reversal. In a narrow-band group of narcotics addicts (Osberg & Berliner, 1956), differences in behavior descriptions occurred as a result of special group characteristics.

Schutz (1958) offers another model in which there are one or two reversals. These deviations are difficult to explain and may be accepted simply as differences in the sequencing of some behaviors. The "time limited contract" in a study by Stoller (1968a) was a special characteristic that led to independence from the leader and allowed the leader in turn to become a member sooner than predicted by the model in this text.

Table 5.4 gives the impression that except for some intermingling gaps there seems to be a fairly wide range of behaviors represented across categories. As compared with two-stage studies there are proportionally fewer gaps and a wider distribution of behavioral descriptions. The average number of descriptions is about equal, seventeen for two-stage studies and eighteen for three-stage studies. The degree of correspondence between our model and three-stage studies is remarkable, especially with regard to the diversity of theoretical approaches. Elimination of contaminating variables developing from special group characteristics, together with consideration of the difficulty in the conversion of behavioral descriptions, strengthens our belief that the model in this text provides a good representative flow of events.

Four-Stage Models

Of the seventeen studies conceptualizing a four-stage model (see Table 5.6), those of Thorpe and Smith (1953) and Tuckman (1965) were concerned primarily with a developmental process. Thorpe and Smith represent a therapy orientation, but their work was with a special population—drug addicts. Tuckman, on the other hand, represents a T-group orientation. The work of these authors in describing behaviors is less comprehensive than most of the other authors who focus primarily on group growth and development. However, these two authors do cover a wide distributional range.

Neither study includes much commentary on events comprising the middle range of issues. The flow described by Tuckman agrees with the authors' model more than does the one proposed by Thorpe and Smith. In fact, there appears to be a greater degree of correspondence between Tuckman's model and the model presented in this book than with any other of the four-stage models.

There are several obvious reversals or disagreements between the sequence of events described by Thorpe and Smith and the one proposed in our model. There is good correspondence between the two models on events occurring near the end of the group. The real departure seems to be on those events that occur in the beginning of a group. Thorpe and Smith's model is narrow-band in that their work is based on drug addicts; the differences seem to be due primarily to special population characteristics. Generally speaking, as a group, drug addicts are mistrustful and have a tendency to blame others for their condition.

These two characteristics tend to postpone the development and expression of some behaviors ordinarily expected to occur earlier. For example,

Table 5.6. Behavioral Characteristics of Four-Stage Studies

Cohen-Smith Phases	1	2	3	4	5	6	7	8	9	10
Behavioral Characteristics	1-4	5-16	17-43	44-59	60-68	69-90	91-101	102-122	123-135	136-144
Studies										
Barron and Krulee (1948) T-Group	1	1,1,1,1 1,2	1,1,1,1,1 2,2,2,2,2 2,3,4	1,2,2,2	1,1		2,3,3,3 4,4	2,2,2,2 2,3,3,3 3,4	2,2,3 3,3,4 4	4,4
Battegay (1966) Therapy		1	2,3				4,4	2,2,3,4	3	
Cooper, E.C. (1968) N-B* - Therapy			2,2,2,2 2,2,2,3 3,3	2,2,3,3	1,2,3	1	1,4	2,2,2,2 3,3,3,3 3,3,3,4	4	3
Dreikurs (1957) Therapy		3	3	2,2	1		3	1,3,3,3 4,4,4,4 4,4,4,4	4	
Geller (1962) Therapy	2	1,1,1 2,2,2 3	1,1,1,1,1 1,1,1,2,2 2,2,2,2,2 3,3,3,3,3	1,1,2,2		1,1	4	4,4,4	4,4,4	

*N-B = narrow-band studies
**Studies with primary focus on group growth and development

Table 5.6. (cont.)

Cohen-Smith Phases	1	2	3	4	5	6	7	8	9	10
Behavioral Characteristics	1-4	5-16	17-43	44-59	60-68	69-90	91-101	102-122	123-135	136-144
Studies										
Gleuck (1968) T-Group								1,2,2,3 4,4	3,3	4
Hadden (1968) Therapy	1	2	2	2,2		4		2,3,3,4 4	3	
Shambaugh and Kanter (1969) N-B* - T-Group		1,2,2	1,1,1,2 2,2,2,2 3,3,4	1,1,4	2,4,4		2,3,4	2,2,2,3 3,3,4,4 4	4,4	3
Mann (1953) Therapy		1	1,1,1,2					1,2,3,3 4,4	3	
Mann and Semrad (1948) Therapy	1	1	1,2,2	2				2,2,2,2 3,3,3		4
Miller (1967) N-B*		1		2				4		4
Modlin and Faris (1956) N-B* - Task	1		1,1,2 2,2,3	3	2,3	3,3,3,4	1,3,3 4,4	2,3,3	1,1,1,3 3,4,4	3

*N-B = narrow-band studies
**Studies with primary focus on group growth and development

Table 5.6. (cont.)

Cohen-Smith Phases	1	2	3	4	5	6	7	8	9	10
Behavioral Characteristics	1-4	5-16	17-43	44-59	60-68	69-90	91-101	102-122	123-135	136-144
Studies										
Schindler (1958) Therapy			2		4	1		2,3,4		
Shellow, Ward, and Rubenfeld (1958) Therapy		1,1	1,1,1,2 2,2,2,3 3,4	1,1,2	2,3,4	2	4	2,2,4,4 4	4,4	
Thorpe and Smith (1953)** N-B*	3	3,3	1,1,1,3				2	4,4,4,4	4	
Tuckman (1965)** T-Group		1,1,2 3	1,2,2	2,2		1,3	3	3,4	4,4	
Wolf (1949) Therapy	1	1	2,2,2,3		2,3			1,2,2,3 3,3,4	4,4	

*N-B = narrow-band studies
**Studies with primary focus on group growth and development

behaviors associated with covert appraisal and testing through a lack of trust take longer to resolve. Adjustment to the group situation and acceptance of each other along with acceptance of responsibility take longer for the drug addict to achieve. So there seems to be a logical basis for the differences between the two models.

The seventeen four-stage studies in Table 5.6 are composed of three with a T-group orientation, ten with a therapy group orientation, and four narrow-band groups. This indicates that most of the work on development done by four-stage theorists has been carried out by those authors who have a therapy orientation, as is also true of three-stage conceptualizations of group development. On the average, twenty-one behavioral events are described by four-stage authors. This average is higher than for three-stage studies, which in turn was slightly higher than for two-stage models. Thus it seems to be true that the more stages conceptualized, the greater the number of behaviors noted.

Inspection of the study profiles in Table 5.6 indicates less correspondence between the model in this text and four-stage models than there is between our model and two- and three-stage studies. These four-stage studies cover a wider range of behaviors than do the two- or three-stage studies. But gaps and proportionally more reversals remain. In terms of frequency of behavioral descriptions falling in each category (see Table 5.7 and Figure 5.1) the same patterns are noted as those that emerged from the two- and three-stage studies. There is some representation across all categories but with a bimodal distribution, more heavily weighted toward the end of group life. Decreased defensiveness and increased experimentation is stressed, followed by behaviors related to members' search for position/definition: primary group transferences/countertransferences. The least emphasis is placed on acquaintance and termination.

Regarding the categories lightly touched on and the gaps in the flows, it seems that with a greater than average number of behavior descriptions there is a tendency for more clustering around the popularized or dominant themes. One possible explanation for the exaggerated emphasis placed on behaviors associated with defenses lies in the majority representation of therapy group studies in the three- and four-stage authors.

The special characteristics of narrow-band studies have some effect on the expected flow as predicted by our model. One example is the study of spouses under stress (wives of hemodialysis patients) by Shambaugh and Kanter (1969). In this case the seeming denial of hostilities and need for independence and assumed responsibilities may have been influencing factors leading to an alteration of flow.

Another narrow-band study, by Shellow, Ward, and Rubenfeld (1958), involved juvenile delinquents whose suspiciousness and sociopathy seemed to demonstrate the effects of special group characteristics on the normally expected flow.

Table 5.7. Four-Stage Studies—Frequency of Behavior-Description Entries

Cohen-Smith Phases	1	2	3	4	5	6	7	8	9	10	Total Across Categories
Behavioral Characteristics	1-4	5-16	17-43	44-59	60-68	69-90	91-101	102-122	123-135	136-144	
Studies											
Totals	7	31	95	27	17	12	22	101	33	8	353
Total 1st Stage	5	18	29	7	4	5	3	4	3		78
Total 2nd Stage	1	8	44	16	5	1	3	28	2		108
Total 3rd Stage	1	5	19	3	4	4	8	33	10	3	90
Total 4th Stage			3	1	4	2	8	36	18	5	77

Number of Four-Stage Studies: 17
Mean Behavioral Descriptions: 21

Modlin and Faris's work (1956) was based on professional hospital psychiatric staff who were members of a group in which there was a task orientation. In the group the flow was slightly altered from that of our model. Some of the behaviors described deviated from the expected flow. These behaviors are related to more explicit goals. Furthermore, the members' roles are well defined and based on the external structure.

Because of methodological artifact, some reversals are readily explainable, others are not. It is becoming apparent that narrow-band reversals are easier to explain than are differences in other theoretical orientations. Concrete situational characteristics provide a sounder basis for predicting deviations from the expected. Differences in terms of different theoretical approaches are not as easily explained.

Models with More than Four Stages

There are only three studies incorporated in this survey that hypothesize more than four stages. (See Table 5.8). Two of these are direct attempts at describing a developmental flow. Of these three studies one involves a T-group orientation, one involves an encounter group orientation, and one involves a therapy group orientation. One author hypothesizes five stages, one six stages, and another twelve stages. They describe an average of thirty-seven behavioral descriptions, which is considerably more than the average for two-, three-, or four-stage studies. As the number of stages increases, there is also an increase in the average number of behavioral descriptions: seventeen for two stages, eighteen for three stages, twenty-one for four stages, thirty-seven for more than four stages. This trend leads to the hypothesis that there is a positive correlation between the number of stages an author conceptualizes and the comprehensiveness with which he views the group developmental process.

Observation of the flow of behavioral descriptions in Table 5.8 indicates that there is some agreement on sequencing, but it is not quite as pronounced as for the two-, three-, and four-stage profiles. While a wide distributional range is present, the distribution is uneven. In fact, all three distributions are skewed. Martin and Hill (1957), assuming a therapy orientation, and Rogers (1967), with an encounter orientation, place heavy emphasis on decreased defensiveness and increased experimentation and on group potency. Martin and Hill also emphasize behaviors associated with distributive leadership. On the other hand, Rogers does not offer a single behavioral description related to distributive leadership.

In accordance with the model presented in this book, Martin and Hill, and Rogers are concerned with issues occurring near the end of group life. This is in striking contrast with the work by Semrad and Arsenian (1951).

Table 5.8. Behavioral Characteristics of Studies with More than Four Stages

Cohen-Smith Phases	1	2	3	4	5	6	7	8	9	10
Behavioral Characteristics	1-4	5-16	17-43	44-59	60-68	69-90	91-101	102-122	123-135	136-144
Studies										
Martin and Hill (1957)** Therapy		1,1	1,2,2,2 2,4,5	1,4,4, 4,5		3,4	1,1,2,3 3,4,4,5 5,5,6,6 6,6,6	2,2,3,3 3,3,4,6 6	3,3,3 3,5,6 6,6,6	6
Rogers (1967)** Encounter-Therapy	1	1,1,1 1,1	1,1,3	1,2,3		3		3,4,4,5 5,6,7,8 9,9,9,9 11,12	4,10 10,11 11	
Semrad and Arsenian (1951) T-Group	1,1	1,1,1	1,1,1,1,1 1,2,2,3,3 3,4,4,4,5 5	3,3,4	5	1	5	4,5,5	4,4	4

**Studies with primary focus on group growth and development

They discuss events or behaviors related to primary group transferences. The Semrad and Arsenian study was based on data collected from groups whose goal was the teaching of group dynamics through group process.

These groups were comprised of hospital staff, including psychologists, social workers, nurses, psychiatrists, residents, and graduate students. Group composition and a training emphasis were significant aspects of these groups. These factors could have slowed the process or directed greater attention to issues as they occurred. The fact that there was an attempt to teach group members how to conduct groups might account for more time spent on intellectualizing the process as it occurred. This would have enabled members to improve their understanding of the interaction and be cognizant of leadership intervention choices.

The group composition and environment would also have tended to make members guarded, suspicious, constrained, and defensive. This might have tended to retard the group and would seem to explain the considerable emphasis on members' search for position/definition: primary group transferences/countertransferences. It is quite possible that the lack of emphasis on decreased defensiveness and increased experimentation, in striking contrast to most other studies reported, could be due to the group's not really reaching this stage of development. (See Table 5.9.)

It is interesting to note that a proportionally higher number of studies (two out of three) conceptualizing more than four stages of group development are primarily concerned with sequence-of-growth phenomena. If an individual is interested primarily in doing work in group growth and development, he seems more likely to propose more stages of development and more behavioral descriptions. The two two-stage studies that focus on developmental process average approximately forty behavioral descriptions. Even though the Bennis and Shepard (1956) study is classified as having two stages, each of these two stages has three substages. Bennis and Shepard are really describing six segments of group life. In this respect, they are moving in the direction of a more comprehensive look at a complex process and are attempting to isolate more analyzable components.

Summary

In most cases it seems that a two-stage ("beginning and end") concept of group growth and development and a three-stage ("beginning, middle, and end") concept are both oversimplified. This reduction of a highly complex process of group interaction to two or three phases, as reflected in the literature, may be due to an inability to deal with group phenomena because of inadequate methodology. The authors feel, however, that this oversimplification represents a disservice.

Table 5.9. Studies with More than Four Stages—Frequency of Behavior-Description Entries

Cohen-Smith Phases	1	2	3	4	5	6	7	8	9	10	Total Across Categories
Behavioral Characteristics	1-4	5-16	17-43	44-59	60-68	69-90	91-101	102-122	123-135	136-144	
Studies											
Totals	2	10	20	10	0	3	15	25	15	3	103
Total 1st Stage	2	10	6	2	0	0	2	0	0	0	22
Total 2nd Stage	0	0	6	1	0	0	1	2	0	0	10
Total 3rd Stage	0	0	4	3	0	2	2	5	4	0	20
Total 4th Stage	0	0	1	3	0	1	2	4	2	0	13
Total 5th Stage	0	0	3	1	0	0	3	2	1	2	12
Total 6th Stage	0	0	0	0	0	0	5	4	4	1	14

Table 5.9. (cont.)

Cohen-Smith Phases	1	2	3	4	5	6	7	8	9	10
Behavioral Characteristics	1-4	5-16	17-43	44-59	60-68	69-90	91-101	102-122	123-135	136-144
Studies										
Total 7th Stage	0	0	0	0	0	0	0	1	0	1
Total 8th Stage	0	0	0	0	0	0	0	1	0	1
Total 9th Stage	0	0	0	0	0	0	0	4	0	4
Total 10th Stage	0	0	0	0	0	0	0	0	2	2
Total 11th Stage	0	0	0	0	0	0	0	1	2	3
Total 12th Stage	0	0	0	0	0	0	0	1	0	1

Number of Studies with More than Four Stages: 3
Mean Behavioral Descriptions: 34

Within our model there is a bimodal frequency distribution of behavioral events described by studies in the literature. (See Table 5.10 and Figure 5.1.) Most attention was given to decreased defensiveness and increased experimentation, followed by behavioral events associated with members' search for position/definition: primary group transferences/countertransferences. However, there was behavioral representation from the literature in all ten categories.

There is a clear trend indicating agreement on a described behavioral flow between the majority of studies reported in the literature and our model. Of course, a number of gaps and reversals in behavioral representation occurred. Most of these discrepancies can be explained in terms of special characteristics, features, or emphases in the studies where gaps or reversals occurred.

Even though many reversals could be explained in terms of study idiosyncrasies, a number of others seemed to be due to methodological artifact. One example relevant to reversals is the problem of converting or translating the behavior described by an author in order to match it with a behavioral description categorized in our model. Due to vagueness or unclear contextual meaning it was necessary to force-fit some described behaviors, thereby increasing the probability of error. It is believed that inescapable, occasional mismatching may have caused some unwarranted and misleading reversals. Very few reversals seemed to be due to basic theoretical differences in approach.

From the inspection of the tables containing the study profiles, it is evident that a few theme categories are poorly represented by the behavioral descriptions taken from the literature. This may reflect author bias, research limitations, the nature and composition of the groups studied, trainer style, therapeutic orientation, or unintended omission.

The preponderance of research focuses on the search for position/definition, transferences, and defenses. Whether intentional or unintentional, many other important aspects of group life seem neglected. Our model suggests that some other salient issues needing attention are the acquaintance process, sharpened interactions, norm crystallization/enforcement, defensive unification, distributive leadership, and termination. (See Table 5.11.)

Based on type of theoretical orientation to groups (see Table 5.12) or author emphasis on developmental sequence as a primary focus (see Table 5.13), an attempt was made to select some of the reasons for either the bimodal or skewed frequency distributions. No consistent pattern emerged except for a much higher percentage of skewed distributions for narrow-band groups than for other types of groups. (See Table 5.12.) Narrow-band groups also seemed to have more reversals than other types of groups.

Listing those studies with specific emphasis on development and then dividing these according to theoretical orientation (see Table 5.13) revealed

A Theory of Group Growth and Development 213

Table 5.10. Summary of All Studies—Frequency of Behavior-Description Entries

Cohen-Smith Phases	1	2	3	4	5	6	7	8	9	10
Behavioral Characteristics	1-4	5-16	17-43	44-59	60-68	69-90	91-101	102-122	123-135	136-144
Studies										
Grand Total	20	90	231	83	27	66	71	256	109	22	975

Table 5.11. Breakdown of Studies According to Theoretical Orientation and Number of Stages Conceptualized

Number of Stages	T-Group	Other Growth Groups	Therapy Groups	Narrow-Band Groups	Total
Two Stages	2	1	0	6	9
Three Stages	5	3	10	2	20
Four Stages	3	0	10	4	17
More than Four Stages	1	1	1	0	3
Total	11	5	21	12	49

Table 5.12. Breakdown of Studies According to Theoretical Orientation and Type of Distribution*

Studies	Even	Skewed	Bimodal	Dispersed	Total
T-Group	6	3	3		12
Other Growth Groups		3		1	4
Total T-Group and Other Growth Groups	6	3	6	1	16
Therapy	6	1	7	2	5	21
N-B Groups	2	4	3	3	12
Total	14	4	17	5	9	49

*Note: These are studies that do *not* focus particularly on phase or stage progression in group growth and development. They speak of specific behaviors at certain points in the life of the group but do not conceptualize concerning them. Therefore, some inferences have been made by Cohen and Smith.

no consistent pattern that might differentiate groups with this focal emphasis from all other studies included in the survey. Based on the totals of all groups, it was noted that approximately half the distributions were skewed toward the later phases of group life. This helps to explain why the greatest emphasis was placed on those behaviors categorized as being related to decreased defensiveness and increased experimentation. Only three out of the forty-nine studies displayed distributions skewed toward the early phases of group life.

Table 5.13. Breakdown of Studies Focusing on Group Growth and Development According to Theoretical Orientation and Type of Distribution

	Distribution				
Studies	Even	Skewed	Bimodal	Dispersed	Total
T-Group	4	1	1		6
Other Growth Groups		1		1	2
Total T-Group and Other Growth Groups	4	1	2	1	8
Therapy		1		1	2
N-B Groups		1	1	1	3
Total	4	1	4	3	13

In attempting to compare other models of group growth and development with our model, some artifacts were noted. These artifacts were those inherent in studies selected for review or those associated with the method of comparison. Some studies were based on the observation of a single group; others seemed to have some primary concern besides developmental phenomena.

Another problem encountered was time dimension. Groups studied and reported in the literature varied considerably in length. Sessions lasted from a few days to many months. T-groups tend to have a clearly limited time span at the outset while therapy groups are often open ended from the beginning.

The classification of some studies by number of stages was occasionally a problem. For example, although Bennis and Shepard described two phases, each phase contained three subphases. Although the model in this text classifies the study as having two stages, a tenable argument could be made for classifying it as having six segments or stages of group life.

A problem previously mentioned is the one of matching behavioral descriptions contained in our model with those given in various studies. In most cases a match could be made. However, there were times when an educated force-fit was made. There were other times when an "equivalence" decision could not be made and the description was not included. Contributing to these problems of matching were idiosyncracies, lack of behavioral context, or vagueness in the description of behavior. In the cases where behavioral descriptions were matched but not entirely equivalent, reversals or interrupted distributional sequences may have resulted. In order to avoid biasing study flow profiles in favor of our model, the judges who matched behaviors were not knowledgeable about the model.

To establish a useful theory of group growth and development, it is necessary to distinguish clearly between the descriptive and prescriptive elements of such a theory. Bennis and Shepard (1956), through the incorporation of "barometric events," and Fiebert (1968) attempt this but do not adequately separate descriptions of events from prescribed interventions. The major value of integrating descriptive with prescriptive elements in developing an intervention theory is effectively realized only after separating the descriptive from the prescriptive elements.

There is no model of group growth and development in the literature surveyed that is specific enough in relating to concrete group experiences. Bennis and Shepard (1956) candidly point out that they did not reproduce the concrete group experience from which their theory was drawn. They do come close though, through their use of a narrative presentation of events during the life of a hypothetical group. However, in addition to being specific, a good theory of group growth and development should be comprehensive. It should offer a sufficient number of descriptive statements to cover a wide range of behavioral occurrences found throughout the life of a group.

Few, if any, of the studies could be called comprehensive. There has been a tendency to oversimplify developmental group processes; future work should attempt to come to grips with these complexities.

Only one other author, Tuckman (1965), proposed a model of group growth and development that is able to incorporate or subsume a variety of diverse groups within its descriptive framework. Tuckman's model, as well as the one in this text, presents a developmental framework that is related to a variety of groups regardless of their theoretical orientation.

The ability of a model of developmental phenomena to relate to concrete group experience provides a basis for meeting the remaining four criteria. Incorporation of specific behavioral events or descriptions makes such a model researchable. These basic components provide a necessary part of the methodology for its own evaluation. By virtue of specific behavioral components such a model should be heuristic and helpful to the practitioner. It should also be effective in providing tools for training, as the prospective group leader or therapist would be much less bewildered by vague generalities. Because of a lack of relation to specific behaviors, nearly all of the current models in the literature fall short of meeting these criteria.

Generally speaking, the comparison of a number of developmental models with our model reveals an agreement with its proposed sequential flow of behavioral events. This relationship seems to hold regardless of individual problems and diverse theoretical orientations to group process, and, in many cases, it is true even for groups with special characteristics.

A number of variables such as group size, composition, environment, goals, and style of leadership probably result in idiosyncratic developmental flows. However, most groups still support our hypothesis that a number of dominant theme topics must be dealt with to some extent and that the sequencing of events across all groups will be much the same.

CHAPTER 6

Some Questions and Answers and an Experience

This book has attempted to present an approach to group leadership that is effective across a wide spectrum of diverse group orientations. We have demonstrated, for example, the utilization of the Critical-Incident Model in the psychoanalytic, nondirective, encounter, and T-group approaches. There remains one other area in which the values, design strategies, and suggested technologies of the group leader become most integrated and evident. In the answers to the probing questions asked by advanced graduate students in training to become group leaders, some of the subtleties of leadership emerge, as well as some of the distinguishing features of our specific orientation. This chapter is a personal answer to the questions most often asked, in an attempt to stimulate and guide further evaluation of the reader's orientation to these issues.

The questions, grouped into four categories, relate to the basic concerns of trainees. The questions in the first category, The Special Nature of Groups, deal with issues ranging from the value of groups as a medium for change to specific questions concerning group process and the place of the democratic ethic in groups.

The second category, Theory: Its Role in Design Strategy and Interventions, attempts to clarify the authors' belief that leadership interventions are most effective when based on an explicit personal theory of change and communicated to the group at appropriate times via planned theory inputs (PTI's) and spontaneous theory inputs (STI's).

Leadership and Interventions in Special Circumstances, the third category, attempts to summarize our concept of leadership and also to answer some specific concerns of trainees, that is, some "What if?" questions, presenting our theoretical rationale for specific designs and interventions.

The final category of questions, Leadership and Authority, receives little attention in some groups; however, since our orientation is the T-group and our focus is on process in order to effect change, this issue does arise in various forms at different stages of group life. Dealing with authority and other kinds of conflict is considered essential to both personal and group growth.

The "experience" at the end of this chapter is an account of a critical incident in a T-group that involved the issue of authority. It illustrates clearly the underlying issues and the process of resolution.

THE SPECIAL NATURE OF GROUPS

1. *Your approach to change has to do, in some manner, with groups. Why groups? What is so special about groups? If you have a theory of change and your goal is to induce or create a change, why use the group?*

For many people, it is necessary to establish a special kind of world where things can happen—a world in which they are not alone, where the presence of others is intensely felt and studied. We try to establish a learning process by bringing about a very human experience, a very warm experience. There seems little doubt that people in groups go through some kind of pain, confrontation, and struggle—not as ends in themselves but rather in the service of personal growth and creativity. It should be noted, however, that intensity of emotional expression must not automatically be equated with "significance" or "importance." To indulge oneself in "a sauna bath of emotions" may be an interesting activity, but it does not guarantee growth or maturity by itself.

A grand theater is not required, just a group situation in which the participants know that they can take on a situation, a problem of reality in the environment, work through it with guidance, and win. In an important sense, the group is a sort of human Rorschach or field of forces in the context of which the individual defines himself by working through ambiguities. Individual members are encouraged to use their talents and abilities much more effectively through the supportive medium of the group process.

The essence of the group process, as we see it, is that an individual is encouraged to have a personal growth experience and to acquire certain knowledge, skills, and values—within a framework that tries to foster generalization from the small group to the biggest group of all, society.

2. *It would appear that you advocate and practice a certain faith in the group process—at times an almost religious faith. This approach seems especially apparent in the newer growth groups stressing closeness and intimacy. Is this type of faith really necessary?*

It appears to be a type of faith primarily because it involves a commitment to the application of a certain theory of change. There is a certain religious quality to belief systems. It is exciting to be committed—turned on and tuned in— to a particular theory of change, whether religious or secular. It really could be something as old-fashioned as a "noble goal"—to gather people into a group; to believe that within that group it is possible to love, to relate, to be open and honest; to believe that it is possible to help change the world sensibly and realistically. As for the newer growth groups that focus on disclosure and intimacy, they seem to require that certain members go through certain "rites of passage," involving, in some cases, an almost religious conversion.

3. *Is it necessary, as a sort of maturation process, that groups go through these "rites of passage?"*

We think this is true. In a religious model (Judaism, for example), you are circumcised, then bar mitzvahed (confirmed), then married, then you have children, and so on. Each is a ritual, whether religious or secular, taking one through a part of the life cycle. A group has a life—it is born—when people come together. Then it matures and develops certain rites. We are aware that there is a danger in reifying the group process, but there is a greater danger in ignoring certain inevitable group processes. A rite of passage is, innately, neither good nor bad; it is simply an outward sign of maturation as defined by whatever society one happens to be born into. The rites of passage in a group would be those occasions in which members experience a sense of shared growth—when each person begins to realize that this is more than just a collection of individuals, that a miniature society is being created with all the problems of the real world reflected in its workings.

If we, as members of a given group, can begin to understand the conflicts, frustrations, and principles involved in working together harmoniously and productively, perhaps there is hope in trying to tackle the problems of society as a whole. It is a good, decent start to making things better.

4. *You have mentioned "group style" at various times, in connection with groups evolving and changing. Are there "group styles" that evolve, and are they connected and predictable?*

We feel quite certain that one of the interesting things that you can always rely on happening in a group is that the group will change in an evolutionary way. Moreover it will grow, at times unevenly. At one stage, members may be able to handle information exchange adequately but still be exhibiting a child-like dependency or an inability to resolve conflict, while during the same stage they may be able to give and receive feedback very appropriately. The competent leader must be able to recognize and selectively deal with each of these distinctive group functions.

It has been our experience that groups go through a limited number of (distinct) stages in their evolutionary growth. Within different stages, there would appear to be one or more "group styles" characteristic of such stages. In the beginning stages, for example, when members have completed the business of getting acquainted, they begin testing each other out, exhibiting the first major signs of subtle conflict. At first, the group style is one of "sharpshooting" or taking "pot shots" at each other. One group member will say or do something that one or more other members will sharply criticize. It is as if members were jumping in and out from behind trees, shooting and being shot at.

The group often passes into a second style best described as "battleship," since all the guns of the group swing as one unit and focus on one group member at a time. This style usually evolves because one or more members may be dominating and/or deviant, thus encouraging group solidification in order to "understand and deal with" this member. We have often pointed out the analogy of the guns swinging around the circle, looking for the next target.

A typical next style to be developed is one termed "psychoanalysis" or "dissection." This style is the first (although naive) group attempt, among members, to be helpful to one another. It usually involves group members encouraging the "patient" to tell about his early life. Questions to this member are usually started with "Why did you . . . "; then the group gives plausible and rational explanations for the member's present concerns based on earlier experiences. This is not usually very helpful to the member, since he has undoubtedly heard these explanations many times previously, and, moreover, it has little effect on changing his current behavior.

Both the "battleship" style and the "psychoanalysis" style arouse enough anxiety and frustration in the group to bring about a split between those members who would feel safer exploring a concrete *task* and those members who would prefer to continue emphasizing *process;* this is potentially a crisis period for the group and is sometimes characterized as a conflict between "personals," i.e., those who wish to explore feelings and relationships, and "structurals," i.e., those members who wish to avoid feelings and personal relationships and deal instead with objective, well-structured, concrete tasks.

When this conflict has been successfully managed, the subsequent T-group styles are essentially those involved in disclosure, intimacy, and mutual support for personal growth. It should be mentioned, however, that certain types of encounter groups automatically begin their activities with an orientation toward feelings and away from tasks. In these situations, the "split" mentioned above will seldom arise, since members enter with expectations of experiencing a certain class of personally oriented events.

In therapy groups that contain resistant members, this same split usually emerges in a more subtle form: several members will prefer to discuss nonpersonal, superficial, there-and-then events, while other members will prefer to discuss personal events in the here-and-now. Beginning group leaders, at this point, are often puzzled as to the "correct" approach. We are sure that there is no one "right" approach, but rather a multiplicity of approaches from which the group leader must choose that which most nearly meets the needs and goals of the group in managing such conflicts.

5. *You have mentioned values many times. If there is going to be a leader, and there are participants in a group, how does "democracy" come about? What is the role of "democracy" in the group?*

A democratic leader cannot function autonomously. He has to function within a framework that permits the democratic ethic to be applied. Perhaps it may best be thought of as an approach to some ideal type, since we never quite reach a pure democracy. We are not even sure we would want to do so. A leader has to operate within certain realities that may be in conflict with democracy at times, while at the same time supporting the existence of individuals and groups whose value orientations are antithetical to democracy. In one narrow sense, then, the leader really sows the potential seeds for his own destruction. He must help make it possible for people to grow and develop and even to work against the democratic ethic, at times, if it is necessary. Within this framework, the group leader can make it possible for a group to work and move toward its farthest limits of creative potential.

This orientation is more than just an ideological value system. It has the practical effect of creating an atmosphere in which all group members feel concerned and important—and hence involved. This tends to free group members sufficiently to encourage attempts at new problem-solving behaviors, while at the same time developing a respect for alternate points of view. The democratic value system appears especially suited to bringing this effect about in the majority of instances. As members practice the democratic ethic with increasing maturity, including the increasing sharing of leadership functions, differences between the leader and group members decrease and the group as a whole advances more toward the democratic ideal.

We want our job as leaders to change in the group. It is a sign of maturity and growth when group members are able to take over and share the functions of leadership. When this state of "distributive leadership" has been reached, we have a distinct feeling of accomplishment. But we would not want to lose our sense of involvement—the feeling that we can intervene or initiate action at any time that seems to make sense.

It is certainly true that the leader must deal with significant differences in people, but if he persists in the application of the democratic process and is technically competent, he should be able to communicate to enough of the group what is going on at any given time. The group can learn from this and will not be likely to settle on extreme solutions. In a sense, each person has to struggle with his own sense or interpretation of the meaning of values, which is not a cognitive issue alone.

Ideally, if a democratic ethic is operating in the group, change emerges more slowly, provisionally, with more exasperation. Impatience is increased because members cannot impose solutions on others, but out of the process grow inevitable safeguards against the destruction of the work already accomplished. If such diversity of resources and open sharing is encouraged, a solid core of strength will develop to guard against attempts to subvert the goals of the group.

THEORY: ITS ROLE IN DESIGN STRATEGY AND INTERVENTIONS

6. *Can the group be considered a social field against which a person can see himself?*

Yes. The group, in this sense, becomes a sort of projective device against which each member interprets both his own behavior as well as other group members' behavior. The individual is faced, at least in the initial stages of the group, with an ambiguous situation within which he can find no definitive rules, no "right answers." It is from this struggle that group identity and personal maturity finally emerge.

There is still another sense in which the group can be considered under the concept of "field": specifically, the use of "force-field analysis" as a structural intervention. You can, for example, look at a group situation in terms of a field of "forces," just as in physics. You can identify certain forces as having certain valences. Of course the simplest attachment of valence is plus or minus, positive or negative valence. The relationship among these helping or hindering forces is such that there is usually some kind of result—which we observe as behavior.

To take a concrete example, suppose a group were blocked or at an impasse. We might well conceptualize the situation as one in which the impasse is the result of helping and hindering forces of approximately equal strength. In effect, what we want to do is to break up the "equilibrium" in order to help the group move toward some new configuration—what may be called a "change goal." In order to do this, we identify both the hindering and helping forces in the group; this and other steps in the intervention are carried out by both the members and the leader. We then take each of the hindering forces and treat it as a change goal in its own right, that is, in terms of forces that tend to help or hinder its achievements. We then set about trying to reduce the hindering forces, while at the same time giving support and reinforcement to the helping forces. Finally, in looking at this sequence, we usually come up with behavior prescriptions of what to do, operationally. That is the last step, because once members have reasonable alternatives, they are usually able to choose paths to other goals.

This orientation toward change goals is, of course, a matter of the leader's personal preference. One could just as easily translate the intervention strategy just described into another theoretical framework. In behavior modification terms, for example, the leader would first analyze the strength of the opposing behavior patterns. He would then break the complex opposing behaviors into more simple component parts in a sort of programmed approach. Finally, a procedure of shaping through successive approximations to a desired goal is instituted by reinforcing helping behaviors and extinguishing hindering behaviors. The terminology we employ does not appear to be nearly so important as the need to apply systematic methods of change and to record the results.

7. *What is the purpose of "design strategy" in groups?*
Design strategy may be seen as a continuum, from those groups that are so programmed that each move or sequence is predetermined to those groups that have no established plan other than to work with whatever the group chances to discuss each time it meets.

While both extremes do serve some special functions, neither rigid programming in which the group member must fit the system nor a loose design in which no planning is given and the system must fit all group members is entirely satisfactory. In the first instance, rigid programming cannot meet the needs of idiosyncratic and personal problems in the group; and, in the latter instance, the group is not always mature enough to determine which areas are important and which areas are irrelevant, especially during the beginning stages.

There must be a guided maturational process—which is the purpose of design strategy. Design strategy aids the group leader in facilitating the emergence of certain situations that, from research, past experience, and a knowledge of the needs of the group, will provide the appropriate learning opportunities important to all members. The following example will perhaps make these points clearer: a group composed of top-level management people might well be concerned with issues of authority, conflict, and decision making. Design strategy, for this group, might focus on an integrated sequence of discussions, activities, theory inputs, and structural interventions focused on these needed areas of interest.

Another group might well be composed of artists, musicians, and writers concerned with self-awareness, personal growth, and creativity. In this latter instance, a different design strategy would be utilized consisting of discussions and activities designed to stimulate these areas. In between these extremes are many areas of overlap.

It is clear that the group leader needs to acquire a wide range of techniques and approaches for effective group leadership. Practically speaking, there are two structural parts of a design strategy—time and content. The time element simply breaks a session down into a sequence of events that may be productive; the word "may" is used to indicate that a group leader should use a design that is flexible enough to shift its focus onto a number of related issues.

For example, the leader may decide to start the group by a brief ten-minute theory input on decision making. Perhaps he hopes the group will spend the next forty minutes discussing this, with a period of roughly ten minutes for a summing-up at the conclusion of the group. Let us imagine, however, that a personal problem of a group member emerges and must be dealt with before further progress is to be made. In this instance, the leader must shift to a design strategy that will provide help in managing the individual problem in such a way that it also allows for movement of the group.

The content aspect of design strategy requires that the group leader (a) be aware of the needs and purposes of the groups, (b) be aware of the recent group "themes," and (c) design a strategy that will incorporate both of these preceding factors.

Design strategy is more than simply conducting a series of activities and labeling it *post hoc* a "design strategy." It is important that the group leader actually record his design strategy as well as the consequences of certain types of design strategy. Did the group go forward or stop? Did the design increase the depth of discussion or cause a shift to a different level? It is not enough to initiate and carry out a design strategy; there must be continuous evaluation so that the effectiveness of interventions can be increased.

8. *Theory seems to be a very important part of the group process. How is it integrated with such things as structural interventions? What is the purpose of having theory?*

There are two aspects of theory as it applies to groups. The first deals with the particular design strategy the group leader utilizes to conceptualize his vision of how groups evolve and develop. This can range from no systematic theory at all, that is, simply starting a group and assuming it has some innate wisdom to discover its own way, to a well-programmed plan of operation.

Theory, in some form, would seem to provide the opportunity to develop procedures and techniques that may then be verified or rejected as they are tested. What each group leader vitally needs is a personal theory of group growth and development that will allow him systematically to test and "operationalize" his leadership. Otherwise, each group meeting becomes a chance, unpredictable, random occurrence, not related or generalizable to any other group or any other setting. This is hardly realistic.

The other aspect of theory deals with the participants. Theoretical knowledge should be an essential part of the group process, not an option. It is tied in with the integrated triad of knowledge, skills, and values that each participant should strive to acquire as a result of group participation. Hopefully, each participant should leave the group with more than just a warm feeling and a fuzzy thought that something important must have happened. There should be some attempt cognitively to understand the experience, to give the participants some understanding of group dynamics that they may carry to other groups. There is a certain harsh sterility associated with knowledge devoid of feeling, but there is futility and even potential danger in raw emotion divorced from knowledge.

Theory can serve many purposes in a group. It may help explain what is going on in terms of conceptual issues, such as the development of norms and standards; it may help to diagnose some deficiencies by comparing problem-solving processes of that group with a model; it can encourage the acting out of different points of view. These functions—and others—give theory an important place in group life.

9. *How much planning should be given to the theory inputs presented to a group—how much preplanning?*

In general, a great deal of care should be given to theory inputs: "mini-lessons" relating experiences to concepts. A leader should ideally be familiar enough with group theory and group design that he has at his fingertips a wide spectrum of applicable and relevant concepts easily grasped by the group. This is not to say that the group should be inundated by concepts in place of experience. Rather, there should be a balance between members' experience of some important phenomena and the application of a relevant concept. In groups that have gone through an especially difficult session in which emotions have reached an intense but satisfying level, it may be well to delay theory inputs until the beginning of the next session, in order not to run counter to the supportive mood or atmosphere.

Continuous discriminating judgment must be used in achieving a healthy balance between theory and experience. A group, for example, that is composed of university professors who might be predisposed toward a cognitive, intellectual level of functioning might, initially, be handled best by interventions that emphasize the affective qualities of their experiences. In a similar manner, a group that has had previous experience in nonintellectual, noncognitive, and emotional activities that excluded what did not deal with affect might have its "growth needs" served best by interventions that provide members with theories and concepts so that the early emphasis is on understanding affect and process. In both types of groups, the leader has the responsibility for effectively blending both experience and theory (affects and cognitions) in a manner that provides both intense involvement in the group and wide generalizations to other groups.

Generally speaking, a theory input can assume many forms. The leader can, for example, briefly interrupt the ongoing group activity with a conceptual input of one or two sentences; e.g., "Several members have made serious suggestions for the group to consider and we've pointedly ignored each one. That's been called the 'plop-flop' phenomenon." In other instances, the theory input may last from a few minutes to a formal presentation of twenty minutes or so.

There are two things to keep in mind, however: first, any theory input, regardless of length, effectively stops the ongoing activity. Thus it must be presented at a point of minimum dysfunctional interruption. Secondly, the aim is to have the theory input (a) help members to understand the phenomena at hand, and (b) provide a stimulus for further discussion and exploration.

It is sometimes preferable to plan long theory inputs either at the very beginning of a group session or at the end. In the former case it serves to bridge the gap between earlier sessions and the present session, as well as point toward areas the group might wish to explore. In the latter case, it provides a framework in which to summarize and understand what has transpired in the group, and it gives a sense of closure or unity. It is important, however, that the leader not allow himself to be placed in the role of a professional explainer and summarizer and, thus, to do the main work of the group.

LEADERSHIP AND INTERVENTIONS IN SPECIAL CIRCUMSTANCES

10. Some group leaders propose abdication of their leadership position in order to be "just another member." There must be a continuum here, but how do you feel about this issue?

There is a continuing debate involved here. Our position is that a leader is there for a purpose. He has specialized skills, talents, techniques, and experiences which place him in a position to facilitate personal growth and creativity. It is not a position he should hastily abdicate due to a false sense of "wanting to be human" or "wanting to be just another member of the group." In any case, an abdication is an artificial pronouncement, since one can renounce only the position of leader—not the responsibility. Even as a "member," the leader must choose to intervene, help, guide the group appropriately, and retard or accelerate discussion of certain areas.

This question may be, in one sense, a reflection of the old concerns among directive and nondirective therapists: should we lead or should we follow? The distinction is largely artificial, since a continuum of "directiveness" seems to exist. Even Carl Rogers, in his debate with B. F. Skinner, admitted that nondirective therapists do subtly guide and direct the therapy. The same analogy would seem to hold for group leadership. It is not certain or proved that a naive group could function effectively without any type of guidance by an experienced leader. Even if this were the case, would it not be quicker, safer, and more efficient to employ appropriate leadership skills? Allowing members to struggle and resolve their own problems, totally or even largely on their own, with greater time, expense, and pain, is no more "humane" or useful than providing members with a skilled guide.

11. What is the most important function of a group leader, as you see it?

The primary job of the group leader is to work continuously for the integration of knowledge, skills, and values . . . of knowing, doing, feeling. If a group leader becomes too absorbed in one as opposed to the others, then he is doing himself and the group a disservice. Every person at times separates his feelings somewhat from what is really going on and from what he is doing because it takes a lot of effort to bring out and utilize real feelings in connection with things that happen to you from day to day. Rather than having a person say, "These are things I know and do here" and "Over there are my feelings," the group leader helps to integrate these into a framework where such knowledge, skills, and values are functionally interdependent. He must have specific skills, techniques, and designs, of course, but all these are built on a particular group approach or orientation.

Our particular society has been criticized for emphasizing knowing and thinking at the expense of personal feelings. It is as if we are often limited by the very attributes that have made humans the dominant species—our intellect. It is often observed that members enter groups significantly alienated from any experience of true, undiluted affect, a situation akin to having been overinsulated from emotional stimuli in the world—a sort of joyless "deliberation" concerning the living of their lives.

The major function of the group leader, in these instances, is to help develop an atmosphere of group support that will allow such individuals to get in touch with their feelings (both positive and negative) and to experiment with more productive life styles. On the other hand, there are members who may be termed "sensitivity heads," who drift from group to group, seeking intense emotional experiences, but who are not sure what to do with them once they emerge and are unable to understand or conceptualize when and why such experiences arise in other groups.

The group leader should help these individuals integrate the experience of intense affect with a knowledge of interpersonal and group processes and with skills that increase their leadership and membership effectiveness. Thus the experience of affect becomes more than an idiosyncratic event and, therefore, more generalizable to the "real world."

The effective group leader tries to help provide those experiences most needed by individual members. A "narrow" group orientation that overemphasizes affect or intellect as a matter of policy would be ignoring the extremely important variable of individual differences.

12. *What are some of the unique problems new group leaders or leaders-in-training might be expected to encounter?*

One of the most anxiety-arousing problems facing new group leaders is a direct threat to their competence and ability. This may often come from an especially aggressive group member who, in an intense encounter, challenges the leader's abilities. The beginning leader, unsure of his new position, may easily be drawn into an emotional retaliation and lose control of the situation. This is not to say that the leader should never allow himself to become angry. It is necessary, however, to use that anger in the service of the group: to be aware of what is happening and to avoid being drawn into a defeating "win-lose" situation. The new leader should be aware that often a personal challenge is simply a surface issue, hiding more important underlying issues involving feelings about authority, society, father, etc.

A second, relatively unique, problem facing the new group leader is the attempt to seduce him into membership. In essence, the group states, "You're a great guy, so great, in fact, that we'd like to get to know you better as a member. Why don't you just tell us all your secrets and become one of us. We really like you." The new leader should be aware that this apparent "adoration" may be an attempt to remove the threat of leadership. As a "member," the leader would carry less importance, less ability to probe, and hence less anxiety and threat. If the compliment is legitimate, it should be treated in the manner in which we usually receive compliments. If, however, it is an attempt to seduce the leader into membership, it should be brought to the attention of the group.

Another likely major problem facing the beginning group leader is the temptation to act in ways that will please or impress the group members. The requirements of being a group leader, like those of a therapist, demand that decisions be made that often are not pleasing, but are necessary and important for effective group growth. It is not an easy situation, because group participants can be clever, even unintentionally, in trying to control the leader's behavior.

We would propose two basic summary assumptions. One is to act genuinely, and the second is to act in the best professional terms for the group. But the most important advice is to get in there, get involved, and stay with it.

13. *How do you know whether to intervene during a long period of silence or whether to let it continue?*

There are several different types of silence. Each has its own "sound" and purpose. In the beginning stages of a group there is the awkward, anxiety-based silence that continues to grow in intensity because no one "knows" what to talk about, no one wants to be the center of attention, and each member tries to avoid disclosing himself. The leader must be comfortable enough with himself to be free of the group's anxiety. A comfortable attitude of patient, calm expectation on the part of the leader is a good stance to adopt.

Silence, in the beginning stages, then, is seen as a generator of anxiety which, in turn, motivates member involvement and participation. A consistent interruption of the silence, by the leader, would short-circuit the anxiety build-up within the group and establish a precedent of excessive dependency upon the leader to do the group's work.

Another qualitatively different type of silence often arises immediately following the first intimate, personal statement or behavior by a group member. This, too, is an awkward silence, full of anxiety over how to respond and embarrassment over what was said. In this instance, however, the leader should step in with (a) support for the disclosed group member, and (b) recognition of the intensity of feelings shared by other group members. In this strategy, the leader both "models" the desired member behavior for the future and legitimizes the expression of strong feeling by encouraging its discussion. To remain silent in such a situation would result in punishment for the member who disclosed himself and an inhibiting anxiety on the part of other group members who might wish to behave similarly.

A third type of silence may arise when a group has made a significant step forward and, having resolved an issue, hesitates to go forward into deeper areas. Instead, members begin casting about for irrelevant topics to discuss. These topics, however, are punctuated by longer and longer periods of silence. In these instances, a leader might simply interpret these silences to the group in conjunction with what has just occurred in the group. The anxiety in these silences seldom rises above a moderate level.

Finally, there are those silences that follow an especially successful learning experience for one or more members. It might be the emergence of an important insight or the exhilaration of a "peak" experience. Regardless of the content of this kind of experience, there usually follows what we call the "human silence of comfort and contentment." The members somehow sense that something meaningful and important has touched them, and they will often sit for relatively long periods of silence, feeling quite comfortable and "alive." In these instances, the leader may not wish to add any comments or behavior that might break the mood. Often, this may prove to be a good breaking point for the group, offering members a chance for personal reflection.

In general, if a group grows and matures successfully together, there should be a high tolerance for the presence of silence and, as for wine, an appreciation of its many forms and qualities.

14. *What can a leader do when an intervention he attempts does not register with the group—in cases where the intervention is "on target" and in cases where the intervention is "off target?"*

Often a leader will make an intervention that is rapidly considered and then utilized by the group. At other times, the group may seem "not to hear" the intervention; that is to say, it does not register for some reason. Perhaps there will be only polite, token acceptance with no real consequences for the group. At other times, there may be open rejection of the intervention.

In these instances, the leader must as objectively as possible attempt to ascertain the validity of his observation. Whether the intervention is "off" or "on target" must be based on reasons separate from the personal ego needs of the leader. If the intervention is wrong, the leader should be able to accept this fact as useful feedback from the group—a point from which to examine the basis for his incorrect assumption. If the intervention is judged to be correct, the leader should stick with the intervention even if the group temporarily rejects it. This does not mean forcing the acceptance of an intervention in a harsh, punitive manner. It does mean saying something like this: "A few minutes ago, I suggested that such and such might be happening, and it was rejected. I think the rejection is important and, because I feel its importance for the group, I would like to call your attention to it for further discussion."

The fact that the group avoided the intervention—and the reasons they avoided it—may be very important in terms of the future growth of the group and should be pursued.

15. *How can a leader know when an issue is finished or completed? How can he know whether to set aside an issue as irrelevant or whether to let it "mature" and deal with it later? How do you handle a situation in which a group attempts to avoid an issue completely?*

When a decision has been made on some issue, a consensus of feeling expressed, and a commitment to the process made, the issue is finished. On the other hand, if decisions have been "railroaded" through, or various members have not been taken into consideration, or there is an undertone of frustration and hostility, the issue needs to be further explored and resolved. An issue may be said to be irrelevant if it does not further the progress of the group and does not seem to deal with either surface or underlying issues in the group.

The leader should be aware, however, that the surface discussion of an issue that may seem irrelevant may actually be serving to help the group avoid dealing with a more intense and personal issue. It would seem wise, in these instances, to point out these observations to the group and watch for any change in behavior.

There are some issues, of course, that emerge in different form throughout the life of the group. The issue of leadership-membership is one, and the issue of acquaintance-intimacy is another. When a group has accomplished a significant step forward in intimacy, it is generally felt to be unwise to push immediately for more intense disclosure and intimacy. Rather, the group should be allowed to move on to other relevant issues, while the just-finished process in one area is allowed to "sink in" and be absorbed possibly as a new group norm. Later, the issue may arise again and further steps may be taken with the issue.

16. *What are the problems involved in dealing with members who are overly defensive or uninvolved observers? How do you change these types of sets?*

As with anxiety and silence, there are several different types of defensiveness and uninvolvement. In one type of defensiveness, the member responds to feedback in a hostile manner. In this case, rather than comment directly upon the member's defensiveness, essentially confronting him, we prefer to shift into a discussion of the difficulties involved in being both a giver and a receiver of feedback. The giver of feedback is faced with the problem of taking a certain risk, of exposing his feelings and judgment, all of which may make him vulnerable to other people's responses. On the other hand, the receiver is in a binding situation with his own self-image. One of the things that gets in the way of both giving and receiving feedback is a sense of aloneness.

Indifference or uninvolvement can also result from a more subtle underlying feeling of defensiveness. In this instance, we might resort to the use of, say, a structural intervention—in which we can indicate to the group that one of the clear things going on is that some of the people have a feeling of being with it, and some do not. We would probably ask the people who are involved to come into the middle of the group and those who feel uninvolved to sit on the outside. The members in the middle would then discuss, for a few moments, what might account for some of the differences. After a period of time, those who feel uninvolved are asked to talk about their uninvolvement. This gives each subgroup a chance to look at the opposite orientation and to become involved in managing the differences. This is often helpful in resolving differences.

Another type of defensiveness is associated with risk—uncertain situations in which the member does not know either the kinds of outcomes that are possible or the probabilities of their occurrence. When the member asks for certainty, we try to help him and the group explore the alternatives realistically. But when the "chips are down," it still amounts to deciding to take a risk—creative risk taking. Because members of the group, with the help of the leader, develop and structure this atmosphere as they go along, there *can* be a genuine kind of comfort in risk taking that can come about as a result of expressing these personal feelings in a sharing atmosphere.

17. *How do you decide when to "open someone up" and when to "keep him closed?" How do you accomplish the latter?*

We strongly disagree with the orientation that allows members to be "opened up" and made vulnerable just for the sake of opening them up. "Opening up" a member, to us, means more than just getting behind some defenses and eliciting some intense emotions. In its full sense, opening someone up means exposing him to a wider range of choices and alternatives than he was previously aware of. It means allowing him to be more spontaneous in his emotional expression and yet at the same time preserving a "creative discipline" over his behavior. Surely we have learned from individual therapy that one does not remove something from the patient without helping him substitute one or more positive alternatives in its place. If this is what is meant by "opening up," we concur with its use and results.

On the other hand, the group leader may also come across certain personality types that may make "opening up" unwise or unfeasible. In the first category are those disturbed individuals who, at best, are making marginal adjustments to life. Their controls are tenuous and uncertain, with large expenditures of energy given to maintaining their defenses. To penetrate these brittle defenses might expose the individual to more affect than he could handle.

It is conceivable that his already weak personality controls might well be destroyed. Whether we give such individuals labels such as "schizoid" or "hysteric" is unimportant compared to the proper recognition and handling of defenses.

Under the second category of "unfeasible" would fall all those individuals who exhibit a rigid personality structure so insulated and defended from new experiences that any change is likely to be minor and too involved for the time period of the group. This is not to say that these individuals cannot be changed, but with ten or more other members in the group seeking change, the time and effort involved with one such individual may be prohibitive. Wilhelm Reich graphically described an encased "body armor" that has solidified with time. Perhaps the best we can do, in such cases, is try to implant an idea or two in any possible cracks in the armor.

In terms of actual treatment, it is best to screen potential group members for possible disturbances and then recommend proper therapeutic treatment. At least this would seem to hold for disturbed individuals whose participation in a T-group would be unwise. Those members whose participation would be limited by their rigid character structure should be apprised of the realistic limitations of the group. If a disturbed person has slipped by screening and is already in the group, we would suggest the following guidelines until proper action can be taken: (1) be supportive of the individual and do not "expose" him to the group, (2) avoid prolonged encounters between this member and any other, and (3) use cognitively oriented, group-level, low-intensity interventions in dealing with his behavior.

18. *How should relatively deep personal problems, such as homosexuality, be dealt with when a person brings them up in the group?*

When a participant in a group brings up a problem of a serious personal nature, we would certainly try to treat it with the appropriate relevance it deserves. The key phrase to keep in mind, however, is "appropriate relevance." There are obviously some problems the group *qua group* is able to handle quite well. An example might be a person who wishes to test in the group his leadership abilities as evaluator.

There are other problems the group can handle only in part—the part that relates to the group and its functional abilities. In this instance, feelings of alienation from others springing from deep feelings of inadequacy, for example, may only be partially handled by the group—perhaps only that aspect dealing with interpersonal closeness. The remainder of the problem may be too deep-seated and chronic for the group successfully to change.

Finally, there are those problems that are destructive for and irrelevant to the group, such as those individuals who attempt to use the group as an arena for "game playing." The individual, in this instance, attempts to engage the group more or less continually in seemingly endless, circular discussion of his problems. Moreover, there is no real desire for help, but rather a need to flaunt the illness as a neurotic badge. The group will recognize this self-defeating and nonproductive behavior in time, but as a group leader one has both the responsibility and relatively the greatest power to prevent this situation.

In general, then, it is best to test what the tone of the group is at the time and try to evaluate (a) whether the problem is relevant for the group, i.e., whether the group can adequately deal with it, and (b) if it is relevant, whether it will be destructive for the group or the individual. One of the things that a group is afraid of, initially, is the handling of trauma. Just like an individual, the group needs to build up a background of experience in order to gain a sense of maturity with regard to confidence in handling the relevant problems of any group member. Members should ideally develop this maturity within a framework that is relative to the ongoing group processes.

19. *How do you feel about participants getting together outside of the group? And what about participants who attempt to bring up certain problems with the leader after the group?*

It is difficult, if not impossible, to legislate activities that occur outside the group session. In a "live-in" program it seems inevitable that some group members, stimulated by the work of the group, will form informal clusters that may often last several hours after the formal group has broken for the night. The feeling of exhilaration and involvement is to be encouraged; it is the attempt to continue with and to resolve certain issues outside the formal group setting that must be discouraged.

We believe that there are certain issues, problems, and conflicts that, for optimum learning, must be dealt with when all members are present in a formal group setting. In addition, there are certain personal problems of individual members that should be pursued only with the guidance and direction of a trained group leader. Uncontrolled attempts at probing, examination of ego defenses, and problem solving may create only more defensive pressure in the individual or, at worst, drive him from the group with heightened anxiety and no tangible benefits.

When a participant is concerned enough to approach the group leader with a personal problem, following any group session, it is the responsibility of the group leader to evaluate the problem within the context of the following question: "Is this a problem that is capable of being handled by the group in the time period allotted?" The group may not have developed the maturity, techniques, or values to handle a problem concerning, for example, an emerging homosexuality.

In such instances, we strongly recommend that the group leader suggest that the issue be taken up with a professional therapist or that he inform the individual that, due to time limitations (if this is the case), the issue will probably not be explored to the member's satisfaction. This needs to be done with considerable sensitivity and support.

In addition, there are certain issues that may be of special concern to one group member but that may be irrelevant to group needs and concerns and the concerns of other individual members. Let us imagine, for example, that a member approaches the leader with problems involving black militancy, women's liberation, or student power. These are legitimate issues of group concern so long as the group has reached a stage where members are capable of doing more than just giving their opinions on the topic.

In these instances, the wisdom of the group usually will prevail and the concerned individual should have no hesitation in presenting these issues. If they are irrelevant to the particular stage the group is in and the issues with which it is wrestling, such issues will be discarded or postponed. This is not to say that these issues do not have a "general" relevance, but rather that certain maturational processes must occur in a group *prior* to effective group problem solving.

The general recommendation, then, would be to bring up all problems in the group for consideration by the group, unless they are judged detrimental to the individual or to the group. The group is usually enriched by working on them.

LEADERSHIP AND AUTHORITY

20. *Is it always necessary for a group to struggle with an authority problem?*

The authority problem probably exists along a continuum, from those groups whose major concern—both in the community and in the small group—is that of leadership, control, and authority-related problems, to those groups at the other end of the continuum whose major concern may be in areas relatively unconcerned with authority, such as personal growth and creativity groups. In these latter groups it is understandable why relatively little time or effort is devoted to exploration of authority problems.

Another factor is the "group style" of the leader. There are those leaders whose intervention approach and personal style act as a stimulus for authority issues to develop in the group. A third factor is the stated purposes of the group. The purposes of some groups would be well served by eliciting and working through authority problems. For other groups, eliciting and trying to deal with authority problems may be somewhat artificial and produce irrelevant expenditures of group energy.

21. *How can a leader be sure when it is an authority issue that is emerging in a group?*

There seem to be several rather clear indications when members are having mixed feelings about authority. There are generally three main types. One type is illustrated when, in an automated way, a person just gives in to authority and wants to be told what to do every step of the way, thus signifying a reaction of overdependence. A second type is illustrated by just the reverse reaction, in which a member rejects most of what the leader does or says regardless of its value—a reaction of counterdependence. The final type is reflected by those members who cannot decide which "side to join," and so they withdraw for a while to become the "nonparticipating" members.

The occurrence of these kinds of issues suggests that perhaps some of the leader's statements or actions have touched on some rather sensitive areas. It becomes very important that the leader ask the group to reflect upon and deal with what is going on, since the kinds of issues that the group is running away from may well come up again and again. The manner in which these issues are dealt with will set the stage for how well the group is able to deal with even more intense issues at later times.

22. *Sometimes a member will challenge the authority of the leader in both direct and indirect ways, for example, in the tone of his voice, his posture, or the nature of his statement or question. How do you feel about these situations and how do you handle these confrontations?*

We feel it is important to exert appropriate leadership in the group. It is of critical importance for the leader to choose how help might be given most effectively. At the same time, it is obvious that the leader has to assess his priorities in order to choose the best means of help. It is a disservice to a group member to treat his "authority challenge" as a simple request for information.

And yet, the group leader should not be manipulated into a debate or argument that is essentially nonproductive and that represents a "win-lose" situation. If it is a legitimate request for information, an answer should be given. But if it is a challenge to authority, it should be recognized as such and dealt with as a learning experience. This circumstance may then provide the leader with a living example, in the group, of how conflict may arise and be worked through. This model of conflict presupposes that collaboration leads to a situation where no one "loses" and where all the conflicting parties may "win."

It is difficult to specify the exact operations or techniques that may be used, since these will vary widely depending on the stage of the group and the individuals who are involved. (Concrete responses to many such authority issues can be found in the *Manual*.)

Generally speaking, it is advisable for the beginning group leader not to react too quickly or intensely to what may seem to be a personal attack. A knowledge of group dynamics should provide the leader with some support and objectivity during this phase. Although leadership approaches vary, our preference is for the group leader generally to accept the criticism or challenge openly without defensiveness or punishing rebuttal. This stance, particularly in the beginning stages of group life, encourages other, less assertive, members to discuss their feelings openly.

An immediate rebuttal or attempt at justification by the leader, at these times, would tend to inhibit further discussion by other members. At a later stage of openness, however, it is desirable for the leader to engage the challenging member more directly in an attempt to resolve the conflict in a mutually facilitating manner. Often this will be resolved quickly and in a manner that is instructive to the other members.

At other times, however, the leader must be prepared for the lack of resolution and/or the emergence of this same issue in future sessions. While there are no guarantees of instant success in these complex problems, we believe a commitment to process will, in the long run, help achieve the most important individual and group goals. Group leadership still is, by and large, a subtle blend of prior experience, current feelings, and skillful techniques.

AN EXPERIENCE

"The Chair and the Johnson Grass: Authority and Murder in a Sensitivity Training Group" is an account of part of the life of one group in a week-long laboratory in interpersonal relations.[1] It is a vivid description of critical events involving many implicit and explicit phenomena and concerns that tend to arise in such groups. In particular, the symbolic meanings of events and the member-member and member-leader interactions that characterized them are highlighted. Love, power, and belonging are dramatically and sometimes painfully illustrated as major driving forces and areas of conflict. How the leader becomes personally involved and yet retains his perspective as an important intervener is clearly revealed in the passionate encounters of group members with each other and with him.

The Chair and the Johnson Grass: Authority and Murder in a Sensitivity Training Group[2]

By VICTOR MALLENBAUM and ARTHUR M. COHEN

Often I wonder about reality. What, if anything, in the life of my group is real and what is merely a game? What that is real outside of the group, becomes unreal in the group? And what that is unreal outside of the group, becomes real in the group? Can the unreal become real and can the real become unreal?

---

[1]This laboratory program was under the direction of Leadership Development Programs, Inc., Atlanta, Georgia.

[2]From *Voices: The Art and Science of Psychotherapy*, Spring 1973, 9(1), 40-45. Special permission for the use of this article has been granted by the editor.

The following episode, which took place at a sensitivity training laboratory, is an example of the confusion of the real and unreal and the merging of group life and the outside world. This group was composed of 12 participants: four white males, four white females, four black males, plus a trainer and intern. I cannot help but believe it was all real because it happened; people responded to it and people made it happen.

For years I have been bothered by a peculiar back problem. Because of this, upon entering a room I immediately seek out a soft chair with a fairly straight back and, preferably, with arm rests. The first time I entered this training room was no exception. I found the only chair in the room that suited my needs and immediately took possession of it. From that point on I always took that particular seat and thought nothing more about it.

Two days later I entered the training room a few minutes late and immediately headed for "my" chair. Shock of shocks, I stopped short. There was Arlene, all 4'11" and 95 pounds of her, filling the chair as if it were made to order just for her body. Filled with self-composure and buttressed by years of faking, unperturbedly I sat on the chair adjacent to "my" place of comfort. I have been told that my interventions are always given twice, once by my facial expression and again when I make the intervention explicit to the group. I do not know what my face was saying to the group at that moment but I do know what I felt: *worried*—that I might suffer the consequences of sitting on that hard chair for two hours. I was also about to tell Arlene why I needed that chair and ask her for it but my request was stymied by a voice from the group. "Boy, Vic, I guess Arlene is the boss now. She has the chair."

My back or the group—that was the question—whether to suffer the slings and arrows of torment that night or to stop the group from exploring a vital issue. But I had learned my lesson well, all in the service of the group, and so I responded, "I guess I lost my position with the chair, but I don't really feel any different."

Somehow, Joe missed the second half of my statement, which was meant to reinstate myself in the ambiguity of the position I had held up to that point. He shouted, "You sure as hell have, but Arlene's not getting it."

"Do you want it?" I asked.

"Yes!"

"Well, what are you going to do about it?"

I was really rather pleased with Joe's outburst. He had been one of the less potent members of the group and impressed me as being a backwoods preacher who would be afraid to try the big time ministry, although he certainly had the potential for it.

"I am going to get it," said Joe. At that point he rushed toward Arlene and demanded that she vacate the chair. She refused and appeared to fill it even more completely than she had before. Joe told her he would take it from her and she dared him to do so. He then perched himself on the arm of the chair

and sat there with one buttock on and one buttock off. A rather inane argument followed which went something like this:
Joe: "You will get off the chair."
Arlene: "No, I will not."
Joe: "Yes, you will."
Arlene: "No!!"
Joe: "I am going to stay here until you do."
Arlene: "You will be there forever."

At that point I said, "Joe, if you will notice your position on the chair right now, you might recognize it is the same half-assed position you have been taking all week."

Joe: "But this time I am not giving up. I am staying right here."

Arlene: "Well, nothing is going to get me out of this chair."

It was quite interesting that Joe did not respond to my intervention, which was aimed at the wishy-washy life style he had been exhibiting all during the week. Apparently he was not ready to hear what I had said, or possibly it might take an intervention of a different kind and of a higher intensity.

At this point the group was becoming quite active in a thumb-moving manner, signalling either death or life to the battler who seemed victorious at the moment. Others egged on the two battlers. As all of this was going on I noticed that Sam was sitting very quietly with a rather smug grin on his face. This smug expression was to remain on his face during all of the action that shortly would be taking place.

After some ten or fifteen minutes of the battling, cheering and booing, the bedlam subsided and the group was undoubtedly as bored with the "struggle" as I was. Rushing over to Joe, I exclaimed, "That's it Joe, you were within reach of your goal, but now you've lost your right to it. You don't deserve to be in that chair." I then grasped Joe bodily and began pulling him off the arm of the chair. The man must chop trees as a hobby. He was as strong as a bull. I am not. The message is that he resisted. We wrestled for what seemed an hour to me. Poor Arlene, she was being crushed beneath us. Some members of the group joined in and together we pushed Joe into another chair.

As I collapsed into another chair I heard Joe say, "By God, Vic, you are strong!" Selective perception triumphs again. Joe did not even realize that it took four of us to get his buttock off the arm of the chair. Very probably he wanted me to defeat him physically in order that he retain his image of me as the ultimate authority in the group. But that issue was not to be brought to light at this time as Sam suddenly jumped out of his place, ambled over to Arlene, picked her up in his arms and very unceremoniously placed her on the floor next to his chair. He then took his seat and said, "Joe, the chair is yours now, take it." Joe did.

After a minute had passed, I said to Joe, "Well, now that you are in the chair how do you feel?"

"Not as good as I thought I would," he answered.
"I feel damn good," interjected Sam.
"Of course you do," I said. "You just raped a white woman and castrated a white man. You have come closer to acting out what you have been doing verbally all week. You have been raping the white women by telling them how incompetent they are and how low they are and you just put Arlene on the floor. She can't get much lower. And, you have been castrating the white men by making them feel guilty about your position and then manipulating them into doing what you want. That is your chair and you know it. You took it and you just put a white dummy into it to do your bidding. That is the way to operate and it is about time we saw it."

"Well, if the white guy is dumb enough to fall for it, that's his bag. It is about time he did something for me anyway. And, I'll tell you, Vic, before I'm through, he'll be doing a hell of a lot for me. He'll be crawling to me."

The session ended about this time, in a stunned silence.

It may be important for me to relate some of my impressions of Sam before this incident. These impressions were confirmed later in the history of the group. I felt he was one of the most intelligent people I had ever met, also one of the shrewdest and most ruthless. In my fantasy, I saw him as the Robespierre of the Black Revolution. Hostility fairly shone from his eyes, yet beneath it I sensed a cry for help. It seemed that he was not completely satisfied with the mask of hostility and hatred with which he covered himself. I sensed a will to live and taste of the joys of life within him.

The next episode took place that evening as the participants and the staff of the laboratory were sitting around the social hall enjoying each other's company. At one point I was sitting and chatting with Art, the director of the program. Sam joined us and while seemingly ignoring me began talking to the director, but his words were unmistakably meant for me.

"I have a certain theory, Art," said Sam. "I believe that every man is born with certain natural enemies. Like the Chief of Police, downtown, is my natural enemy. Now these enemies you're born with, you can't do anything about so you just learn to live with them and you know you always have to be on guard about them. But these are enough for any man to handle. You can't afford any more.

"Then there are enemies that I make along the way, like Vic here. He's not my natural enemy. He's a made enemy. So those you got to get rid of. You know what Johnson Grass is? It's a type of grass you can't just mow down or use weedkiller on. It'll just grow right back. You have to completely uproot it. Pull it out by its roots and destroy it that way. That's what I got to do to Vic, just completely uproot him and destroy him."

I am not sure whether I remained silent because I was completely dumbfounded, scared, or amazed; or if it was just good breeding which dictated that I not interfere with a conversation between two people. I would like to believe it was the latter but I know nobody else would believe it. At any rate, I did remain silent at that time and made a mental note to lock my door that night.

The next morning as we entered the group room Arlene was perched very comfortably on my therapeutic chair and my first fantasy was that she would be killing me much more effectively than Sam. It was then that in an "Ah-Ha!" flash I felt I knew what Sam was feeling and my fears dissipated. But I wasn't to be given the opportunity of taking a deep breath and relaxing in my newly found ease. Sam started off immediately by saying, "I wasn't kidding last night, Vic. I am going to kill you."

"You have to, Sam," I said. "You have to kill me, but you won't. You have to kill me because I see into your little game. I see the way you manipulate other people and I point it out, and I'll always be there to point it out to you. The only way you can stop me is by killing me, but you are not going to do it because a part of you wants it to be pointed out. A part of you wants to say, 'Sam, you are a phoney.' You are afraid to do it directly so you use guilt, sympathy, or whatever the hell you can to manipulate other people to do what you want. No, I won't stop, Sam, and you will have to kill me; but you won't because you need me too much and you know it."

"Goddamn you, Vic. Don't you have any racial hangups? You know, we either shuffle our feet or we carry blades. Doesn't it get to you? What will? Shit, I can kill. That's why I left home. I almost killed my two little brothers. No, I didn't want to kill them. I know it is not their fault. Their goddamn father is white. Shit, do I hate that bastard. My own brothers, half white. Shit, do you know what that does to me? My own kid brothers."

"Do you want me to feel sorry for you because the big leader of the Black Freedom Movement has half-white brothers? And, if I do feel sorry for you, then what—do you put me back in that chair and figure you can start pulling strings? Well, I don't care what color your brothers are and how much you hate their white father. But you couldn't castrate him, could you? And you will find a hell of a lot of white men you won't be able to castrate."

"No! I can't castrate you. Shit, maybe I could if I wanted to, but I don't want to. What the hell can I do to you?"

"Tell me about your mother."

"Goddamn, what are you doing to me? What the hell do you want from me? She's my mama, damn it. How the hell could she let a white cock into her? How could she do that to me—to everyone? What the hell do you want me to talk about her for? The hell with her."

"Who do you hate worse, Sam, your mother or the white guy?"

"Him, her! Shit, I don't know. I hate them both. I should have killed them both. What the hell do I want from my brothers. It's not their fault. Goddamn it, she's not Black. She's a Nigger. God, I don't really want to castrate no white dudes. I want my mother to be Black. Why can't she be Black?"

During this encounter Sam had gone from his usual smugness to anger, then to rage, and finally into uncontrolled sobbing. After a moment I sat down beside him and put my arms around him and he buried his head in my shoulder and cried for a while longer. When his sobbing subsided he said, "Well, you just castrated me, Vic."

"No," I answered, "I can't castrate you. Only you can castrate you. I think maybe you have been doing that. What do you really want, Sam?"

"I just want to be Black."

"To me you are as Black as the ace of spades," said one of the Black members of the group.

"And beautiful, too," said a white girl.

"Maybe, I'll feel that way, some day. I can't stay now. I got to be alone. I'll be back. I'll see you all soon."

With that Sam left the room and the group spent the rest of the session going through some "mourning rites" at the loss of Sam. But these rites were different from those I had seen in the past. They were something akin to what happens to the devoutly religious who are certain, beyond any doubt, that they will see their beloved departed again, but the next meeting will be in heaven.

The feeling was fairly accurate. I don't claim to know what heaven is like and what happened the next morning was never in any clergyman's description of the great beyond. But perhaps it was a little higher.

It was the last meeting of our group and again Sam started off. "You bastard, Vic, I called my brothers last night. First time I have spoken to them in two years. We must have spoken for over an hour and it's a long, long distance to there. I ought to charge you for the call. Oh! What am I shitting about. I wanted to tell them I am still alive and I am still their brother and I love them. And I did it. And I haven't felt this good in as long as I can remember. Maybe I am even turning Black."

At this point the entire group gathered around Sam and gave him one of the warmest hugs I have ever seen.

We then spent the rest of the session trying to complete all the other work that had been going on in the group along with the Chair and the Johnson Grass.

Here I must ask myself, what was real in the episodes of the group described above? Was the chair really a throne? To me it was simply the place to sit that would cause me the least discomfort and in thinking about it I realize it was far from a throne. It was rather a shoddy looking, torn up armchair with the stuffing coming out of it from all directions.

But there in the group it was indeed a throne, a place of honor and glory. It was the place in which the "leader" sat, and although the leader did not lead in the traditional sense of the word, the group members brought with them from their life experiences the concept of "leader." This was real on the outside. What was also real on the outside was that the chairman of the board has his special place to sit, the clergyman has his special seat, the president has his special seat, and no one dare usurp any of them. This was brought to the group with the participants. Therefore the leader of their group "should" have his own special chair. But their leader did not "lead" and so all of his potency was transferred to the chair and the chair became a symbol of power in this group. The chair, as a throne, was real to the members of the group. One did usurp this symbol of authority. Others fought for it. Each member's "will to power," in Adlerian terms, was manifested in various ways which were highly indicative of their life styles. It is obvious that under other conditions and in other circumstances the chair would have been nothing more than another shabby piece of furniture. Had my back not been as it was, and had I sat in different chairs or on the floor, the chair would have remained nothing but a chair. But the situation of the leader not being a traditional leader was real and the fact that he always sat on that chair was real. That the group members wanted an authority figure in the group was also real and the fact that they were willing to transfer "authority" to the chair or to anyone who occupied the chair was very real as well as very frightening.

If we were to transfer the chair to the world outside the group, no doubt it would only be a chair. But if we were to transfer a situation of ambiguous leadership to the world, what symbols would be chosen for authority and who would be allowed to utilize these symbols and to occupy the position of authority? World history and conjecture from what is observed in groups lead us to not very optimistic conclusions. What was seen in the group, its members choosing a chair as a symbol of authority was real. The pig's head in *The Lord of the Flies* was real. The number of choices people may make in moments of existential anxiety over "Where are we going?" and "Who is going to get us there?" are infinite. The fear of meaninglessness implied in those questions is real and the ways that fear is dealt with are also real and are infinite. Unfortunately not all the ways chosen are positive or constructive. Joe's failure to remove Arlene from the chair was not growth producing for him, for the group, or for Arlene. Sam's setting Joe up as a puppet government was not enhancing for the group, nor did it serve Sam's own real desires. Yet a model of what the group brought into that room with them was completely real within that room and was also real outside of that room.

Sam came into the room hating his brothers and the white man who was their father, and that was real. But Sam left the room loving his brothers and that too was real. I don't believe that Sam learned to love his brothers in that room. I believe that he had been carrying that love with him for all those years but he didn't recognize it. It took something of the reality of the group to help Sam face the reality of his love outside of the group. Sam's hatred and love of me in the group was real but it did not exist in reality before the group for he had never seen me before. Whatever feeling Sam has for me today and I have for him is real and it is outside of the group, but it was born within the group.

So, I conclude as I began. The group is real. It is the world in miniature but with one difference. In the group the members are encouraged to recognize their feelings, their needs and their desires, and to build their community without negating their own individualities.

A Selected Bibliography

Ackerman, N. W. What constitutes intensive psychotherapy in a child guidance clinic? *American Journal of Orthopsychiatry*, 1945, *15*, 711–720.

Ackerman, N. W. The training of case workers in psychotherapy. *American Journal of Orthopsychiatry*, 1949, *19*, 14–24.

Ackerman, N. W. Some structural problems in the relations of psychoanalysis and group psychotherapy. *International Journal of Group Psychotherapy*, 1954, *4*(2), 131–145.

Ackerman, N. W. Group psychotherapy with a mixed group of adolescents. *International Journal of Group Psychotherapy*, 1955, *5*(3), 249–260.

Ackerman, N. W. (Ed.). *Family process.* New York: Basic Books, 1970.

Adler, A. [*Social interest: A challenge to mankind*] (J. Linton & R. Vaughan, Trans.). New York: Capricorn, 1964.

Allport, F. H. *Social psychology.* Boston: Houghton Mifflin, 1924.

Allport, F. H. *The group fallacy in relation to social science.* Hanover, N.H.: The Sociological Press, 1927.

American Psychiatric Association. Encounter groups and psychiatry. *Task Force Report 1.* Washington, D.C.: Author, 1970.

Appley, D. G., & Winder, A. E. *T-groups and therapy groups in a changing society.* San Francisco: Jossey-Bass, 1973.

Argyris, C. *Interpersonal competence and organizational effectiveness.* Homewood, Ill: Irwin-Dorsey, 1962.

Argyris, C. T-groups for organizational effectiveness. *Harvard Business Review*, 1964, *42*(2), 60–74.

Argyris, C. Speech delivered at Georgia State University, November 9, 1972.

Axline, V. M. *Dibs: In search of self: Personality development in play therapy.* Boston: Houghton Mifflin, 1964.

Ayllon, T., & Arzin, N. *The token economy: A motivational system for therapy and rehabilitation.* New York: Appleton-Century-Crofts, 1968.

Bach, G. R. *Intensive group psychotherapy.* New York: Ronald Press, 1954.

Bach, G. R. Observations on transference and object relations in the light of group dynamics. *International Journal of Group Psychotherapy*, 1957, 7(1), 64–76.

Bach, G. R. The marathon group: Intensive practice of intimate interaction. *Psychological Reports*, 1966, *18*(3), 995–1002.

Bach, G. R. Group and leader phobias in marathon groups. *Voices: The Art and Science of Psychotherapy*, 1967, 3(3), 41–46.

Bach, G. R., & Deutsch, R. M. *Pairing: How to achieve genuine intimacy.* New York: Wyden, 1970.

Back, K. W. *Beyond words: The story of sensitivity training and the encounter movement.* New York: Russell Sage, 1972.

Bales, R. F., & Strodtbeck, F. Phases in group-problem-solving. *Journal of Abnormal and Social Psychology*, 1951, 46, 485–495.

Bandura, A. *Principles of behavior modification.* New York: Holt, Rinehart and Winston, 1969.

Banet, A. G., Jr. Therapeutic intervention and the perception of process. In J. W. Pfeiffer & J. E. Jones (Eds.), *The 1974 annual handbook for group facilitators.* La Jolla, Ca.: University Associates, 1974.

Barret, M. L., Hunt, V. V., & Jones, M. H. Behavioral growth of cerebral palsied children from group experience in a confined space. *Developmental Medicine and Child Neurology*, 1967, 9(1), 50–58.

Barron, M. E., & Krulee, G. K. Case study of a basic skill training group. *Journal of Social Issues*, 1948, 4(2), 10–30.

Battegay, R. The verbal exchange in the therapeutic group. *Group Psychotherapy*, 1966, *19*(3–4), 166–175.

Bebout, J., & Gordon, B. The value of encounter. In L. N. Solomon & B. Berzon (Eds.), *New perspectives on encounter groups.* San Francisco: Jossey-Bass, 1972.

Benne, K. D. From polarization to paradox. In L. P. Bradford, J. R. Gibb, & K. D. Benne (Eds.), *T-group theory and laboratory method: Innovation in re-education.* New York: John Wiley, 1964. (a)

Benne, K. D. History of the T-group in the laboratory setting. In L. P. Bradford, J. R. Gibb, & K. D. Benne (Eds.), *T-group theory and laboratory method: Innovation in re-education.* New York: John Wiley, 1964. (b)

Benne, K. D. *A conception of authority: An introductory study.* New York: Russell & Russell, 1971.

Bennis, W. G., & Shepard, H. A. A theory of group development. *Human Relations*, 1956, 9, 415–437.

A Selected Bibliography 247

Berg, C. *The casebook of a medical psychologist.* London: George Allen & Unwin, 1948.

Berkovitz, I. H. (Ed.). *Adolescents grow in groups: Clinical experiences in adolescent group psychotherapy.* New York: Bruner/Mazell, 1972.

Berlin, J. I., & Wyckoff, L. B., Jr. Program learning for personal and interpersonal improvement. *Acta Psychologia,* 1964, *23,* 313–321.

Berne, E. *Transactional analysis in psychotherapy: A systematic individual model of social psychiatry.* New York: Grove, 1961.

Berne, E. *Principles of group treatment.* New York: Oxford University Press, 1966.

Berzon, B., Pious, C., & Farson, R. The therapeutic event in group psychotherapy: A study of subjective reports by group members. *Journal of Individual Psychology,* 1963, *19*(2), 204–212.

Berzon, B., & Solomon, L. Research frontier: The self-directed therapy group: Three studies. *Journal of Counseling Psychology,* 1966, *13*(4), 491–497.

Bierer, J. Modern social and group therapy. In N. G. Harris (Ed.), *Modern trends in psychological medicine.* London: Hoeber, 1948.

Bierer, J., & Evans, R. J. *Innovations in social psychiatry.* London: Avenue Publishing, 1969.

Bieri, J. Cognitive complexity-simplicity and predictive behavior. *Journal of Abnormal and Social Psychology,* 1955, *51,* 263–268.

Bion, W. R. Experiences in groups, I. *Human Relations,* 1948, *1,* 314–320.

Blake, R. R., Mouton, J. S., Barnes, L. B., & Greiner, L. E. Breakthrough in organization development. *Harvard Business Review,* 1964, *42*(6), 133–155.

Blumberg, A. Laboratory education and sensitivity training. In R. T. Golembiewski & A. Blumberg (Eds.), *Sensitivity training and the laboratory approach: Readings about concepts and applications* (2nd ed.). Itasca, Ill.: F. E. Peacock, 1973.

Bonner, H. *Group dynamics: Principles and applications.* New York: Ronald Press, 1959.

Borenzweig, H., & Dombey, D. The uses of social group work in a vocational training program. *Journal of Rehabilitation,* 1969, *35*(1), 30–32.

Boring, E. G. *A history of experimental psychology* (2nd ed.). New York: Appleton-Century-Crofts, 1950.

Bosco, A. *Marriage encounter: The rediscovery of love.* St. Meinrad, Ind.: Abbey Press, 1972.

Bowers, N. D., & Soar, R. S. *Evaluation of laboratory human relations training for classroom teachers.* (Studies of Human Relations in the Teaching-Learning Process: V, Final Report, U.S. Office of Education.) Columbia, S.C.: University of South Carolina, 1961.

Bradford, L. P. Trainer intervention: Case episodes. In L. P. Bradford, J. R. Gibb, & K. D. Benne (Eds.), *T-group theory and laboratory method: Innovation in re-education.* New York: John Wiley, 1964.

Bradford, L. P. Biography of an institution. *Journal of Applied Behavioral Science,* 1967, 3(2), 127-143. (a)

Bradford, L. P. The formation of achievement attitudes among lower class Negro youth (Doctoral dissertation, University of Michigan, 1967). *Dissertation Abstracts,* 1967, 28(1-A), 293-294. (b)

Bradford, L. P., Gibb, J. R., & Benne, K. D. (Eds.). *T-group theory and laboratory method: Innovation in re-education.* New York: John Wiley, 1964.

Bradford, L. P., Lippitt, G. L., & Gibb, J. R. Human relations training in three days. *Adult Leadership,* 1956, 4(10), 11-26.

Buber, M. [*I and thou*] (R. G. Smith, Trans.). New York: Charles Scribner's, 1937.

Buchanan, P. C. *Evaluating the effectiveness of laboratory training in industry.* Washington, D.C.: National Training Laboratories and National Education Association, 1965.

Bugental, J. F. T. The existential crisis in intensive psychotherapy. *Psychotherapy: Theory, Research and Practice,* 1965, 2(1), 16-20. (a)

Bugental, J. F. T. *The search for authenticity: An existential-analytic approach to psychotherapy.* New York: Holt, Rinehart and Winston, 1965. (b)

Burrow, T. N. *Science and man's behavior: The contribution of phylobiology* (W. E. Galt, Ed.). New York: Philosophical Library, 1953.

Burton, A. (Ed.). *Encounter: Theory and practice of encounter groups.* San Francisco: Jossey-Bass, 1969.

Burton, A. *Interpersonal psychotherapy.* Englewood Cliffs, N.J.: Prentice-Hall, 1972.

Byron, G. G., Lord. *The works of Byron.* London: John Murray, 1840.

Cahn, M. M. Poetic dimensions of encounter. In A. Burton (Ed.), *Encounter: Theory and practice of encounter groups.* San Francisco: Jossey-Bass, 1969.

Campbell, J. D., & Dunnette, M. D. Effectiveness of T-group experiences in managerial training and development. *Psychological Bulletin*, 1968, 70(2), 73–104.

Carkhuff, R. R., & Berenson, B. G. *Beyond counseling and therapy*. New York: Holt, Rinehart and Winston, 1967.

Carter, W. W. Group counseling for adolescent foster children. *Children*, 1968, 15(1), 22–27.

Cassirer, E. (Ed.). *The renaissance philosophy of man*. Chicago: University of Chicago Press, 1954.

Cholden, L. Group therapy with the blind. *Group Psychotherapy*, 1953, 6(1–2), 21–29.

Clark, J. V. Authentic interaction and personal growth in sensitivity training groups. *Journal of Humanistic Psychology*, 1963, 3, 1–13.

Clark, T. C., & Miles, M. B. Human relations training for school administrators. *Journal of Social Issues*, 1954, 10(2), 25–39.

Coch, L., & French, J. R. P., Overcoming resistance to change. *Human Relations*, 1948, 1, 512–532.

Cohen, A. M., & Smith, R. D. The critical incident approach to leadership intervention in groups. In W. G. Dyer (Ed.), *Modern theory and methods in group training*. New York: Van Nostrand Reinhold, 1972.

Cohn, R. C. Psychoanalytic or experimental group psychotherapy: A false dichotomy. *Psychoanalytic Review*, 1969, 56(3), 333–345. Also in C. J. Sager & H. S. Kaplan (Eds.), *Progress in group and family therapy*. New York: Brunner/Mazel, 1972.

Coleman, J. C. *Abnormal psychology and modern life*. Glenview, Ill.: Scott, Foresman, 1964.

Comte, A. *Cours de philosophie positive* (5th ed.). Paris: Librairie C. Reinwald, Schleicher Freres, 1907–08. (Originally published, 1842.)

Conze, E. *Buddhism: Its essence and development*. New York: Harper & Row, 1959. (a)

Conze, E. (Ed. & trans.). [*Buddhist scriptures.*] Baltimore: Penguin, 1959. (b)

Cooley, C. H. *Social process*. New York: Charles Scribner's, 1918.

Cooper, B. An analysis of the quality of behaviors of principals as observed and reported in six critical incident studies. *Journal of Education Research*, 1963, 56(8), 410–414.

Cooper, C. L. *T-groups: A survey of research*. London: Wiley Interscience, 1971.

Cooper, E. C. A therapy process for the adult stutterer. *Journal of Speech and Hearing Disorders*, 1968, *33*(3), 246–260.

Corsini, R. J. *Methods of group psychotherapy*. New York: McGraw-Hill, 1957.

Cox, H. G. *The secular city: Secularization and urbanization in theological perspective*. New York: Macmillan, 1965.

Cutts, N. B. *Group leadership style and patient-perceived empathy, congruence and positive regard*. Unpublished doctoral dissertation, Georgia State University, 1972.

Darwin, C. The origin of the species. In R. M. Hutchins (Ed.), *Great books of the Western World* (Vol. 49). Chicago: Wm. Benton, Encyclopedia Britannica, 1952. (Originally published, 1859.)

Davis, S. A. An organic problem-solving method of organizational change. *Journal of Applied Behavioral Science*, 1967, *3*(1), 3–21.

Denny, A. Theater of encounter. *Personal Growth*, July 1974, *21*, 9–11.

Deutsch, M. Field theory in social psychology. In G. Lindsay & E. Aronson (Eds.), *The handbook on social psychology* (Vol. 1). Reading, Mass.: Addison-Wesley, 1968.

Dreikurs, R. Group psychotherapy and the third revolution in psychiatry. *International Journal of Social Psychiatry*, 1955, *1*(3), 23–32.

Dreikurs, R. Group psychotherapy from the point of view of Adlerian psychology. *International Journal of Group Psychotherapy*, 1957, *7*, 363–375.

Dreikurs, R. *Children: The challenge*. New York: Hawthorne, 1964.

Dreikurs, R. *Psychodynamics, psychotherapy and counseling: Collected papers* (Rev. ed.). Chicago: Alfred Adler Institute, 1967.

Dreikurs, R., et al. (Eds.). *Adlerian family counseling: A manual for counseling centers*. Eugene, Ore.: University of Oregon Press, 1959.

Durkheim, E. [*The rules of sociological method*] (8th ed.). (E. G. Catlin, Ed., and S. A. Solovay & J. H. Mueller, Trans.) Glencoe, Ill.: Free Press, 1938.

Durkin, H. E. Towards a common basis for group dynamics: Group and therapeutic processes in group psychotherapy. *International Journal of Group Psychotherapy*, 1957, *7*(2), 115–130.

Durkin, H. E. *The group in depth*. New York: International Universities Press, 1964.

Dyer, W. G. An inventory of training interventions. *Human Relations Training News*, 1963, *7*(1), 4–5.

Egan, G. *Encounter: Group processes for interpersonal growth.* Monterey, Ca.: Brooks/Cole, 1970.

Egan, G. Contracts in encounter groups. In J. W. Pfeiffer & J. E. Jones (Eds.), *The 1972 annual handbook for group facilitators.* La Jolla, Ca.: University Associates, 1972.

Eliot, T. S. *The wasteland.* New York: Boni & Liveright, 1922.

Ellis, A. What is psychotherapy? *Annual of Psychotherapy*, 1959, *1*, 1–51.

Ellis, A. Objectivism: The new religion. *Rational Living*, 1967, *2*(2), 1–6.

Ellis, A. Rational emotive therapy. *Journal of Contemporary Psychotherapy*, Winter 1969, *1*(2), 82–90. (a)

Ellis, A. A weekend of rational encounter. In A. Burton (Ed.), *Encounter: Theory and practice of encounter groups.* San Francisco: Jossey-Bass, 1969. (b)

Ellis, A. *Growth through reason.* Palo Alto, Ca.: Science & Behavior Books, 1971.

Ellis, A. *Humanistic psychotherapy: The rational-emotive approach* (E. Sagarin, Ed.). New York: Julian Press, 1973.

Endore, S. G. *Synanon.* New York: Doubleday, 1968.

Erikson, E. H. *Childhood and society.* New York: Norton, 1950.

Etzioni, A. *Modern organizations.* Englewood Cliffs, N.J.: Prentice-Hall, 1964.

Etzioni, A. *The active society.* New York: Free Press, 1968.

Eyseneck, H. S. *Experiments in behavior therapy: Readings in modern methods of treatment of mental disorders derived from learning theory.* Oxford: Pergamon Press, 1964.

Ezriel, H. A psycho-analytic approach to the treatment of patients in groups. *Journal of Mental Science*, 1950, *96*, 744–747.

Fast, J. *Body language.* New York: M. Evans, 1970.

Fiebert, M. S. Sensitivity training: An analysis of trainer intervention and group process. *Psychological Reports*, 1968, *22*(8), 829–838.

Fisher, S. *Body experience in fantasy and behavior.* New York: Appleton-Century-Crofts, 1970.

Fisher, S. *Body consciousness: You are what you feel.* Englewood Cliffs, N.J.: Prentice-Hall, 1973.

Flanagan, J. C. *The aviation psychology program in the Army Air Forces* (AAF Aviation Psychology Program Research Report No. 1). Washington, D.C.: U.S. Government Printing Office, 1947. (a)

Flanagan, J. C. Personnel psychology. In W. Dennis (Ed.), *Current trends in psychology.* Pittsburgh: University of Pittsburgh Press, 1947. (b)

Flanagan, J. C. The critical incident technique. *Psychological Bulletin,* 1954, *51*(4), 327–358.

Flanders, N. A., & Bales, R. F. Planning an observation room and group laboratory. *American Sociological Review,* 1954, *19,* 771–781.

Forer, B. R. Use of physical contact. In L. N. Solomon & B. Berzon (Eds.), *New perspectives on encounter groups.* San Francisco: Jossey-Bass, 1972.

Foulkes, S. H., & Anthony, E. J. *Group psychotherapy: The psychoanalytic approach* (2nd ed.). Baltimore: Penguin, 1965.

Fox, J. The systematic use of hypnosis in individual and group psychotherapy. *International Journal of Clinical and Experimental Hypnosis,* January 1960, *8*(1), 109–114.

Frank, J. D. Some determinants, manifestations, and effects of cohesiveness in therapy groups. *International Journal of Group Psychotherapy,* January 1957, *7*(1), 53–63.

Frank, J. D. *Persuasion and healing.* Baltimore: Johns Hopkins University Press, 1961.

Frank, J. D. Training and therapy. In L. P. Bradford, J. R. Gibb, & K. D. Benne (Eds.), *T-group theory and laboratory method: Innovation in re-education.* New York: John Wiley, 1964.

French, J. R. P., Sherwood, J. J., & Bradford, D. L. Change in self-identity in a management training conference. *Journal of Applied Behavioral Science,* 1966, *2*(2), 210–218.

Freud, S. Group psychology and the analysis of the ego. In R. M. Hutchins (Ed.), *Great books of the Western World* (Vol. 54). Chicago: Wm. Benton, Encyclopedia Britannica, 1952. (Originally published, 1921.)

Friedlander, F. The impact of organizational training laboratories upon the effectiveness and interaction of ongoing work groups. *Personnel Psychology,* 1967, *20*(3), 289–307.

Friedman, P. H. Personalistic family and marital therapy. In A. A. Lazarus (Ed.), *Clinical behavior therapy.* New York: Brunner/Mazel, 1972.

Frost, S. E. *Basic teachings of the great philosophers: A survey of basic teachings.* New York: Doubleday, 1962.

Fung, Y. L. [*A history of Chinese philosophy*] (D. Bodde, Trans.). Peiping: Henri Vetch, 1937.

Gazda, G. M. (Ed.). *Basic approaches to group psychotherapy and group counseling.* Springfield, Ill.: Charles C Thomas, 1968.

Geller, J. J. Parataxic distortions in the initial stages of group relationships. *International Journal of Group Psychotherapy*, 1962, *12*(1), 27–34.

Gibb, J. R. Climate for trust formation. In L. P. Bradford, J. R. Gibb, & K. D. Benne (Eds.), *T-group theory and laboratory method: Innovation in re-education*. New York: John Wiley, 1964. (a)

Gibb, J. R. Communication and productivity. *Personnel Administration*, 1964, *27*(1), 8–13. (b)

Gibb, J. R. The present status of T-group theory. In L. P. Bradford, J. R. Gibb, & K. D. Benne (Eds.), *T-group theory and laboratory method: Innovation in re-education*. New York: John Wiley, 1964. (c)

Gibb, J. R. Sensitivity training as a medium for personal growth and improved interpersonal relationships. *Interpersonal Development*, 1970, *1*, 6–31. (a)

Gibb, J. R. TORI community. In G. Egan (Ed.), *Encounter groups: Basic readings*. Belmont, Ca.: Wadsworth, 1970. (b)

Gibb, J. R. Effects of human relations training. In A. E. Bergin & S. L. Garfield (Eds.), *Handbook of psychotherapy and behavior change*. New York: John Wiley, 1971.

Gibb, J. R. Meaning of the small group experience. In L. N. Solomon & B. Berzon (Eds.), *New perspectives on encounter groups*. San Francisco: Jossey-Bass, 1972.

Gibb, J. R. The message from research. In J. E. Jones & J. W. Pfeiffer (Eds.), *The 1974 annual handbook for group facilitators*. La Jolla, Ca.: University Associates, 1974.

Gibb, J. R., & Gibb, L. M. Emergence therapy: The TORI process in an emergent group. In G. M. Gazda (Ed.), *Basic approaches to group psychotherapy and group counseling*. Springfield, Ill.: Charles C Thomas, 1968. (a)

Gibb, J. R., & Gibb, L. M. Leaderless groups: Growth-centered values and potentials. In H. A. Otto & J. Mann (Eds.), *Ways of growth: Approaches to expanding awareness*. New York: Grossman, 1968. (b)

Gibb, J. R., & Gibb, L. M. Role freedom in a TORI group. In A. Burton (Ed.), *Encounter: Theory and practice of encounter groups*. San Francisco: Jossey-Bass, 1969.

Gibb, L. M., & Gibb, J. R. *Effects of the use of participative action groups in a course in general psychology*. Paper presented at the meeting of the American Psychological Association, Washington, D.C., 1952.

Ginott, H. G. *Group psychotherapy with children: The theory and practice of play therapy*. New York: McGraw-Hill, 1961.

Glasser, W. *Reality therapy: A new approach to psychiatry.* New York: Harper & Row, 1965.

Gleuck, W. F. Reflections on a T-group experience. *Personnel Journal,* 1968, *47*(7), 500–504.

Goldberg, C. *The human circle: An existential approach to the new group therapies.* Chicago: Nelson-Hall, 1973.

Goldfarb, A. Relationship to diagnostic group (Part II of *The use of the critical incident technique to establish areas of change accompanying psychotherapy*). Unpublished master's thesis, University of Pittsburgh, 1952.

Golembiewski, R. T., & Blumberg, A. The laboratory approach to organization change: The "confrontation design." *Journal of the Academy of Management,* 1968, *11*(2), 199–210.

Golembiewski, R. T., & Blumberg, A. (Eds.). *Sensitivity training and the laboratory approach: Readings about concepts and applications.* Itasca, Ill.: F. E. Peacock, 1970.

Golembiewski, R. T., Corrigan, S. B., Mead, W. R., Mungenrider, R., & Blumberg, A. Integrating disrupted work relations: An action design for a critical intervention. In R. T. Golembiewski & A. Blumberg (Eds.), *Sensitivity training and the laboratory approach: Readings about concepts and applications* (2nd ed.). Itasca, Ill.: F. E. Peacock, 1973.

Gordon, T. *The airline pilot: A survey of the critical requirements of his job and of pilot evaluation and selection procedures* (Civil Aeronautics Administration, Division of Research, Report No. 73). Washington, D.C.: U.S. Government Printing Office, 1947.

Gordon, T. *The development of a standard flight-check for the airline transport rating based on the critical requirements of the airline pilot's job* (Civil Aeronautics Administration, Division of Research, Report No. 85). Washington, D.C.: U.S. Government Printing Office, 1949.

Gordon, T. *Group centered leadership: A way of releasing the creative power of groups.* Boston: Houghton Mifflin, 1955.

Gordon, T. *Parent effectiveness training.* New York: Wyden, 1970.

Gottschalk, L. A., & Pattison, E. M. Psychiatric perspectives on T-groups and the laboratory movement: An overview. *American Journal of Psychiatry,* 1969, *126*(6), 823–839.

Greiner, L. E. *Organization change and development.* Unpublished doctoral dissertation, Harvard University, 1965.

Grotjahn, M. The process of maturation in group psychotherapy and in the group therapist. *Psychiatry,* 1950, *13*, 63–67.

Gunther, B. *Sense relaxation below your mind.* New York: Macmillan, 1968.

Gunther, B. Sensory awakening and relaxation. In H. Otto & J. Mann (Eds.), *Ways of growth: Approaches to expanding awareness.* New York: The Viking Press, 1969.

Gunther, B. *What to do till the Messiah comes.* New York: Macmillan, 1971.

Gustaitis, R. *Turning on.* New York: Macmillan, 1969.

Hacon, R. J. *Management training: Aims and methods.* London: English Universities Press, 1961.

Hadden, S. B. Group psychotherapy for sexual maladjustments. *American Journal of Psychiatry,* 1968, *125*(3), 327–332.

Haley, J. *Strategies of psychotherapy.* New York: Grune & Stratton, 1963.

Haley, J. Beginning and experienced family therapists. In A. M. Ferber, M. Mendelsohn, & A. Napier (Eds.), *The book of family therapy.* New York: J. Aronson, 1972.

Hall, C. S., & Lindzey, G. *Theories of personality.* New York: John Wiley, 1957.

Hampden-Turner, C. M. An existential "learning theory" and the integration of T-group research. *Journal of Applied Behavioral Science,* 1966, *2*(4), 367–386.

Hanson, P. G., Rothaus, P., Johnson, D. L., & Lyle, F. A. Autonomous groups in human relations training for psychiatric patients. *Journal of Applied Behavioral Science,* 1966, *2*(3), 305–324.

Hare, A. P. *Handbook of small group research.* New York: Free Press, 1962.

Harris, J., & Joseph, C. *Murals of the mind: Image of a psychiatric community.* New York: International Universities Press, 1973.

Harrison, R. L. Research on human relations training: Design and interpretation. *Journal of Applied Behavioral Science,* 1971, *7*(1), 71–85.

Harrison, R. L., & Lubin, B. Personal style, group composition and learning. *Journal of Applied Behavioral Science,* 1965, *1*, 286–301.

Heine, C., Lubin, B., Perlmutter, J., & Lubin, A. Negotiating for group and trainers: The open marketplace. *Social Change,* 1974, *4*(2), 3–6.

Herbert, E. L., & Trist, E. L. The institution of an absent leader by a students' discussion group. *Human Relations,* 1953, *6*, 215–248.

Hill, L. B. On being rather than doing in group psychotherapy. *International Journal of Group Psychotherapy,* 1958, *8*(2), 115–122.

Hill, W. F. Hill Interaction Matrix (HIM): A conceptual framework for understanding groups. In J. E. Jones & J. W. Pfeiffer (Eds.), *The 1973 annual handbook for group facilitators.* La Jolla, Ca.: University Associates, 1973.

Hobbes, T. *Leviathan.* New York: Liberal Arts Press, 1958. (Originally published, 1651.)

Hobbs, N. Nondirective group counseling. *Journal of the National Association of Deans of Women,* March 1949, *12*(3), 114–121. Also in C. R. Rogers, *Client-centered therapy.* Boston: Houghton Mifflin, 1951.

Hobbs, N. Client centered therapy. In J. McCary & D. E. Sheer (Eds.), *Six approaches to psychotherapy.* New York: Dryden Press, 1955.

Horwitz, L. Transference in training groups and therapy groups. In R. T. Golembiewski & A. Blumberg (Eds.), *Sensitivity training and the laboratory approach: Readings about concepts and applications* (2nd ed.). Itasca, Ill.: F. E. Peacock, 1973.

House, R. J. T-group education and leadership effectiveness: A review of the empiric literature and a critical evaluation. *Personnel Psychology,* 1967, *20,* 1–32.

Houts, P. S., & Serber, M. (Eds.). *After the turn on, what?: Learning perspectives on humanistic groups.* Champaign, Ill.: Research Press, 1972.

Howard, J. *Please touch.* New York: McGraw-Hill, 1970.

Hume, D. Concerning human understanding. In R. M. Hutchins (Ed.), *Great books of the Western World* (Vol. 35). Chicago: Wm. Benton, Encyclopedia Britannica, 1952. (Originally published, 1748.)

Hyman, H. H., & Singer, E. An introduction to reference group theory and research. In E. P. Holland & R. G. Hunt, *Current perspectives in social psychology* (3rd ed.). New York: Oxford University Press, 1971.

Jackson, D. D. The managing of acting out in a borderline personality. In A. Burton (Ed.), *Case studies in counseling and psychotherapy.* New York: Prentice-Hall, 1959.

Jacobs, M. An holistic approach to behavior therapy. In A. A. Lazarus (Ed.), *Clinical behavior therapy.* New York: Brunner/Mazel, 1972.

Jaensch, E. *Grundformen Menschlichen Seins.* Berlin: O. Elsner, 1929.

Jaensch, E. *Eidetic imagery and typological methods of investigations: Their importance for the psychology of children, the theory of education, general psychology and the psychophysiology of human personality.* Westport, Conn.: Greenwood Press, 1970.

Jaffe, S. L., & Sherl, D. J. Acute psychosis precipitated by T-group experiences. *Archives of General Psychiatry,* 1969, *21,* 443–448.

James, M., & Jongeward, D. *Born to win: Transactional analysis with Gestalt experiments.* Reading, Mass.: Addison-Wesley, 1971.

James, W. *The principles of psychology.* New York: Henry Holt & Co., 1890.

Janov, A. *The primal scream: Primal therapy, the cure for neurosis.* New York: Putnam, 1970.

Johnson, D. L., Hanson, P. G., Rothaus, P., Morton, R. B., Lyle, F. A., & Moyer, R. Follow-up evaluation of human relations training for psychiatric patients. In E. H. Schein & W. G. Bennis (Eds.), *Personal and organizational change through group methods.* New York: John Wiley, 1965.

Jones, E. *The life and work of Sigmund Freud.* New York: Basic Books, 1953.

Jones, J. E. Types of growth groups. In J. W. Pfeiffer & J. E. Jones (Eds.), *The 1972 annual handbook for group facilitators.* La Jolla, Ca.: University Associates, 1972.

Kadis, A. L., et al. *A practicum of group psychotherapy.* New York: Harper & Row, 1963.

Kaplan, H. I., & Sadock, B. J. (Eds.). *Sensitivity through encounter and marathon* (H. I. Kaplan & B. J. Sadock, Eds., *Modern Group Books,* Vol. 4.). New York: J. Aronson, 1972.

Kaplan, S. R., & Roman, M. Phases of development in an adult therapy group. *International Journal of Group Psychotherapy,* January 1963, *13,* 10–26.

Kassebaum, G., Ward, D., & Wilner, D. *Prison treatment and parole survival: An empirical assessment.* New York: John Wiley, 1971.

Katz, D. *Animals and men: Studies in comparative psychology.* New York: Longmans, Green, 1937.

Katz, D. *[Gestalt psychology: Its nature and significance]* (R. Tyson, Trans.). New York: Ronald Press, 1950.

Khanna, J. L. *A discovery learning approach to inservice training.* Paper presented at the meeting of the American Psychological Association, San Francisco, 1968.

Kierkegaard, S. *Fear and trembling.* Princeton, N.J.: Princeton University Press, 1941.

King, C. H. Activity group therapy with a schizophrenic boy: Follow-up two years later. *International Journal of Group Psychotherapy,* April 1959, *9*(2), 184–194.

Klapman, J. W. *Group psychotherapy.* New York: Grune & Stratton, 1946.

Klaw, S. Two weeks in a T-group. *Fortune,* 1961, *64,* 114–117.

Koch, S. An implicit image of man. In L. Solomon & B. Berzon (Eds.), *New perspectives on encounter groups.* San Francisco: Jossey-Bass, 1972.

Koffka, K. [*The growth of the mind: An introduction to child psychology*] (2nd ed.) (R. M. Ogden, Trans.). New York: Harcourt Brace Jovanovich, 1928.

Koffka, K. *Principles of Gestalt psychology.* New York: Harcourt Brace Jovanovich, 1935.

Kohler, W. *Gestalt psychology.* New York: H. Liveright, 1929.

Krantzler, M. *Creative divorce.* New York: M. Evans, 1973.

Kuriloff, A. H., & Atkins, S. T-group for a work team. *Journal of Applied Behavioral Science*, 1966, 2(1), 63–69.

Lakin, M. *Interpersonal encounter: Theory and practice in sensitivity training.* New York: McGraw-Hill, 1972.

Lakin, M. Some ethical issues in sensitivity training. In R. T. Golembiewski & A. Blumberg (Eds.), *Sensitivity training and the laboratory approach: Readings about concepts and applications* (2nd ed.). Itasca, Ill.: F. E. Peacock, 1973.

Landau, M. Group psychotherapy with deaf retardates. *International Journal of Group Psychotherapy*, 1968, 18(3), 345–351.

Lazarus, A. A. Group therapy of phobic disorders by systematic desensitization. *Journal of Abnormal and Social Psychology*, 1961, 63, 504–510.

Lazarus, A. A. Behavior therapy in groups. In G. M. Gazda (Ed.), *Basic approaches to group psychotherapy and group counseling.* Springfield, Ill.: Charles C Thomas, 1968.

Lazarus, A. A. Group treatment for impotence and frigidity. *Sexology*, 1969, 36, 22–25. (a)

Lazarus, A. A. The inner circle strategy: Identifying crucial problems. In J. Krumboltz & C. Thorensen (Eds.), *Behavioral counseling: Cases and techniques.* New York: Holt, Rinehart and Winston, 1969. (b)

Lazarus, A. A. *Behavior therapy and beyond.* New York: McGraw-Hill, 1971.

Lazarus, A. A. *Clinical behavior therapy.* New York: Brunner/Mazel, 1972. (a)

Lazarus, A. A. The relation of theory to technical practice with special reference to eclecticism. *Multi Modal Behavior Therapy* (Behavioral Sciences Tape Library, Tape #4). Leonia, N.J.: Sigma Information, 1972. (b)

Lazell, E. W. The group treatment of dementia praecox. *Psychoanalytic Review*, 1921, 8, 168–179.

LeBon, G. *The crowd: A study of the popular mind.* London: T. F. Unwin, 1896.

Levitsky, A., & Simkin, J. Gestalt therapy. In L. N. Solomon & B. Berzon (Eds.), *New perspectives on encounter groups.* San Francisco: Jossey-Bass, 1972.

Lewin, K. Forces behind food habits and methods of change. *Bull International Research Council,* 1943, *108,* 35–65.

Lewin, K. *Resolving social conflicts: Selected papers on group dynamics* (G. W. Lewin, Ed.). New York: Harper & Row, 1948.

Lewin, K. *Field theory in social science: Selected theoretical papers* (D. Cartwright, Ed.). New York: Harper & Row, 1951.

Liberman, R. Behavioral approaches to family and couple therapy. *American Journal of Orthopsychiatry,* January 1970, *40*(1), 106–118. (a)

Liberman, R. A behavioral approach to group dynamics: I—Reinforcement and prompting of cohesiveness in group therapy. *Behavior Therapy,* 1970, *1,* 141–175. (b)

Liberman, R. A behavioral approach to group dynamics: II—Reinforcing and prompting hostility to the therapist in group therapy. *Behavior Therapy,* 1970, *1,* 312–327. (c)

Lieberman, M. A. Behavior and impact of leaders. In L. N. Solomon & B. Berzon (Eds.), *New perspectives on encounter groups.* San Francisco: Jossey-Bass, 1972.

Lieberman, M. A., Lakin, M., & Whitaker, D. S. Problems and potential of psychoanalytic and group dynamic theories for group psychotherapy. *International Journal of Group Psychotherapy,* April 1969, *19*(2), 131–141.

Lieberman, M. A., Yalom, I. D., & Miles, M. B. The impact of encounter groups on participants. *Journal of Applied Behavioral Science,* 1972, *8*(1), 29–50.

Lieberman, M. A., Yalom, I. D., & Miles, M. B. *Encounter groups: First facts.* New York, Basic Books, 1973.

Lipkin, S. Notes on group psychotherapy. *Journal of Nervous and Mental Diseases,* 1948, *107,* 459–479.

Locke, J. *An essay concerning human understanding* (Vols. 1 & 2). Oxford: Clarendon Press, 1894.

Locke, N. M. *Group psychoanalysis: Theory and technique.* New York: New York University Press, 1961.

London, P. *The modes and morals of psychotherapy.* New York: Holt, Rinehart and Winston, 1964.

Lubin, B., & Eddy, W. B. The laboratory training model: Rationale, method, and some thoughts for the future. *International Journal of Group Psychotherapy*, 1970, *20*, 305–339. Also in R. T. Golembiewski & A. Blumberg (Eds.), *Sensitivity training and the laboratory approach: Readings about concepts and applications* (2nd ed.). Itasca, Ill.: F. E. Peacock, 1973.

Luchins, A. S. *Group therapy: A guide.* New York: Random House, 1964.

Luft, J. *Group processes: An introduction to group dynamics.* Palo Alto, Ca.: National Press, 1963.

Luft, J. *Of human interaction.* Palo Alto, Ca.: National Press, 1969.

Mallenbaum, V., & Cohen, A. M. The chair and the Johnson grass. *Voices: The Art and Science of Psychotherapy*, Spring 1973, *31*, 40–45.

Mann, J. Group therapy with adults. *American Journal of Orthopsychiatry*, 1953, *23*, 332–337.

Mann, J., & Semrad, E. V. The use of group therapy in psychosis. *Journal of Social Casework*, 1948, *29*, 176–181.

Marrow, A. J. *The practical theorist: The life and work of Kurt Lewin.* New York: Basic Books, 1969.

Marsh, L. C. Group therapy by the psychological equivalent of the revival. *Mental Hygiene*, 1931, *15*, 328–349.

Martin, J. C., & Hill, W. F. Toward a theory of group development: Six phases of therapy group development. *International Journal of Group Psychotherapy*, 1957, *7*, 20–30.

Martinson, R. Solidarity under close confinement: A study of the freedom riders in Parchman Penitentiary. *Psychiatry*, 1967, *30*, 132–148.

Maslow, A. H. *Toward a psychology of being* (2nd ed.). New York: D. Van Nostrand, 1968.

Maslow, A. H. *The farther reaches of human nature.* New York: The Viking Press, 1971.

Massarik, F. Standards for group leadership. In L. N. Solomon & B. Berzon (Eds.), *New perspectives on encounter groups.* San Francisco: Jossey-Bass, 1972.

May, R. *Man's search for himself.* New York: Norton, 1953.

May, R. *Love and will.* New York: Norton, 1969.

May, R. *Power and innocence: A search for the sources of violence.* New York: Norton, 1972.

May, R., Angel, E., & Ellenberger, H. F. (Eds.). *Existence: A new dimension in psychiatry.* New York: Basic Books, 1958.

Mayer, A. Uber einzel und Gesamleistung des Schulkindes. *Arch. f. d. Ges. Psychol.*, 1903, *1*, 276–416.

McCorkle, L. W., Elias, A., & Bixby, F. L. *The Highfields story: An experimental treatment project for youthful offenders.* New York: Holt, Rinehart and Winston, 1958.

McDougall, W. *The group mind.* New York: Putnam's Sons, 1920.

McLellan, D. S., Sondermann, F. A., & Olson, W. C. *The theory and practice of international relations* (3rd ed.). Englewood Cliffs, N.J.: Prentice-Hall, 1970.

McLuhan, M. *Understanding media: The extensions of man.* New York: McGraw-Hill, 1964.

McLuhan, M., & Quentin, F. *The medium is the massage.* New York: Bantam, 1967.

McLuhan, M., & Watson, W. *From cliche to archetype.* New York: The Viking Press, 1970.

Meiers, J. I. Origins and development of group psychotherapy. *Sociometry*, 1945, *8*, 499–534.

Mellett, T. P. *Differences among therapists* (Part III of *The use of the critical incident technique to establish areas of change accompanying psychotherapy*). Unpublished master's thesis, University of Pittsburgh, 1952.

Meumann, E. *[Psychology of learning: An experimental investigation of the economy and technique of memory]* (J. W. Baird, Trans.). New York: Appleton-Century-Crofts, 1913.

Miles, M. B. Human relations training: How a group grows. *Teacher's College Record*, 1953, *55*, 90–96.

Miles, M. B. Human relations training: Processes and outcomes. *Journal of Counseling Psychology*, 1960, *7*(4), 301–306.

Miles, M. B. Changes during and following laboratory training: A clinical experimental study. *Journal of Applied Behavioral Science*, 1965, *1*, 215–242.

Mill, C. R. (Ed.). *Twenty exercises for trainers.* Washington, D.C.: NTL/Learning Resources Corporation, 1972.

Mill, J. *Analysis of the phenomena of the human mind.* London: Longmans, Green, Render & Dyer, 1869.

Mill, J. S. Representative government. In R. M. Hutchins (Ed.), *Great books of the Western World* (Vol. 43). Chicago: Wm. Benton, Encyclopedia Britannica, 1952. (Originally published, 1861.)

Miller, J. C. Effects of leadership style and meeting sequence on emotional responses in smoking groups (Doctoral dissertation, Yale University, 1967). *Dissertation Abstracts*, 1967, *28*(1–B), 341–342.

Miller, N. E. *Psychological research on pilot training* (AAF Aviation Psychology Program Research Report No. 8). Washington, D.C.: U.S. Government Printing Office, 1947.

Mills, T. M. *The sociology of small groups.* Englewood Cliffs, N.J.: Prentice-Hall, 1967.

Mintz, E. Time-extended marathon groups. *Psychotherapy: Theory, Research and Practice*, 1967, *4*(2), 65–70.

Mintz, E. *Marathon groups: Reality and symbol.* New York: Appleton-Century-Crofts, 1971.

Modlin, H. C., & Faris, M. Group adaptation and integration in psychiatric team practice. *Psychiatry*, 1956, *19*, 97–103.

Moreno, J. L. A note on sociometry and group dynamics. *Sociometry*, 1952, *15*(3–4), 364–366.

Moreno, J. L. *Foundations of psychotherapy* (J. L. Moreno, *Psychodrama*, Vol. 2.). New York: Beacon House, 1959. (a)

Moreno, J. L. The scientific meaning and the global significance of group psychotherapy. *Alta Psychotherapeutica et Psychosomatica, Orthopaedagog*, 1959, *7*, 148–167. (b)

Moreno, J. L. Lien entre la psychiatric et la sociologie (The concept of role: Bond between psychiatry and sociology). *Evolution Psychiatrique*, 1962, pp. 327–337.

Moreno, J. L. The actual trends in group psychotherapy. *Group Psychotherapy*, 1963, *16*, 117–131.

Morgan, C. T., & King, R. A. *Introduction to psychology* (3rd ed.). New York: McGraw-Hill, 1966.

Moustakas, C. E. *Creativity and conformity.* New York: D. Van Nostrand, 1967.

Mowrer, O. H. *The new group therapy.* New York: D. Van Nostrand, 1964.

Mullan, H. The nonteleological in dreams in group psychotherapy. *Journal of Hillside Hospital*, 1956, *5*, 480.

Mullan, H., & Rosenbaum, M. *Group psychotherapy: Theory and practice.* New York: Free Press, 1962.

Murphy, M. H. Education for transcendence. *Journal of Transpersonal Psychology*, 1969, *1*(2), 21–32.

Muuss, R. E. *Theories of adolescence.* New York: Random House, 1962.

Nadler, E. B. Social therapy of a civil rights organization. *Journal of Applied Behavioral Science*, 1968, 4(3), 281–298.

Nagay, J. A. *The airline tryout of the standard flight-check for the airline transport rating* (Civil Aeronautics Administration, Division of Research Report No. 88). Washington, D.C.: U.S. Government Printing Office, 1949. (a)

Nagay, J. A. *The development of a procedure for evaluating the proficiency of air route traffic controllers* (Civil Aeronautics Administration, Division of Research Report No. 83). Washington, D.C.: U.S. Government Printing Office, 1949. (b)

Naranjo, C. B. Contributions of Gestalt therapy. In H. A. Otto & J. Mann (Eds.), *Ways of growth*. New York: Grossman, 1968.

Nath, R. *Dynamics of organizational change: Some determinants of managerial problem solving and decision making competencies*. Unpublished doctoral dissertation, Massachusetts Institute of Technology, 1964.

National Training Laboratories Institute for Applied Behavioral Science. *Feedback and the helping relationship* (NTL Institute Reading Book). Washington, D.C.: Author, 1967.

National Training Laboratories Institute for Applied Behavioral Science. *Standards for the use of the laboratory method in NTL Institute programs*. Washington, D.C.: Author, 1969.

Neitzsche, F. W. [*Thus spake Zarathustra: A book for all and none*] (T. Common, Trans.). Edinburgh: T. N. Foulis, 1909.

Noyes, A., & Kolb, L. *Modern clinical psychiatry*. Philadelphia: W. B. Saunders, 1964.

O'Banion, T., & O'Connell, A. *The shared journey: An introduction to encounter*. Englewood Cliffs, N.J.: Prentice-Hall, 1970.

Osberg, J. W., & Berliner, A. K. The developmental stages in group psychotherapy with hospitalized narcotic addicts. *International Journal of Group Psychotherapy*, 1956, 6(1–4), 436–446.

Otto, H. A. (Ed.). *Human potentialities: The challenge and the promise*. St. Louis, Mo.: Warren H. Green, 1968.

Otto, H. A., & Mann, J. (Eds.). *Ways of growth*. New York: Grossman, 1968.

Park, R. E., & Burgess, E. W. *Introduction to the science of sociology* (3rd ed., rev.). Chicago: University of Chicago Press, 1969.

Parloff, M. B. Group therapy and the small-group field: An encounter. *International Journal of Group Psychotherapy*, 1970, 20(3), 267–304.

Paterson, J. G. Group supervision: A process and philosophy. *Community Mental Health Journal*, 1966, *2*(4), 315–318.

Peberdy, G. A. Hypnotic methods in group psychotherapy. *Journal of Mental Science*, 1960, *106*, 1016–1020.

Perls, F. S. *Gestalt therapy verbatim* (J. O. Stevens, Ed.). Moab, Utah: Real People Press, 1969.

Perls, F. S., Hefferline, R., & Goodman, P. *Gestalt therapy: Excitement and growth of the human personality.* New York: Dell, 1951.

Perls, L. One Gestalt therapist's approach. In J. Fagan & I. Shepherd (Eds.), *Gestalt therapy now.* Palo Alto, Ca.: Science & Behavior Books, 1970.

Pigors, F., & Pigors, P. J. W., *The incident process: Case studies in management development* (2nd ed.). Washington, D.C.: Bureau of National Affairs, 1957.

Plato. [*The laws*] (Vol. V) (G. Burgis, Trans.). London: Oxford University Press, 1960. (Original date, c. 348 B.C.)

Polansky, N., Lippitt, R., & Redl, F. An investigation of behavioral contagion in groups. *Human Relations*, 1950, *3*, 319–348.

Porter, L. A longer look at feedback. *Social Change*, 1974, *4*(3), 1–2.

Powdermaker, F., & Frank, J. D. Group psychotherapy with neurotics. *American Journal of Psychiatry*, 1948, *105*, 449–455.

Powdermaker, F., & Frank, J. D. *Group psychotherapy.* Cambridge, Mass.: Harvard University Press, 1953.

Pratt, J. H. *A year with Osler, 1896–1897: Notes taken at his clinics in the Johns Hopkins Hospital.* Baltimore: John Hopkins University Press, 1949.

Preston, H. O. *The development of a procedure for evaluating officers in the United States Air Force.* Pittsburgh: American Institute for Research, 1948.

Raskin, N. J. The development of nondirective therapy. *Journal of Consulting Psychology*, 1948, *12*, 92–110.

Reddy, W. B. Screening: Selection of participants. In L. N. Solomon & B. Berzon (Eds.), *New perspectives on encounter groups.* San Francisco: Jossey-Bass, 1972.

Reich, W. [*Character-analysis*] (3rd ed.) (T. P. Wolfe, Trans.). New York: Noonday Press, 1949.

Rhyne, J., & Vich, M. A. Psychological growth and the use of art materials: Small group experiments with adults. In A. J. Sutich & M. A. Vich (Eds.), *Readings in humanistic psychology.* New York: Free Press, 1969.

Roethlisberger, F. J., & Dickson, W. J. *Management and the worker: An account of a research program.* Cambridge, Mass.: Harvard University Press, 1939.

Rogers, C. R. *Counseling and psychotherapy: Newer concepts in practice.* Boston: Houghton Mifflin, 1942.

Rogers, C. R. *Client-centered therapy.* Boston: Houghton Mifflin, 1951.

Rogers, C. R. A process conception of psychotherapy. *American Psychologist,* 1958, *13,* 142–149.

Rogers, C. R. *On becoming a person.* Boston: Houghton Mifflin, 1961.

Rogers, C. R. The interpersonal relationship: The core of guidance. *Harvard Educational Review,* Fall 1962, *32*(4), 416–529.

Rogers, C. R. The process of the basic encounter group. In J. F. T. Bugental (Ed.), *Challenges of humanistic psychology.* New York: McGraw-Hill, 1967.

Rogers, C. R. *Carl Rogers on encounter groups.* New York: Harper & Row, 1970.

Rogers, C. R., & Stevens, B. *Person to person: The problem of being human: A new trend in psychology.* Walnut Creek, Ca.: Real People Press, 1967.

Rolf, I. Structural integration: Gravity, an unexplored factor in more human use of human beings. *Systematics,* 1958, *1*(1), 3–20.

Rose, S. *Treating children in groups: A behavioral approach.* San Francisco: Jossey-Bass, 1972.

Rosenbaum, M. Group psychotherapy and psychodrama. In B. P. Wolfman (Ed.), *Handbook of clinical psychology.* New York: McGraw-Hill, 1965.

Rossides, D. W. *Society as a functional process: An introduction to sociology.* Toronto: McGraw-Hill of Canada, 1968.

Rothaus, P., Johnson, D. L., Hanson, P. G., & Lyle, F. A. Participation and sociometry in autonomous and trainer-led patient groups. *Journal of Counseling Psychology,* 1966, *13*(1), 68–76.

Rouse, W. H. D. *Gods, heroes and men of ancient Greece.* New York: New American Library, 1957.

Rousseau, J. J. Social contract. In R. M. Hutchins (Ed.), *Great books of the Western World* (Vol. 38). Chicago: Wm. Benton, Encyclopedia Britannica, 1952. (Originally published, 1762.)

Rubin, I. The reduction of prejudice through laboratory training. *Journal of Applied Behavioral Science,* 1969, *3*(1), 29–50.

Sager, C. J., & Kaplan, H. S. (Eds.). *Progress in group and family therapy.* New York: Brunner/Mazel, 1972.

Sargent, W. *Battle for the mind.* London: Heinemann, 1957.

Sarlin, M. B., & Altshuler, K. Z. Group psychotherapy with deaf adolescents in a school setting. *International Journal of Group Psychotherapy,* July 1968, *18*(3), 337–344.

Satir, V. *Conjoint family therapy: A guide to theory and technique.* Palo Alto, Ca.: Science & Behavior Books, 1964.

Schein, E. H., & Bennis, W. G. *Personal and organizational change through group methods: The laboratory approach.* New York: John Wiley, 1965.

Schilder, P. The analysis of ideologies as a psychotherapeutic method, especially in group treatment. *American Journal of Psychiatry,* November 1936, *93*(3), 601–617.

Schilder, P. Results and problems of group psychotherapy in severe neurosis. *Mental Hygiene,* 1939, *23*, 87–98.

Schilder, P. *Brain and personality: Studies in the psychological aspects of cerebral neuropathology and the neuropsychiatric aspects of the motility of schizophrenics.* New York: International Universities Press, 1951. (a)

Schilder, P. *Psychoanalysis: Man and society.* New York: Norton, 1951. (b)

Schilder, P. *Psychotherapy* (2nd ed.). New York: Norton, 1951. (c)

Schindler, R. Bifocal group therapy. In J. Masserman & J. L. Moreno (Eds.), *Progress in psychotherapy.* New York: Grune & Stratton, 1958.

Schmuck, R. A. Helping teachers improve classroom group processes. *Journal of Applied Behavioral Science,* 1968, *4*(1) 401–435.

Schutz, W. C. *Firo: A three dimensional theory of interpersonal behavior.* New York: Holt, Rinehart and Winston, 1958.

Schutz, W. C. *Joy: Expanding human awareness.* New York: Grove Press, 1967.

Schutz, W. C. *Here comes everybody: Bodymind and encounter culture.* New York: Harper & Row, 1971.

Schutz, W. C. *Elements of encounter.* Big Sur, Ca.: Joy Press, 1973.

Schutz, W. C. Not encounter and certainly not facts. In J. W. Pfeiffer & J. E. Jones (Eds.), *The 1974 annual handbook for group facilitators.* La Jolla, Ca.: University Associates, 1974.

Schutz, W. C., & Seashore, C. Promoting growth with nonverbal exercises. In L. N. Solomon & B. Berzon (Eds.), *New perspectives on encounter groups.* San Francisco: Jossey-Bass, 1972.

Semrad, E. V., & Arsenian, J. The use of group processes in teaching group dynamics. *American Journal of Psychiatry,* 1951, *108*, 358–363.

Shambaugh, P. W., & Kanter, S. B. Spouses under stress: Group meetings with spouses of patients on hemodialysis. *American Journal of Psychiatry*, 1969, *125*(7), 923–936.

Shellow, R. S., Ward, J. L., & Rubenfeld, S. Group therapy and the institutionalized delinquent. *International Journal of Group Psychotherapy*, 1958, *8*(1–4), 265–275.

Sherif, M., & Sherif, C. W. *Groups in harmony and tension: An integration of studies on intergroup relations.* New York: Harper & Row, 1953.

Sherif, M., et al. *Intergroup conflict and cooperation: The Robbers' Cave experiment.* Norman, Okla.: Oklahoma University Institute of Group Relations, 1961.

Sikes, M. P., & Cleveland, S. Human relations training for police and community. *American Psychologist*, October 1968, *23*(10), 766–769.

Simmel, G. The metropolis and mental life. In K. H. Wolff (Ed.), *Die Grosstadt*. Dresden: Zahn & Jaenesch, 1903.

Simmel, G. *The sociology of Georg Simmel.* Glencoe, Ill.: Free Press, 1950.

Siroka, R. W., Siroka, E. K., & Schloss, G. A. *Sensitivity training and group encounter: An introduction.* New York: Grosset & Dunlap, 1971.

Skinner, B. F. *Science and human behavior.* New York: Macmillan, 1953.

Slavson, S. R. *The practice of group therapy.* New York: International Universities Press, 1947.

Slavson, S. R. *Analytic group psychotherapy with children, adolescents, and adults.* New York: Columbia University Press, 1950.

Slavson, S. R. *A textbook in analytic group psychotherapy.* New York: International Universities Press, 1964.

Smith, M. E. Comparison of certain personality traits as rated in the same individuals in childhood and fifty years later. *Child Development*, 1952, *23*(3), 159–180.

Smith, W. M. Observations over the lifetime of a small isolated group: Structure, danger, boredom and vision. *Psychological Reports*, 1966, *19*(2), 457–514.

Solomon, L. N., & Berzon, B. (Eds.). *New perspectives on encounter groups.* San Francisco: Jossey-Bass, 1972.

Sorrells, J. Groups, families and the karass. In L. N. Solomon & B. Berzon (Eds.), *New perspectives on encounter groups.* San Francisco: Jossey-Bass, 1972.

Spencer, H. *First principles* (2nd ed.). New York: Appleton-Century-Crofts, 1899.

Speth, E. W. *Function of age and education* (Part I of *The use of the critical incident technique to establish areas of change accompanying psychotherapy*). Unpublished master's thesis, University of Pittsburgh, 1952.

Spiegel, J. P. *Messages of the body.* Riverside, N.J.: Free Press, 1974.

Standal, S. W., & Corsini, R. J. (Eds.). *Critical incidents in psychotherapy.* Englewood Cliffs, N.J.: Prentice-Hall, 1959.

Stanford, G. Human relations training in the classroom. In R. T. Golembiewski & A. Blumberg (Eds.), *Sensitivity training and the laboratory approach: Readings about concepts and applications* (2nd ed.). Itasca, Ill.: F. E. Peacock, 1973.

Stefflre, B., & Matheny, K. B. *The function of counseling theory.* Boston: Houghton Mifflin, 1968.

Stephenson, R. M., & Scarpitti, F. R. *Group interaction as therapy: The use of the small group in corrections.* Westport, Conn.: Greenwood Press, 1974.

Stock, D. A survey of research on T-groups. In L. P. Bradford, J. R. Gibb, & K. D. Benne (Eds.), *T-group theory and the laboratory method: Innovation in re-education.* New York: John Wiley, 1964.

Stoller, F. H. The long weekend. *Psychology Today,* 1967, *1*(7), 28–33.

Stoller, F. H. Accelerated interaction: A time-limited approach based on the brief, intensive group. *International Journal of Group Psychotherapy,* 1968, *18*(2), 220–235. (a)

Stoller, F. H. Focussed feedback with video tape: Extending the group's functions. In G. M. Gazda (Ed.), *Innovations to group psychotherapy.* Springfield, Ill.: Charles C Thomas, 1968. (b)

Stoller, F. H. Marathon group therapy. In G. M. Gazda (Ed.), *Innovations to group psychotherapy.* Springfield, Ill.: Charles C Thomas, 1968. (c)

Stoller, F. H. Marathon groups: Toward a conceptual model. In L. N. Solomon & B. Berzon (Eds.), *New perspectives on encounter groups.* San Francisco: Jossey-Bass, 1972.

Stoute, A. Implementation of group interpersonal relationships through psychotherapy. *Journal of Psychology,* 1950, *30,* 145–156.

Sutherland, J. D. Notes on psychoanalytic group therapy. I—Therapy and training. *Psychiatry,* 1952, *15,* 111–117.

Telschow, E., Gorlow, L., & Hoch, E. L. *The role of the group leader in nondirective psychotherapy.* Ed.D. project, Teachers College, Columbia University, 1950.

Theodorson, G. A. Elements in the progressive development of small groups. *Social Forces,* 1953, *31,* 311–320.

Thomas, H. F. Encounter: The game of no game. In A. Burton (Ed.), *Encounter: Theory and practice of encounter groups*. San Francisco: Jossey-Bass, 1969.

Thorne, F. C. Principles of personality counseling. Brandon, Vt.: *Journal of Clinical Psychology*, 1950.

Thorpe, J. J., & Smith, B. Phases in group development in the treatment of drug addicts. *International Journal of Group Psychotherapy*, 1953, 3(1), 66–78.

Triplett, N. The dynamogenic factors in pacemaking and competition. *American Journal of Psychology*, 1897, 9, 507–533.

Tuckman, B. W. Developmental sequence in small groups. *Psychological Bulletin*, 1965, 63(6), 384–399.

Van Dusen, W., Hare, A. P., & Hill, L. B. The theory and practice of existential analysis. *American Journal of Psychotherapy*, 1957, 11(2), 310–322.

Van Meulenbrouck, M. Serial psychodrama with alcoholics. *Group Psychotherapy and Psychodrama*, 1972, 25(4), 151–154.

Walton, R. E. How to choose between strategies of conflict and collaboration. In R. T. Golembiewski & A. Blumberg (Eds.), *Sensitivity training and the laboratory method: Readings about concepts and applications* (2nd ed.). Itasca, Ill.: F. E. Peacock, 1973.

Ward, L. F. *Dynamic sociology*. New York: Appleton-Century-Crofts, 1883.

Warkentin, J. Marriage: The cornerstone of the family system. In O. Pollak & A. Friedman (Eds.), *Family dynamics and female sexual delinquency*. Palo Alto, Ca.: Science & Behavior Books, 1969.

Watson, R. I. *The great psychologists from Aristotle to Freud* (2nd ed.). Philadelphia: Lippincott, 1968.

Watts, A. W. *Psychotherapy, east and west*. New York: Pantheon Books, 1961.

Webster's new collegiate dictionary (2nd ed.). Springfield, Mass.: G. & C. Merriam, 1960.

Wender, L. The dynamics of group psychotherapy and its application. *Journal of Nervous and Mental Disorders*, 1936, 84, 54–60.

Wertheimer, M. Untersuchungen zur Lehre von der Gestalt II. *Psychol. Forsehung*, 1923, 4, 301–351.

Wertheimer, M. *Productive thinking*. New York: Harper & Row, 1945.

Weschler, I. R., & Reisel, J. *Inside a sensitivity training group* (Monograph of the Institute of Industrial Relations, Series 4). Los Angeles: University of California, 1959.

Whitaker, C. A., & Malone, T. P. *The roots of psychotherapy.* New York: Blakiston, 1953.

Whitman, R. M. Psychodynamic principles underlying T-group processes. In L. P. Bradford, J. R. Gibb, & K. D. Benne (Eds.), *T-group theory and the laboratory method: Innovation in re-education.* New York: John Wiley, 1964.

Wickert, F. *Psychological research on problems of redistribution* (AAF Aviation Psychological Program Research Report No. 14). Washington, D.C.: U.S. Government Printing Office, 1947.

Wile, D. B. Nonresearch uses of the group leadership questionaire (GTQ-C). In J. W. Pfeiffer & J. E. Jones (Eds.), *The 1972 annual handbook for group facilitators.* La Jolla, Ca.: University Associates, 1972.

Williams, M. *The velveteen rabbit or how toys become real.* Garden City, N.Y.: Doubleday, 1958.

Wolberg, L. R. *The technique of psychotherapy* (2nd ed.). New York: Grune & Stratton, 1967.

Wolf, A. The psychoanalysis of groups (Part I). *American Journal of Psychotherapy,* 1949, 3(4), 525–558.

Wolf, A. The psychoanalysis of groups (Part II). *American Journal of Psychotherapy,* 1950, 4(1), 16–50.

Wolpe, J., & Lazarus, A. A. *Behavior therapy techniques: A guide to the treatment of neuroses.* New York: Pergamon, 1966.

Yablonsky, L. *The tunnel back: Synanon.* New York: Macmillan, 1965.

Yablonsky, L. Humanizing groups through psychodrama. *Group Psychotherapy and Psychodrama,* 1972, 25(1), 7–15.

Yalom, I. D. *The theory and practice of group psychotherapy.* New York: Basic Books, 1970.

Yalom, I. D., & Lieberman, M. A. A study of encounter group casualties. *Archives of General Psychiatry,* July 1971, 25, 16–30. Also in R. T. Golembiewski & A. Blumberg (Eds.), *Sensitivity training and the laboratory approach: Readings about concepts and application* (2nd ed.). Itasca, Ill.: F. E. Peacock, 1973.

APPENDIX

Behavioral Characteristics

1. Acquaintance

1. Individuals categorize or pigeonhole one another, with outside roles and statuses often determining inside roles.
2. During the superficial acquaintance process group members get to know one another by sharing names, background, and outside information.
3. Some members lead the discussion enthusiastically, while others respond with little activity or dialogue.
4. Group members size up one another covertly and test each other out. This is known as covert appraisal and testing.

2. Goal Ambiguity and Diffuse Anxiety

5. Members avoid sustained work because of the lack of common goals and values.
6. Members experience confusion, uncertainty, or difficulty in understanding the goals or purposes of the group. Attempts at defining group aims, structures, and modes of function are largely unsuccessful.
7. Trivial or irrelevant topics or issues are discussed.
8. Anxiety is diffuse and is expressed in concerns over the ambiguity of the situation and its unstructured nature. Members seek to reduce this ambiguity.
9. The group members' experience of this anxiety may be of a general or unspecified nature.
10. Members, during this stage, feel very unsure of themselves. Some members may feel helpless to do anything and may become self-deprecating and express inadequacy.

11. A few members may attempt to establish bonds with other members who seem to have similar problems, attitudes, and backgrounds. They identify with those who are in a similar situation.

12. A few members may defend themselves by becoming hesitant to enter into interactions and may resist all attempts to engage them in conversation.

13. These members may engage in autistic, self-centered communication monologues without really hearing or responding to what others have said.

14. Values and attitudes go into a state of flux, because of the new and ambiguous situation.

15. Group members show mistrust of one another by exhibiting caution and conformity.

16. Members become accustomed to being together as a group. They adjust to the group situation.

3. Members' Search for Position/Definition: Primary Group Transferences/Countertransferences

17. Power may shift rapidly during this phase as various assertive members try to influence and/or control the group or engage in leadership struggles. Initiators become leaders; leaders emerge; those group members who take the initiative in interacting tend to become the leaders.

18. Being fearful of the group and involvement on a personal level, some members will continue to engage in considerable intellectualization and generalization.

19. Some members tend to keep the conversation going at all costs and to engage in excessive or overly smooth talking.

20. A member's statement may be related to another's, but his responses are not in the context of the previous speaker.

21. There is indirect discussion of group concerns: group members discuss an outside problem or intellectual concern that indirectly reflects issues in the group; e.g., a group with difficulties in resolving membership or attendance issues may discuss truancy in school children.

22. At this stage of group life, differences begin to emerge in accordance with pre-existing definitional societal ranks and status. These differences give rise to an early form of cleavage in the group, e.g., police vs. community.

23. Projection of blame and responsibility toward the leader and other members becomes more evident.

24. Anxiety over intimacy and attempts at closeness begin to be exhibited. Group members are fearful of disclosing their inner selves.

25. Group members vie with one another for the approval of the leader by seeking to be closest to him and to please him the most.
26. Group members are generally protective toward the leader and his image. They defend him against any and all criticisms, protect him from being hurt, and view him almost as perfect (an expression of dependence).
27. Because of their desire or expectation that the leader will tell them what to do and will take all responsibility for what happens in the group, some members continue to express dependence on the leader.
28. Some members tend to express anger toward the surroundings, the institution.
29. Members engage in resistance, delay, and disruption; i.e., group members may take negative attitudes, change the subject, or delay the actions of the group.
30. Group members may be unwilling or unable to admit they are experiencing negative feelings, even when clear evidence of hostility is pointed out by the leader.
31. A cleavage between dependent and counterdependent members of the group becomes apparent.
32. Members form small partnerships for mutual support.
33. Some members may be absent from the group or show their reluctance to participate in other ways.
34. There is frustration with the way the group is functioning; members are unable to perform effectively on a task, to change their way of operating, or significantly to influence their own fate.
35. Regarding leadership and structure, some group members choose one member of the group to be their leader and structure the situation for them.
36. Increased hostility is expressed toward the leader because of a number of complex factors. The leader is still an outsider and is viewed by members as not being a full member of the group.
37. Members become angry because of their perceived dependence on the leader.
38. Some of the group members may begin to test the strengths and limits of the leader in various ways. They may try to provoke him by seeing if they can shock him by catching some fault or shortcoming.
39. Assertive members may imply (sometimes quite directly) that the leader is incompetent and unnecessary.
40. Relationships and feelings begin to fluctuate rapidly. They range from intense, but brief, linkages to sharp reversals of feelings.
41. Some members engage in inappropriate disclosure, striving to be the center of attention.
42. Members tend to communicate their own needs through their "typical" interpersonal life styles that are introduced as a consequence of the ambiguous situation.

43. Group members respond to the leader (or other members) with feelings and behaviors learned in earlier groups, usually family and other primary group relationships. They tend to transfer primary feelings and modes of relating.

4. Sharpened Affects and Anxieties: Increased Defensiveness

44. Males may clash with one another while females observe, in a controlled acting-out process. Males struggle for leadership; females frequently play more passive roles.
45. Cleavages develop between people who are personally vs. counterpersonally oriented and structured vs. unstructured. Group members are split on every issue they try to deal with and seem unable to agree on anything (cleavage-fragmentation).
46. Members show anxiety concerning their anger and aggressions and the potential loss of ego-defenses on which their self-esteem is built.
47. Fears emerge centering about belonging and acceptance.
48. Scapegoating occurs: individual members of the group are singled out as targets of hostility (anger may be shifted from the leader to other members).
49. Catharsis/tension release involves the release or relieving of emotional tension by an individual or the group through the expression of positive or negative feelings directed toward a specific person. For example, a T-group member may confront the trainer and openly express his resentment or hostility.
50. Another form of tension release occurs when a particularly strong emotional sharing or exchange within the group is followed by a joke or humorous remark. Laughter dissipates the tension.
51. The tensions members experience and the stress they feel as a result of subgroupings and cleavages become difficult to bear, and members express a desire to move toward unity.
52. Group members more specifically identify what discipline or punishment they fear and why they fear it.
53. Group members return to old methods of adaptation in response to difficulties. Regressive behavior to projection displacement to denial of affect may occur. Members may be observed alternating between fight and flight—between sudden attacks and withdrawal or avoidance.
54. As group members are unwilling or unable to talk about feelings and transactions between group members, defensiveness/denial toward the here-and-now occurs. Members talk about things outside of the group; they resist or ignore any attempt by the leader to focus attention on immediate events in the group.

55. Defensiveness/denial of external dangers occurs as group members deny or minimize the real dangers that exist in their external environment.

56. When accused of wrongs, group members deny that they have done anything wrong or that there is any need for them to change: defensiveness/denial of wrongdoing or need to change.

57. Group members attempt to limit their interactions to task-related activities of a conceptual nature.

58. After leadership struggles and changes, original leaders re-emerge.

59. Members cling to old values and attitudes in the face of apparent threats to them.

5. Sharpened Interactions: Growth-Identifying Activities and Reality Strengthening

60. Catalyst roles emerge as some members behave in ways that encourage total member involvement and precipitate group interaction.

61. Group members take a more vigorous part in the interaction.

62. Misunderstandings become sharpened as frequent communication problems occur.

63. Group members share more of their significant personal experiences, including early lives, dreams, and problems.

64. Silent members are actively encouraged to interact with others.

65. Group members may openly engage in a discussion of their concerns about power and leadership in the group.

66. During this phase, relationships between the leader and the individual member are strengthened through a slow process.

67. Reality testing between the leader and members increases and grows stronger.

68. Group members may begin to test their perceptions and assumptions about the leader by verbalizing them and checking them with him.

6. Norm Crystallization/Enforcement-Defensification

69. Norms develop as the group works on and evolves rules and standards for behavior in the group.

70. Group attention stays on interactions and processes within the group, not on outside matters.

71. A norm of participation develops in which participation by the total group becomes a group value.

72. One person may assume the role of disciplinarian who punishes or chastises group members deviating from the group's norms.

73. Group members give support to the emerging role of disciplinarian.

74. Daily routine patterns of working and relating are established.

75. In general, members become self-disciplined and self-regulated.

76. Rapid development of goals and values occurs. Group members quickly settle on goals for the group and the values within which to operate.

77. Because norms are not grossly violated, discipline becomes less harsh.

78. The group begins to develop a unique culture that includes jargon, rituals, a group consciousness and cohesion, rites of passage, group roles, etc.

79. Outside ties are devaluated.

80. Negative reactions to dissension in the group become more frequent.

81. There is a breaking of psychological ties to outside relationships (family) as members form attachments to the group.

82. This may lead group members to view the nonmember outgroup with suspicion, distrust, or hostility.

83. Group members, in describing themselves, may exaggerate their accomplishments or experiences.

84. Those who dissent or refuse to cooperate with the group suffer temporary loss of status.

85. Group members try to effect compromises between any remaining cleavages and factions.

86. To preserve the illusion of greater unity, there is a tendency to gloss over or ignore some disputes among group members.

87. Group members who have aligned themselves with neither the dependents nor the counterdependents begin to speak their views, and other members listen to them.

88. Later in this stage, group punishment becomes harsher because norms are violated more before action is taken.

89. Members tend to concentrate on cooperating on simple tasks. There is an observable willingness to work together on tasks and goals.

90. Individual identity is submerged in the group. Members deny their own identity in pursuit of group unity.

7. Distributive Leadership

91. Members take individual responsibility for their own problems and for what happens to them in the group.

92. An increase in feelings of equality occurs; members accept each other as equals.

93. A more realistic view of the leader emerges. There is acceptance of the leader's role. Group members accept the authority of the leader and his position; he is seen less in black-and-white terms and more as a person.

94. Group members now begin to use the leader more freely as a "skilled resource" who can observe group process and help them deal with emotional issues.

95. There is an integrated autonomy in which group members can assert individuality and independence without threatening group solidarity.

96. In essence the leader is seen as a person and as a member of the group.

97. Members develop and apply observation skills by acting as observers of the group process as well as participants in it, thus becoming more self-regulating and self-determining.

98. Informality prevails. Leadership and structure become functional to whatever the group is doing.

99. There may be a considerable increase in decisions based on consensus through basically rational discussions of the issues involved.

100. When conflict occurs during this state, it is over substantive rather than hidden emotional issues.

101. Formal structure and roles wither. The formalized structure of leadership and decision making ceases to operate; informality prevails; leadership and structure are functional.

8. Decreased Defensiveness and Increased Experimentation

102. There is a dropping of masks and protective facades.

103. Insight into others develops and becomes common.

104. Symptom modification relief, such as absenteeism, occurs with a reduction or disappearance of outside problems.

105. There is diminished aggression. Members experience less anger and show less hostility. A more relaxed informal state seems to characterize this phase.

106. There is a freer flow of feelings and thoughts.

107. Group members are more open in expressing hostility toward one another and in expressing general tensions, angers, and fears, and in working through conflict between one another. As a result, tension is lowered in the group.

108. There is more open, free expression of negative and positive feelings. Fantasies and previously unexpressed thoughts are now discussed.

109. There is an increase in the amount and appropriate application of feedback. Members tell each other their reactions to and perceptions of one another, evaluating each other's group roles.

110. There is an increase in the development of empathy. Members come to understand the feelings of one another and their problems and have a greater insight into each other's differences. A nonjudgmental atmosphere prevails.

111. Less-biased evaluations of the contributions of members and members' questions are seen more frequently. There is less regard for power or status in the group.

112. Insight into others is common. Group members perceive the defenses and the faulty value systems of other group members. They seek to understand the underlying reasons.

113. Members are also able to deal directly with emotional and maintenance issues and are able to separate task from maintenance.

114. The locus of evaluation moves inward. Group members consider their self-evaluation most important.

115. Group members work on personal problems and discuss the problems that bother them both within the group and outside. They are able to share common experiences.

116. Members gain self-awareness and insight and become more aware of their own personal involvement in the group and how it tends to affect their perceptions. They see their own biases and prejudices; they are able to accept these and other aspects of group process without alarm.

117. Members try out new ways of behaving and atypical interpersonal styles.

118. Risk taking emerges as group members express feelings or behave in ways that involve the risk of group hostility, ridicule, or rejection.

119. An increased sense of self-worth and self-confidence occurs as group members value themselves more highly and have greater self-esteem.

120. Personal growth and improved outside relationships occur as members develop new ambitions, reveal increased self-reliance, and have more realistic goals and better interpersonal skills.

121. There is a higher regard for others since members have greater respect and liking for one another as individuals. Having moved beyond their initial impressions or stereotypes to more realistic views of one another they have a more realistic view of group members.

122. Group members show a greater willingness to compromise for the sake of solidarity. Personalities of group members are reorganized and defenses regrouped.

9. Group Potency

123. Group support and reinforcement is given as the group accepts individual members and rewards their positive changes.

124. There is a functional and flexible use of the group. Members are able to choose whether it is appropriate to deal with an issue or ignore it.

125. Purposefulness occurs as members frequently reaffirm their sense of direction.

126. Cooperation and shared responsibility is common as group members work together on their task in a way that demonstrates an acceptance of mutual responsibility for achieving their goals. They have a greater awareness of the problems that face them.

127. Members experience time as prolonged.

128. There is regularity in attendance.

129. There are longer spans of attention to interaction involving interpersonal learnings. Some interaction sequences last for several meetings.

130. Interdependence increases interpersonal solidarity as common goals and the need to work together increase group members' loyalty and affection for one another.

131. There is a greater awareness of the need to work together and an increase in group members' loyalties and affections for one another. The group is integrated and cohesive. Group members are typically responsive, loyal, and accepting toward one another.

132. The group may deal with highly intense interpersonal interactions without becoming defensive or changing the subject.

133. There is an intensification of elation and excitement; members experience intense joy and pleasure.

134. Members become confident that the group will accept them as they are.

135. Members accept the group as a potent change agent for personal growth and verbalize their acceptance.

10. Termination

136. There are expressions of overoptimism about the power of the group. Some members attempt to overestimate the group's potential for resolving their problems.

137. Members are individually and collectively optimistic.

138. Some members may wish to deny the impending termination of the group by expressing disbelief and regret. This is coupled with a verbalized wish to extend the group sessions.

139. As a defense against the pain of separation, some group members withdraw before the group ends.

140. Some members begin to withdraw their involvement in the group and seek some closure.

141. Other members experience happiness over leaving and returning to the "outside" world.

142. Members experience the need to affirm that the group has been valuable to them, and they express these feelings in the form of testimonials.

143. There is a growing sense of completion. Members feel they have completed the task of the group and are now ready to go forward and look to the outside world.

144. Others will wish to explore the mechanics of the transfer of learning.

Indexes

SUBJECT INDEX

Acquaintance process, 163, 164, 168, 169-170
Activities outside of group, 234-235
Aggression, 164, 173, 174
A-groups, 40
Alumni laboratories, 41
American Association of Humanistic Psychology, 50
Animal model, 24
Anxiety, 71, 74, 142, 143, 146, 163, 164-167, 168, 169, 170-171, 172, 173-174, 175, 177, 178, 179, 180, 190, 191, 200, 228, 229, 230, 271, 272, 274
Application of new behavior, 62-63
 See also Practice and application of new behaviors
Asylums, 24
Atypical behavior, 166, 178, 179, 278
Authenticity, 78, 79-80, 199
Authority, 103-108, 145, 165, 175, 176, 235-237
Aviation psychology program, 121

"Barometric" group members, 129-130, 216
Basic assumptions, 58-60
"Battleship" group style, 221

Behavior
 atypical, 166, 178, 179
 change, 71, 74, 75, 161, 183, 184, 223-224
 descriptions of, 184, 185, 186, 187, 190, 193, 199, 200, 201, 205, 207, 209, 212, 215, 216
Behavioral characteristics, 169-217, 271-280
Behavioral events, 156, 185, 186, 191, 193, 205, 209, 212, 216
Behaviors, extinction and reinforcement of, 161
Body armor, 233
Body awareness, 54, 81
Body wisdom, 80-81
Breaking-out intervention, 151-152
BST group, 38-40
Buddhism, 15

Challenge to leadership, 163, 228-229, 236-237, 273
 See also leadership and authority
Change goal, 223
Change within groups, 218-221
Character armor, 48-49
Choice
 group member, 69, 70
 leader, freedom of, 9-10

Choice points, 114, 129-131
Christianity, 15, 16
Cleavage in group, 164, 172, 173, 174, 176, 273, 274, 276
Client-centered therapy, 68, 70, 72, 136
Closeness, 78-79, 164, 167, 170, 172
  See also Warmth, trust, and closeness
Closure, group members' search for, 167, 180, 181, 279
Community groups, 39
Completion of issue, 231
Conditions for learning, 3, 58-63
Conflict, 67, 79, 220-221, 236
Confrontation, 103
Confucianism, 15-16
Connecticut Workshop Project, 37
Controlled observational measures, 122
"Cooling off" process, 109
Counterconditioning, 67
Covert appraisal and testing, 170, 205, 271
Creativity, 81-82
Critical incident
  concept, evolution of, 115-116
  procedure, 119-120
  technique, systematic use of, 119
Critical-Incident Model, 4, 5, 6, 7, 8, 114-154
  guidelines for use of, 129
  outline of, 124-125
Critical incidents, 6
  "The Chair and the Johnson Grass," 237-244
  common problems of, 118
  defined, 114
  directive, 132-133
  encounter group, 132, 148-154
  examples of, 88-89, 90, 91-92, 93, 103-108
  nondirective group, 137-138, 139
  nondirective individual, 135-137, 139
  P.A.C. model, 105-107
psychoanalytic group, 140-143
in school settings, 122
T-group, 144-148

Data, collection of, 122
Decision making, group, 165, 175, 176, 177, 277
Defensiveness, 164, 173-176, 199, 200, 231-232, 275
  decreased, 166, 169, 178-179, 185, 191, 193, 199, 207, 209, 212, 214
Democracy in groups, 222-223
Demonology, 24
Dependence/counterdependence, 163, 164, 168, 172, 236
Dependency, 67, 126, 131, 141, 164, 170, 171, 172, 220
Design strategy, 3, 4, 58, 63-64, 65, 69, 73, 75, 78, 224-225
Developmental processes, 155
Developmental psychology, 155
Developmental stages of groups, 155-217
Diffuse anxiety, 163, 168, 170-171
  See also Goal ambiguity
Directionality, 125
Directive group, 7, 64-67
Disclosure, 61-62, 74, 175, 273
"Dissection" group style, 221
Distributive leadership 2, 73, 176-178, 207, 212, 222
Dominant theme topics
  concept of, 161-181
  behavioral characteristics of, 271-280
Double-bind situation, 49
Drug addicts, studies of, 200, 201
Dynamics, group, 23, 33-34, 72

Eastern philosophy, 15-16, 49
Eclectic approach, 67
Emotional distance, 91
Empiricism, British, 18-20

Encounter groups, 7, 47-49, 51-52, 65, 76-83, 84-86, 148-153, 183, 186, 187, 188, 193, 195, 196, 199, 207, 208, 218
Esalen Institute, 51
Evolution, 21
Evolution of groups, 161, 220-221
Existentialism, 45-47
Exorcism, 24
Experimentation, 62, 167, 169, 191, 193, 199, 205, 207, 209, 214, 277-278

Fading, 2
Faith in group process, 219
False consensus, 170, 173, 174
Family model, 172
  See also Primary group model
Family therapy, 31, 65
Feedback, 60-62, 74, 75, 117, 165, 175, 180, 220, 277
Force-field theory, 34, 36, 59, 223

Game playing, 233
Generalizing from research, 183
Goal ambiguity and diffuse anxiety, 163, 168, 170-171
Goals of therapy, 65
"Great man" question, 182
Greek philosophy, 13-14
Greeks, application of groups by, 14, 27
Group
  approaches, 33-57
  assumptions of authors about, 59-60
  atmosphere, 222
  climate, 126-128
  composition, 31
  growth, 35, 45, 51
  mind, 23, 28
  movement, 35, 45
  phase, 125-126

potency, 179-180
pressure, 80
procedures, intensity of, 31
process (es), 11, 60, 72, 155-156, 162-184, 220
power, 180
psychotherapy, 26-35
  differences from individual psychotherapy, 30
  as social field, 223-224
  stages, 220-221
  styles, 220-221
  systems of concern, levels of, 4
  therapy, 26-35
Group Analytic Society, 31
Group dynamics, 23, 33-34, 72
Group gestalt, 34
Group growth and development, 8, 118, 123, 135
  continuous model of, 160
  criteria for a model of, 157-158
  cyclical model of, 155-156, 159-160
  evolutionary model of, 160-161, 216-217
  four-stage models of, 201-207
  lack of theories of, 156-157, 185
  literature, 156-160
  model of, 113, 156
  models of more than four stages, 70-72
  recycling model of, 160
  sequential discontinuous model of, 160
  study of,
    control of bias in, 186
    criterion for inclusion in, 185
  theory of, 156-158, 216
  three-stage models of, 191, 193, 201
  two-stage models of, 187-191, 192
Group leadership orientation of authors, 4
Group leader, training of, 7
Group Psychotherapy Association, 31

Groups
 applications of, 31, 32, 33, 42
 criticism of, 52-53
 goal-oriented behavior in, 32-33
 growth, 35, 45, 51
  the significant encounter in, 48
 history of, 2, 13-57
 use of the arts in, 54
 uses of, 56
"Growth needs," 226

Hawthorne studies, 39
Here-and-now, 42, 69, 79-80, 100, 181, 221
"Hidden agenda," 96
Hillel's rule, 16
History of groups, 2, 13-57
 Greek philosophy in, 13-14
 hospitals in, 25
 religious influences in, 14-17
Humanistic-existential orientation, 181
Humanistic therapists, 34
Human potential movement, 47
Hypnosis, 35

Impromptu, 30
Incident process, 121-122
Individual responsibility, 68
Industrial revolution, effects of, 18
Insight, 71, 82-83
Intensity of intervention, 4, 102-113
 concentric circle model of, 103-104
Interpersonal-intrapersonal problems, clarification of, 41
Interpersonalization, 163, 164-167, 168, 180, 279
Interpersonal relationships, emphasis on, 29
Intervention
 conceptual type of, 87, 91, 92-99

 experiential type of, 87, 88, 92
 group level, 87, 88-91
 ignored, 230
 individual level, 87, 88-91
 intensity of, 5, 87, 88, 102-113
 intent of, 133-134
 interpersonal level, 87, 88-91
 level of, 5, 87-91
 method of, 123
 problem areas, 117
 response, selection of, 114, 115, 116, 117, 126-133
 structural type of, 87, 88, 100-102
 styles of, 4
 techniques, 76
 timing and rationale of, guidelines for, 65-66
 type of, 5, 87, 88, 91-102
Intervention Cube, 4, 5, 7, 8, 87-88
 comparison of orientations, 154
 uses of, 87, 113
Interventions
 "piggyback," 112, 115
 movement of, 90, 113
Intimacy, 62, 179, 221
 See also Closeness
Islam, 15

Johari Window, 95-96
Judaism, 14, 15, 16
Juvenile delinquents, study of, 205

Knowledge, skills, and values, 3, 38, 60, 144, 225, 227, 228

Laboratory training, 4, 17, 35-45, 72-76
 issues, 43-45
Leader
 directive group, 64-65

freedom of choice of, 9-10
influence of, vii, 1
role of, 11, 74, 76, 94, 116, 123, 126, 177, 222, 227-237, 277
Leaderless groups, 117, 123
Leadership
abdication of, 227
and authority, 104-108, 218-219, 235-236
challenge to, 163, 228-229, 236-237, 273
distributive, 2, 73, 176-178, 207, 222
functions of, 122-123
and interventions in special circumstances, 218, 227-235
responsibility, 227
Leadership Development Programs, Inc., 41
Learning, conditions for, 3, 58-63
Level of intervention, 5
Life style, influence of, 129
Living in the present, See Here-and-now

Marathon group, 55
Manual for group leaders, 7, 8-9, 236
Medical model, 23-25
Members' search for position/definition, 163, 168, 171-173
Mental illness, history and treatment of, 23-31
Molar events, 162
Molecular vs. molar view, 182
Monasteries, 14-16
Mood of group, 126-127

"Narrow-band" groups, 186, 187, 188, 189, 191, 193, 194, 195, 200, 202, 203, 204, 205, 207, 212, 214, 215
National Training Laboratories (NTL), 41, 42, 43, 44, 61

Neurotic member, 233-234
Nondirective group, 7, 32, 68-72
Nonverbal activities, 80, 100
Normatization, 75, 163, 164-167, 168, 170, 171, 173, 175, 176, 177, 178, 179, 180, 275, 276
Norm crystallization, 165, 175-176, 275-276
Norm of participation, 175, 275

"On the spot" theory, 98-99
"Opening up," 232-233

Peak experience, 102, 179, 230
Pecking order, 106
Personalization, 163, 164-167, 168, 180, 279
Personal problems, 233, 234-235
"Personals" vs. "structurals," 221
Philosophy, Greek, 13-14
Physical contact, 78-81
Planned theory input (PTI), 92-98, 218
"Plop-flop," 99, 111-112, 226
Possession, 24
Power, 67, 163, 164-167, 168, 170, 172, 174, 175, 176, 178, 179, 180, 272, 278, 279
Practice and application of new behavior, 62-63
Primary group model, 172-173
Process(es), group, 11, 60, 72, 155-156, 162-184, 220
Protestantism, 21
Psychic causality, 159
"Psychoanalysis" group style, 174, 221
Psychoanalytic groups, 31, 64, 67
Psychodrama, 48
Psychological time vs. chronological time, 179
Psychologist as therapist, 25
Psychology, developmental, 155

Rational-emotive groups, 4, 64
Reality therapy, 67
Religious work groups, 17
Renaissance, 17-18
Representations collectives, 22, 23
Research studies, 117-118
Reversals, 187, 190, 200, 207, 212, 215
Risk taking, 43, 166, 179, 232, 278
"Rites of passage," 220
Role of leader, 11, 94, 123, 126, 177, 222, 227-237, 277
Role playing, 50, 190
Roles, assumption of by group members, 176

Satiation, 67
Scapegoating, 174, 274
Screening of members, 233
Seduction into membership of leader, 165, 175, 229
Sensory awareness, 54, 80-81
Sharing progression, 147-148
Sharpened affects and anxieties, 163, 164, 169, 173-174, 274-275
Sharpened interactions, 165, 174-175, 275
"Sharpshooting" group style, 221
Silence, 229-230
Situational approach in group therapy, 31
Skill groups, 40
Social psychology, emergence of, 26
Social telesis, 22
Sociology, 22-23
Sociometry, 30
Southwest Human Relations Laboratory, 41
Special nature of groups, 218, 219-223
"Split" in groups, 221
Spontaneous theory input (STI), 92, 98-99, 218
Structural integration, 54

Structured experiences, 100-101
Styles of groups, 220-221
Supportive climate, 62, 74
Surface issues, 130-131, 231
Survival concept of behaviors, 161
Synanon, 53, 55

Task-orientation, 100, 101, 221
Temptations of beginning leader, 229
Termination, 162, 167, 168, 180-181, 199, 200, 205, 212, 279-280
T-group, 7, 40, 41, 42, 52, 65, 76, 77, 80, 83, 84-86, 144-148, 149, 181, 182, 183, 186, 187, 188, 189, 191, 193, 194, 195, 196, 201, 202, 203, 204, 205, 207, 208, 214, 215, 218, 221
Theme topics, 163-182
Theory
  application to groups, 225-226
  criteria for group, 157-158
  functions of, 157, 158
  inputs, 226-227
  role in design strategy and interventions, 218, 223-227
Therapy
  client centered, 68, 70, 72, 136
  goals of, 65
  group, 26-35, 84-86
There-and-then, 68
  See also Here-and-now
Third revolution in psychiatry, 32
Time-sampling studies, 122
Trainer, *See* Leader
Training, laboratory, 37-45
Transactional analysis, 64, 65, 66
Transference/countertransference, 163, 171-173, 191, 193, 199, 205, 209, 212, 272
Trephining, 24
Trust, 62, 78, 115
  See also Warmth, trust, and closeness
Type of intervention, 5, 87, 88, 91-102

Unconditional positive regard, 68, 69, 72
Underlying issues, 130-131
Underlying group processes, 162-169
Underlying themes, 161
Uninvolved members, 231-232
Utilitarian philosophy, 20

Values, 69, 78, 222
Velveteen Rabbit, 127-128

Warmth, trust, and closeness, 78-79, 81
Western Training Laboratory, 41, 42
Win-lose situation, 236
World War I, 45
World War II, 25

Zen, 55

NAME INDEX

Ackerman, N. W., 32, 65, 66
Adler, A., 27, 29
Allport, F. H., 23
Altshuler, K. Z., 189
American Psychiatric Association, 52
Angel, E., 46, 47
Anthony, E. J., 31, 33
Appley, D. G., 52, 53
Argyris, C., 43, 68, 191, 194
Aristotle, 19
Arsenian, J., 207, 208, 209
Atkins, S., 118
Axline, V. M., 122

Bach, G. R., 31, 33, 34, 55, 116, 122, 159
Back, K. W., 45
Bales, R. F., 193, 194, 200
Ballard, H. T., 155, 181
Banet, A. G., Jr., 10, 34
Barrett, M. L., 188, 191
Barron, M. E., 202
Battegay, R., 202
Bebout, J., 53
Benne, K. D., 37-42, 60, 72, 89, 100, 116, 117, 159
Bennis, W. G., 8, 53, 160, 182, 184, 187, 188, 191, 209, 215, 216
Berg, C., 133
Berkovitz, I. H., 33
Berliner, A. K., 193, 195, 200
Berne, E., 65, 66, 194
Berzon, B., 116, 117, 123
Bierer, J., 27
Bieri, J., 31
Bion, W. R., 34
Bixby, F. L., 32
Blake, R. R., 42

Blamberg, S., 40
Blumberg, A., 43, 44, 48, 56, 181, 184
Bonner, H., 22, 23, 26, 35
Borenzweig, H., 187, 190
Boring, E. G., 159
Bosco, A., 53
Bradford, D. L., 39, 117
Bradford, L. P., 37, 38, 41, 60, 72, 76, 89, 100, 116, 117, 130, 134, 159, 182
Buber, M., 15
Buchanan, P. C., 117
Bugental, J. F. T., 159
Burgess, E. W., 22
Burrow, T. N., 27, 30
Burton, A., 32, 46, 52, 53, 65, 77, 79
Byron, G. G., Lord, 21

Cahn, M. M., 77
Campbell, J. D., 117, 118, 123
Carter, W. W., 188, 190
Cassirer, E., 17
Cholden, L., 194
Clark, J. V., 159, 182
Cleveland, S., 189
Coch, L., 39
Cohen, A. M., 214, 237
Cohn, R. C., 140, 141
Coleman, J. C., 24, 133
Comte, A., 22, 23, 35
Conze, E., 17
Cooley, C. H., 23, 36
Cooper, B., 122
Cooper, C. L., 117
Cooper, E. C., 202
Corsini, R. J., 6, 27-32
Cox, H. G., 15, 16
Cutts, N. B., 109

Darwin, C., 21
Davis, S. A., 42, 56
Dedrich, C., 55
Denny, A., 54
Deutsch, M., 36, 37
Dewey, J., 36, 37
Dickson, W. J., 39
Dombey, D., 187, 190
Dreikurs, R., 30, 31, 32, 33, 202
Dunnette, M. D., 117, 118, 123
Durkheim, E., 21, 22, 23, 36
Durkin, H. E., 33, 140, 142, 143
Dyer, W. G., 10

Eddy, W. B., 35, 43, 53, 65, 77
Egan, G., 34, 35
Elias, A., 32
Eliot, T. S., 46
Ellenberger, H. F., 46, 47
Ellis, A., 20, 53, 65, 66, 77
Endore, S. G., 55
Erikson, E. H., 160
Etzioni, A., 53
Ezriel, H. A., 34

Faris, M., 203, 207
Fast, J., 54
Fiebert, M. S., 10-11, 123, 159, 160, 181, 184, 194, 216
Fisher, S., 54
Flanagan, J. C., 6, 119-121
Forer, B. R., 80
Foulkes, S. H., 31, 33, 34
Fox, J., 35
Frank, J. D., 26, 33, 51, 195
French, J. R. P., 39, 117
Freud, S., 25, 28, 30, 50, 160
Friedman, P. H., 11
Frost, S. E., 19
Fung, Y. L., 16

Geller, J. J., 202
Gibb, J. R., 37, 38, 42, 72, 77, 83, 89, 100, 116, 117, 157, 159

Gibb, L. M., 77
Ginott, H. G., 32
Glasser, W., 67
Gleuck, W. F., 203
Goldberg, C., 34
Goldfarb, A., 121
Golembiewski, R. T., 43, 56, 181, 184
Goodman, P., 50
Gordon, B., 53
Gordon, T., 32, 33, 121
Gorlow, L., 71
Gottschalk, L. A., 72
Grotjahn, M., 194
Gunther, B., 54, 64, 77-82, 101, 102, 148
Gustaitis, R., 50, 51, 54

Hadden, S. B., 203
Haley, J., 32, 67
Hall, C. S., 158
Halprin, A., 54
Hampden-Turner, C. M., 53, 159, 182
Hare, A. P., 34
Harris, J., 26
Harrison, R. L., 44
Hearn, G., 40
Hefferline, R., 50
Heine, C., et al., 44
Herbert, E. L., 194, 200
Hill, L. B., 34
Hill, W. F., 34, 207, 208
Hillel, 15, 16
Hobbes, T., 19, 20
Hobbs, N., 32, 69, 70, 137, 138
Hoch, E. L., 71
Horwitz, L., 26, 37, 53
House, R. J., 117
Houts, P. S., 10
Howard, J., 51, 80
Hume, D., 20
Hunt, V. V., 188, 191
Huxley, A., 51
Hyman, H. H., 53

Jackson, D. D., 32

Jaensch, E., 50
James, M., 66
James, W., 25, 50
Jones, E., 28
Jones, J. E., 35
Jones, M. H., 188, 191
Jongeward, D., 66
Joseph, C., 26

Kadis, A. L., et al., 29, 31, 33, 34
Kanter, S. B., 203, 205
Kaplan, H. I., 55
Kaplan, H. S., 32
Kaplan, S. R., 8
Kassebaum, G., 32
Katz, D., 50
Kierkegaard, S., 46
King, C. H., 194
King, R. A., 25
Klapman, J. W., 27
Klaw, S., 118
Koffka, K., 50
Kohler, W., 50
Kolb, L., 195
Krantzler, M., 33
Krulee, G. K., 202
Kuriloff, A. H., 118

Lakin, M., 11, 53, 72
Landau, M., 195, 200
Lazarus, A. A., 11, 26, 32
Lazell, E. W., 27, 29
LeBon, G., 28
Levitsky, A., 49
Lewin, K., 35, 36, 37
Liberman, R., 71
Lieberman, M. A., 11, 26, 43, 44, 53, 78, 82, 116, 118
Lindzey, G., 158
Lipkin, S., 32
Lippitt, G. L., 32
Lippitt, R. O., 37
Locke, J., 18, 19, 20
Locke, N. M., 140

Lubin, A., 44
Lubin, B., 35, 43, 44, 52-53, 65, 77
Luchins, A. S., 27
Luft, J., 95

Mallenbaum, V., 237
Malone, T. P., 34
Mann, J., 77, 203
Marquis de Sade, 27
Marrow, A. J., 36
Marsh, L. C., 27, 29
Martin, J. C., 207, 208
Martinson, R., 195, 200
Maslow, A. H., 49, 50, 53
Massarik, F., 33, 42
May, R., 46, 47, 55
Mayer, A., 26
McCorkle, L. W., 32
McDougall, W., 28
McLellan, D. S., et al., 52
McLuhan, M., 53
Mead, G. H., 36
Meiers, J. I., 27
Mellett, T. P., 121
Mesmer, A., 27
Meumann, E., 26
Miles, M. B., 11, 26, 43, 44, 53, 78, 82, 116, 117, 118, 123, 191, 195
Mill, C. R., 11
Mill, J., 20
Mill, J. S., 20, 21
Miller, J. C., 203
Miller, N. E., 120
Mills, T. M., 34
Mintz, E., 55
Modlin, H. C., 203, 207
Moreno, J. L., 27-32, 34, 37, 47, 48
Morgan, C. T., 25
Moustakas, C. E., 76
Mouton, J. S., 42
Mullan, H., 29, 30, 34
Murphy, M. H., 51
Muuss, R. E., 20

Nadler, E. B., 56, 188, 190

Nagay, J. A., 121
Naranjo, C. B., 50
Nietzsche, F. W., 46
Noyes, A., 195

O'Banion, T., 53
O'Connell, A., 53
Osberg, J. W., 193, 195, 200
Otto, H. A., 77, 78, 79, 82

Park, R. E., 22
Parloff, M. B., 56-57
Paterson, J. G., 187, 189, 191
Pattison, E. M., 72
Peberdy, G. A., 35
Perlmutter, J., 44
Perls, F., 47, 50, 54, 64, 182
Perls, L., 47
Pigors, F., 121, 122
Pigors, P. J. W., 121, 122
Pinel, P., 25
Plato, 14, 24
Polansky, N., 32
Porter, L. A., 75
Powdermaker, F., 26, 195
Pratt, J. H., 27, 29
Preston, H. O., 121

Quentin, F., 53

Raskin, N. J., 68
Reddy, W. B., 53
Redl, F., 32
Reich, W., 47, 48, 50
Reinhardt, M., 50
Reisel, J., 118
Rhyne, J., 54, 82
Roethlisberger, F. J., 39
Rogers, C. R., 8, 20, 32, 34, 53, 68, 69, 72, 77, 116, 135, 136, 138, 160, 182, 207, 208, 227
Rolf, I., 53, 54

Roman, M., 8
Rose, S., 33
Rosenbaum, M., 27, 29, 30, 31, 34
Rossides, D. W., 14, 23
Rouse, W. H. D., 14
Rousseau, J. J., 20
Rubenfeld, S., 56, 204, 205
Rubin, I., 54, 56

Sadock, B. J., 55
Sager, C. J., 32
Sarlin, M. B., 189
Satir, V., 32
Scarpitti, F. R., 32
Schilder, P., 30
Schindler, R., 204
Schloss, G. A., 45
Schutz, W. C., 35, 47, 49, 51, 52, 53, 64, 65, 77-80, 82, 101, 148-151, 193, 195, 200
Schwartz, M. S., 34
Seashore, C., 79, 80
Seeman, M., 37
Semrad, E. V., 203, 207, 208, 209
Serber, M., 10
Shambaugh, P. W., 203, 205
Shellow, R. S., 56, 204, 205
Shepard, H. A., 8, 53, 160, 182, 184 187, 188, 191, 209, 215, 216
Sherif, C. W., 41, 42
Sherif, M., 41, 42
Sherwood, J. J., 39, 117
Sikes, M. P., 189
Simkin, J., 49
Simmel, G., 23, 36, 37
Singer, E., 53
Siroka, E. K., 45
Siroka, R. W., 45
Skinner, B. F., 182, 227
Slavson, S. R., 31, 34
Smith, B., 201, 204
Smith, M. E., 122
Smith, R. D., 214
Smith, W. M., 189, 191
Socrates, 14
Solomon, L. N., 116, 117, 123

Sorrells, J., 48
Spencer, H., 22, 23, 35
Speth, E. W., 121
Spiegel, J. P., 54
Standal, S. W., 6
Stanford, G., 32
Stephenson, R. M., 32
Stock, D., 117, 156, 159, 183
Stoller, F. H., 55, 196, 201
Stoute, A., 196
Strasberg, L., 54
Strodtbeck, F., 193, 194, 200
Sutherland, J. D., 34

Tannenbaum, R., 42
Telschow, E., 71
Thelen, H., 40
Theodorson, G. A., 191, 196
Thomas, H. F., 132
Thorne, F. C., 66
Thorpe, J. J., 201, 204
Tonnies, F., 36
Triplett, N., 25
Trist, E. L., 194, 200
Tuckman, B. W., 8, 157, 159, 160 181, 182, 183, 201, 204, 216

Van Dusen, W., 34

Van Meulenbrouck, M., 48
Vich, M. A., 54, 82

Walton, R. E., 53
Ward, D., 32
Ward, J. L., 56, 204, 205
Ward, L. F., 22, 23
Warkentin, J., 32, 77
Watson, R. I., 25
Watson, W., 53
Watts, A. W., 49
Wender, L., 30, 196
Wertheimer, M., 50
Weschsler, I. R., 42, 118
Whitaker, C. A., 34
Whitman, R. M., 191, 196
Wickert, F., 121
Wile, D. B., 10
Williams, M., 128
Wilner, D., 32
Winder, A. E., 52, 53
Wolberg, L. R., 64, 72
Wolf, A., 30, 34, 204
Wolpe, J., 32
Wundt, W., 25, 159

Yablonsky, L., 48, 55
Yalom, I. D., 11, 26, 43, 44, 53, 72, 78, 82, 116, 118